THE SHIP AND RELATED SYMBOLS
IN THE NEW TESTAMENT

THE SHIP AND RELATED SYMBOLS
IN THE
NEW TESTAMENT

by

EARLE HILGERT

Professor of New Testament, Andrews University

WIPF & STOCK · Eugene, Oregon

Wipf and Stock Publishers
199 W 8th Ave, Suite 3
Eugene, OR 97401

The Ship and Related Symbols in the New Testament
By Hilgert, Earle
Softcover ISBN-13: 978-1-7252-8043-4
Publication date 5/7/2020
Previously published by Van Gorcum, 1962

FOREWORD

Christianity, like other religions, has always employed symbols to communicate its message. Yet symbolism, by the very fact that it connotes meaning, rather than denoting it, can only lie on the borderlands of exact communication. Because it often speaks from a level of consciousness which defies literal expression, words are incapable of explaining with complete accuracy all that it intends. The present study is an attempt to explore these borderlands from the standpoint of certain biblical symbols. Many of its results are confessedly tentative. Still, because the New Testament appears to employ such symbols, their explication is a legitimate and necessary hermeneutical undertaking. It is our conviction that the theme of salvation history is set forth in the New Testament, not only literally, but also on this symbolic level.

In this study biblical quotations in English have been made from the *Revised Standard Version* (New York: Thomas Nelson and Sons; New Testament, 1946; Old Testament, 1952) unless otherwise indicated. For the Hebrew Bible we have followed the ninth edition of R. Kittel's *Biblia Hebraica* (1954), for the LXX, the fifth edition of A. Rahlfs' *Septuaginta* (1952), and for the Greek Testament, the 24th edition of E. Nestle's *Novum Testamentum Graece* (1960), all published by the Privileg. Württ. Bibelanstalt, Stuttgart. Quotations from other ancient sources have been taken from standard English translations whenever they were available. All quotations from non-English works not credited to a translation have been translated by the writer.

A number of persons have placed me particularly in debt for their contributions to this study. In its early stages Professor E. R. Goodenough of Yale graciously pointed me to certain source materials; later, the Rev. Lloyd Gaston made valuable criticisms; and throughout Professor Oscar Cullmann of Basel and Paris gave encouragement and advice. Above all others, however, thanks are due Professor Bo Reicke of Basel, under whose guidance this study was carried out and presented as a dissertation for the doctorate in theology. Not only did he first suggest the topic, but throughout showed the warmest friendship, ever standing ready with suggestion, criticism, and counsel.

My appreciation is also extended to the librarians of the University of Basel and the Library of Congress; and to Mrs. Martin Ambs, Mrs. Herbert Kiesler, and Mrs. James Owens, who helped in preparing the manuscript for publication. Particular recognition is due President F. O. Rittenhouse and the Trustees of Andrews University for a grant making possible the publication of this study.

Finally, special thanks are deserved by my wife for her patience in typing the original drafts, and especially for her intelligent interest throughout.

CONTENTS

FOREWORD 5
CHAPTER   I - INTRODUCTION 9

PART I - BACKGROUNDS

CHAPTER   II - NON-JEWISH BACKGROUNDS 15
CHAPTER III - HEBREW AND JEWISH BACKGROUNDS. 26
CHAPTER   IV - SUMMARY OF BACKGROUNDS: THE SHIP AS A
               FIGURE IN THE HELLENISTIC WORLD. 40
EXCURSUS   - THE SYMBOLISM OF THE SEA IN PRE-CHRISTIAN
               LITERATURE 43

PART II - THE NEW TESTAMENT

CHAPTER   V - THE PROBLEM OF SYMBOLISM IN THE GOSPELS 53
CHAPTER   VI - THE STORY OF THE STORM ON THE SEA AND
               THE HEALING OF THE DEMONIAC 72
CHAPTER VII - THE STORY OF JESUS' WALKING ON THE SEA . 91
CHAPTER VIII - THE STORIES OF A MIRACULOUS DRAFT OF FISH 105
CHAPTER   IX - THE SHIP IN THE ACTS, THE EPISTLES, AND THE
               REVELATION 124
CHAPTER   X - CONCLUSION 150
SELECTED BIBLIOGRAPHY. 157

CHAPTER I

INTRODUCTION

From the dawn of man's history, the sea has fascinated and inspired his imagination. In its unpredictable moods he has seen reflected the capricious forces with which his own life must contend; in the ever uncertain outcome of a voyage, he has read the imponderables of human fate; and by the ship and its gear, upon which the seafarer's life depends, he often has symbolized those institutions in which he places his hope of survival, both now and hereafter. It is no wonder, then, that in the literary and archaeological remains of such a seafaring world as the ancient Mediterranean, nautical symbols, and above all, the symbol of the ship, are among the most frequently encountered.[1]

To our knowledge, the first study of the ship as a symbol in early Christianity was that of J. Aleander, *Navis ecclesiam referentis symbolum in veteri gemma annulari insculptum* (1626). Added materials were provided in the eighteenth and nineteenth centuries by several important works on early Christian art,[2] but it has remained for the Roman Catholic scholarship of the twentieth century to undertake a comprehensive study. More than three decades ago, F. J. Dölger provided an introductory contribution,[3] which was followed by Fr. Sühling, particularly from the standpoint of dove and ship in Christian

---

[1] G. F. H. Coenen, *Dissertatio literaria de comparationibus et metaphoris apud Atticos praesertim poetas* (1875), p. 55; H. Blümer, *Über Gleichnis und Metaphern in der attischen Komödie* (1891), p. 163; C. Bonner, "Desired Haven", *Harv. Theol. Rev.*, 34 (1941), p. 49.

[2] E.g. M. A. Boldetti, *Osservazioni sopra i cimiteri de' santi martiri ed antichi cristiani di Roma* (1720); L. Perret, *Catacombes de Rome*, I-VI (1851-55); G. B. de Rossi, *Roma sotteranea*, I-III (1864-77), and articles in *Bullettino di archeologia cristiana* (1863ff.); R. Garrucci, *Storia dell' arte cristiana*, I-VI (1873-81). More recent works in the same area are: J. Wilpert, *Die römischen Mosaiken und Malereien des kirchlichen Bauten vom IV. bis XIII. Jahrhundert*, I-IV (1916); O. Marucchi, *Le catacombe romane* (1933). See also C. M. Kaufmann, *Die sepulkrale Jenseitsdenkmäler der Antike und des Urchristentums* (1900).

[3] F. J. Dölger, *Sol salutis* (1925), pp. 272-286.

archaeology.⁴ H. Leclercq, with characteristic plenitude, also assembled many examples from early Christian art.⁵ However, Dölger's call for a history of the ship symbol remained essentially unanswered until 1941, when H. Rahner began a series of articles in the *Zeitschrift für katholische Theologie* under the general title, "Antenna Crucis."⁶ Bringing together a rich collection of references both from classical and patristic literature, Rahner has undertaken to write a history of the ship as a symbol in the early Church.⁷

In the present investigation, we also have undertaken to study the ship as a symbol in early Christianity. Whereas Rahner's work is essentially a study in patristic theology, we have followed the suggestion of a number of scholars in thinking that the ship may already have played a symbolic role in the New Testament,⁸ and have concentrated our study there.

A word is appropriate here regarding the definition of the term "symbol" as we have employed it. E. R. Goodenough, whose monumental work, *Jewish Symbols* (I-VIII, 1953-58), is concerned with the same kind of symbolism we have studied, offers the following

⁴ Fr. Sühling, *Die Taube als religiöses Symbol im christlichen Altertum* (1930).
⁵ H. Leclercq, "Arche," "Gemme," "Lampe," "Navire," in *Dict. d'arch. chrét.*
⁶ H. Rahner, "Antenna Crucis," *Zeitschr. f. kath. Theol.*, 65 (1941), pp. 123-152; 66 (1942), pp. 89-118; 67 (1942), pp. 196-227; 68 (1943), pp. 1-21;75 (1953), pp. 129-173, 358-410; 79 (1957), pp. 129-169; the series is still in progress; idem, "Navicula Petri," *Zeitschr. f. kath. Theol.*, 69 (1947), pp. 1-35. For further bibliography see especially 65 (1941), p. 124, n. 1; 67 (1942), p. 198, n. 11.
⁷ A number of short studies of individual aspects of the ship symbol, both in classical and in Christian literature have appeared: S. Eitrem, "De servatore mundi navis gubernatore," *Coniect. neotest.*, 4 (1940), pp. 5-8; C. Bonner(n. 1), pp. 49-67; idem, "The Ship of the Soul on a Group of Grave-Stelae from Terenuthis," *Proc. of the Am. Phil. Soc.*, 85 (1941), pp. 84-91; G. Stuhlfauth, "Das Schiff als Symbol der altchristlichen Kunst," *Rivista di arch. christ.*, 19 (1942), pp. 111ff.; E. Peterson, "Das Schiff als Symbol der Kirche," *Theol. Zeitschr.*, 6 (1950), pp. 77-79; K. Goldammer, "Das Schiff der Kirche," *Theol. Zeitschr.*, 6 (1950), pp. 232ff.; R. Mach, *Der Zaddik im Talmud und Midrasch* (1957), Anhang I: "Die nautische Symbolik in der rabbinischen Literatur," pp. 223-241. Of particular importance for classical literature is J. Kahlmeyer, *Seesturm und Schiffbruch als Bild im antiken Schrifttum* (1943).
⁸ This possibility was suggested to me by Bo Reicke (cf. his article, "Die Bedeutung des Gottesvolks-Gedankens für den neutestamentlichen Kirchenbegriff," *Kirchenbl. f. die ref. Schweiz*, 111 [1955], p. 262). It has also been proposed by G. Dehn, *Der Gottessohn* (3d ed., 1932), pp. 108f.; Austin Farrer, *A Study in St. Mark* (1951), p. 87; E. Klostermann, *Das Markus Evangelium* (2d ed.; 1926), p. 53; R. H. Lightfoot, *History and Interpretation in the Gospels* (1934), p. 89; J. Mánek, "Fishers of Men," *Nov. Test.*, 2 (1957), p. 141; Peterson (n. 7), pp. 77ff.; Alan Richardson, *The Miracle Stories of the Gospels* (1956), pp. 92f.

definition: "A symbol is an image or design with a significance, to the one who uses it, quite beyond its manifest content."[9] Such a symbol, of course, need not be graphic; it may take the form of a figure of speech.

Such a definition gives the term "symbol" both a narrower and a broader sense than some legitimately assign it. Thus any word, because it brings to mind objects or ideas that go beyond itself, may be called a symbol, though, if it has no inner connection with that for which it stands, a more precise term for this would be a sign.[10] On the other hand, we do not employ the term "symbol" here in special metaphysical senses such as have been given it by Jaspers[11] and Tillich,[12] for we are concerned not with ideal abstractions, but with graphic designs and literary figures of speech that represent concrete ideas.[13]

Goodenough goes on to point out that "a symbol is an object or a pattern which... operates upon men and causes effect in them, beyond mere recognition of what is literally presented in the given form."[14] Herein lies their power. Because symbols have their roots and their function in the area of connotative, rather than of denotative thinking, they may defy the imposition of logical classifications or the establishment of rational relationships. By virtue of this ambiguity, a good symbol can aid in resolving the contradictions of life. As Goodenough explains, a proper religious symbol presents the paradox of life and death, and life through death, to the believer. This is usually best accomplished by a symbol drawn from nature.[15] A pre-eminent example of such a vitally meaningful symbol is that of the ship, a frail craft of wood, that nevertheless could carry ancient man across wild waves, frought with demonic powers and fateful adventure.[16]

[9] E. R. Goodenough, *Jewish Symbols*, IV (1954), 28; cf. E. Mitzka, "Symbolismus als theologische Methode," *Zeitschr. f. kath. Theol.*, 67 (1943), p. 24.
[10] Goodenough (n. 9), IV, 29; P. Tillich, *Systematische Theologie* (1955), I, 283, applies the same distinction to metaphysical symbols.
[11] K. Jaspers, *Philosophie* (3d ed., 1956), III, 15-17, 128-236.
[12] Tillich (n. 10), I, 281ff., 332ff.
[13] See Goodenough (n. 9), IV, 28, n. 12.
[14] Goodenough (n. 9), IV, 28.
[15] Goodenough (n. 9) IV, 39-41.
[16] Wisdom 14 : 1, 5; Polybius, *Histories* XXI, 31, 6-13; Rahner (n. 6), 66 (1942), pp. 91-94.

PART I

BACKGROUNDS

CHAPTER II

NON-JEWISH BACKGROUNDS

The ship in Egyptian religion

Geographically and economically, the life of ancient Egypt focused on the Nile. Virtually all traffic was by ship.[1] It is not surprising, then, that the ship also played a definite role in religious ceremonial and myth. The gods were exhibited to the people on portable shrines in the form of a ship,[2] and the greater gods possessed real ships for ceremonial journeys. However, from the standpoint of the ship as a religious symbol, chief interest attaches to its funerary use.

Many Egyptian cemeteries were situated on the opposite side of the Nile from the town they served, so that a passage of the river by ship was a necessary part of every funeral.[3] The use of a ship in such ceremonies naturally connected with the notion of the voyage of the soul to the hereafter. In Egypt it was only natural to conceive that the dead would travel by ship to the next world.[4] The early god of the underworld, *Skr*, Sokaris, represented the sun during its nightly journey from west to east, under the world.[5] As

[1] A. Erman, *Die Religion der Aegypter* (1934), pp. 15, 180. Cf. the variety of words in which the ship was used as determinative in hieroglyphic: *pnᶜ*, "upset": an overturned ship; *tȝw*, "breath," "wind," *mḥyt*, "northwind," *dᶜw*, "storm": a sail; *ḥdi*, "to travel northward" (downstream on the Nile): a ship with a prominent rudder; and *ḫnti*, "to travel southward" (up-stream): a ship under full sail (see A. H. Gardiner, *Egyptian Grammar* [1927], pp. 486-487).
[2] Cf. also Apuleius, *The Golden Ass* XI, 16; Pausanias, *Description of Greece* I, 29, 1.
[3] C. Bonner, "The ship of the Soul on a Group of Grave-Stelae from Terenuthis," *Proc. of the Am. Phil. Soc.*, 85 (1941), p. 89; E. A. W. Budge, *The Mummy* (1893), p. 168; ibid. (1925) Pl. XXXVIII; Erman (n. 1), pp. 262f.; Diodorus, *Bibliotheca historica* I, 92.
[4] A similar psychological process may be observed among peoples whose travel was usually by land; in German mythology the dead traveled by wagon (L. Radermacher, *Das Jenseits im Mythos der Hellenen* [1903], p. 76), on horseback (F. Piper, *Mythologie und Symbolik der christlichen Kunst*, I : 1 [1847], 220).
[5] Budge (n. 3), p. 295; Erman (n. 1), pp. 26, 49. Cf. Gardiner (n. 1), p. 459; F. J. Dölger, *Sol salutis* (1925), p. 284, n. 2; Fr. Sühling, *Die Taube als religiöses Symbol im christlichen Altertum* (1930), pp. 249, 250.

the sun set in the west, the Egyptians early concluded that the abode of the dead lay under the world, which consequently was known as "the West," the dead as "the Westerners," and Sokaris as "the first of the Westerners."[6] To reach this Westland, the soul must seek the services of a divine ferryman.[7]

At an early date heavenly islands, in contrast to the underworld, came to be considered as the abode of those dead who had pleased the gods. Only those who were provided with ships at their burial, or were given passage over the waters by a deity, were able to reach them. Often the sun, Re himself, provided the needed transportation by taking the departed soul into his sun-bark. Egyptian mortuary literature contains many prayers and spells intended to aid the soul in gaining entrance to this solar ship.[8]

A very different use of nautical figures appears in *The Instruction of Amen-em-opet*, at latest from the sixth century B.C., and perhaps earlier. Here the sage warns against making false statements to achieve success:

> Be steadfast in thy heart, make firm thy breast.
> Steer not with thy tongue (alone).
> If the tongue of a man (be) the rudder of a boat,
> The All-Lord is its pilot.[9]

This seems to imply that the boat is the person. Just as a rudder guides a ship, so the tongue by its honesty or dishonesty determines the course of life; yet above all stands God whose will and judgment are the ultimate factor.

A number of these uses of the ship in Egyptian religion reappear in Greek, Roman, and early Christian literature and art. Particularly important are the following: death as involving a passage through waters to the next life, the ship as the conveyance of the soul to the hereafter, the divine ferryman, the presence of the soul in a ship with its god, and the connection between this motif and the soul's possession of everlasting life. At the same time, these motifs seem to find little

---

[6] Erman (n. 1), p. 211, another explanation is offered by J. B. Pritchard, *Ancient Near Eastern Texts* (1950), p. 33; see also H. Kees, *Totenglauben und Jenseitsvorstellungen der alten Ägypter* (1926), pp. 30f., 89f.

[7] G. Roeder, *Urkunden zur Religion des alten Aegypten* (1915), p. 220.

[8] Roeder (n. 7), pp. 213, 216, 219, 220, 282-284; Pritchard (n. 6), p. 33.

[9] "The Instruction of Amen-em-opet," xx, 3-6 (ch. 18), in Pritchard (n. 6), pp. 423-424; cf. i, 1, 5-7, 10; iv, 19-v, 1; x, 10f. H. Grapow, *Vergleiche und andere bildliche Ausdrücke im Ägyptischen*, Der Alte Orient, 21 (1920), Heft 1/2, p. 16, interprets the ship in another text as representing the land of Egypt.

if any connection with the ship symbol in the New Testament. More important for the latter is the very different figure of the ship as a human life or person. We would not insist that any of these motifs passed directly from Egypt to the Graeco-Roman and Christian literatures. They are of such a nature that, given somewhat similar environments, they could have arisen quite spontaneously, as, indeed, they doubtless did originally in Egypt. But it is not without significance that the Egyptians – and to a large extent early in their history – were the first to develop them.

The ship as a figure in Mesopotamian art and literature

Like the Nile in Egypt, the Tigris and Euphrates in Mesopotamia were essential to civilization, but they were not the only routes of communication. The gods possessed both ceremonial wagons and ships.[10] Ships also appear in ritual scenes on seals from the middle of the third millenium (Uruk period), but it is impossible to say exactly what these scenes portray.[11]

At an early period in Sumerian art the sun-god is shown seated in his ship. This theme may be traced in a stereotyped pattern on a series of cylinder seals from the Early Dynastic period to the First Dynasty of Babylon.[12] A number of attributes on these seals imply that the journey of the sun in a ship is its nightly journey to the underworld,[13] while the general theme of a ship as the means of conveyance to the netherworld appears repeatedly in Mesopotamian art and literature.[14] Thus the ship was intimately related

---

[10] B. Meissner, *Babylonien und Assyrien* (1925), II, 73; Pritchard (n. 6), p. 334, lines 410 ff. Cf. A. Moortgat, *Tammuz: der Unsterblichkeitsglaube in der altorientalischen Bildkunst* (1949), Pls. 10 a/b, 11; pp. 40ff.; J. B. Pritchard, *The Ancient Near East in Pictures* (1954), No. 103; H. Frankfort, *Cylinder Seals* (1939), p. 124 and Pl. XX f; S. N. Kramer, *Sumerian Mythology* (1944), pp. 60, 66f. and Pl. XIV; G. Widengren, *Mesopotamian Elements in Manichaeism* (1946), p. 100.

[11] Pritchard (n. 10), Nos. 104, 673; Frankfort (n. 10), Pls. III d/e; p. 20: "Ritual scenes on seals of this age (Uruk period) defy even hypothetical explanation."

[12] Pritchard (n. 10), Nos. 676, 677, and p. 330; Frankfort (n. 10), Pls. XIV k, XV j, XV n, XIX e and pp. 67f.; Moortgat (n. 10), Pl. 28a; Kramer (n. 10), Pl. X.

[13] Frankfort (n. 10), pp. 68, 108-110, 136, Pls. XV j/n (same as Moortgat [n. 10], Pl. 28; cf. pp. 90-92), XIX f (same as Kramer [n. 10], Pl. XII; Pritchard [n. 10], No. 686).

[14] L. Woolley, Excavations at Ur (1955), p. 65; Pl. 93; Moortgat (n. 10), p. 62; Pl. 23a; Pritchard (n. 10), No. 105; "The Epic of Gilgamesh," X, ii, 23 (Assyrian Version), in Pritchard (n. 6), p. 91; "A Vision of the Nether World,"

to the idea of descent to the underworld and return to (or achievement of) eternal life. Widengren sees here a "soteriological aspect."

In the Mandaean literature,[15] these motifs portray the ascent of the soul from this world through the sky to "the place of light." This is accomplished in a ship.[16] The Mandaean saviour declares of himself:

> ... I shall deliver my friends, bring them up, and set them up in my ship. I shall clothe them with garments of splendor, and cover them with precious lights. ... I and my disciples will ascend and behold the place of light.[17]

Widengren has argued strongly for the view that this theme of the descent of the saviour, his rescue of souls from this world, and his

in Pritchard (n. 6), p. 109. M. Witzel, *Tammuz-Liturgien und Verwandtes* (1935), pp. 97, Verso III, 17f.; 377, 16-26; 425, 14-23; 427, 13-14; 447, Recto I, 11 (cf. p. 444); 447, Recto II, 7-Verso I, 4; Widengren (n. 10), pp. 100ff.

[15] Since the most important Mandaean texts were translated and published by M. Lidzbarski (*Das Johannesbuch der Mandäer*, I-II [1905, 1915] and *Ginzā: der Schatz oder das grosse Buch der Mandäer* [1925]), there has been much discussion regarding the religious-historical relationships of Mandaism and its significance for the New Testament. See especially R. Reitzenstein, "Das mandäische Buch des Herrn der Grösse und die Evangelienüberlieferung," *Sitzber. Heidelb. Ak. Wiss.*, Phil.-hist. Kl., 1919, 12. Abh.; E. Peterson, "Bemerkungen zur mandäischen Literatur," *Zeitschr. f. nt. Wiss.*, 25 (1926), pp. 236-248; F. C. Burkitt, "The Mandaeans," *Journ. Theol. Stud.*, 29 (1928), pp. 225-235; H. Lietzmann, "Ein Beitrag zur Mandäerfrage," *Sitzber. preuss. Ak. Wiss.*, Phil.-hist. Kl., 27 (1930), pp. 596-608; R. Bultmann, "Die Bedeutung der neuerschlossenen mandäischen und manichäischen Quellen für das Verständnis des Johannesevangeliums," *Zeitschr. f. nt. Wiss.*, 24 (1925), pp. 100-146; *Theol. Litzeitg.*, 56 (1931), cols. 577-580; E. Percy, *Untersuchungen über den Ursprung der johanneischen Theologie* (1939), who sought rather to derive important features of Mandaism from Christianity. T. Säve-Söderbergh, *Studies in the Coptic Manichaean Psalm-Book* (1949); W. Baumgartner, "Der heutige Stand der Mandäerfrage," *Theol. Zeitschr.*, 6 (1950), pp. 401-410; W. F. Albright, "Recent Discoveries in Palestine and the Gospel of John," in W. D. Davies and D. Daube, eds., *The Background of the New Testament and its Eschatology* (1956), p. 154; E. Haenchen, "Aus der Literatur zum Johannesevangelium, 1929-1956," *Theol. Rundsch.*, N.F. 23 (1955), pp. 314-317; H. Schlier, "Zur Mandäerfrage," *ibid.*, N.F., 5 (1933), pp. 1-34. In presenting the Mandaean literature, we do not intend to imply that these texts may be used as sources for the New Testament. Such parallels as exist seem best to be accounted for by both bodies of writings having drawn on a common world of thought; cf. P. Vielhauer, *Oikodome* (1940), pp. 34f.

[16] Lidzbarski, *Das Johannesbuch* (n. 15), pp. 197, 13-15; 203, 14-204, 1; 151-152; 155-156; 161; 162; Widengren (n. 10), p. 97.

[17] Lidzbarski, *Das Johannesbuch* (n. 15), pp. 150, 154. R. Mach, *Der Zaddik in Talmud und Midrasch* (1957), pp. 220f.; 237, n. 4. Cf. pp. 159ff.

transporting them in his ship to the place of light and life is derived from the old Mesopotamian religion. Parallels both of content and of language with Sumerian, Babylonian, and Assyrian texts are so striking, that a relationship appears certain. If Baumgartner is correct that Mandaism is of western origin, but that it early migrated to the east and absorbed Mesopotamian elements,[18] we may be able to account for these distinctly Mesopotamian motifs in the typically Gnostic saviour-myth of the Mandaean literature. It seems clear that one of these authentically Mesopotamian elements is the ship as a vehicle of salvation.

The ship as a symbol in Greek literature and art

Nautical figures are among the most common and the most varied in application of any symbols in Greek litereature. In the following survey, we are concerned with two salient meanings of the ship: 1) as the conveyance of the soul after death; and, 2) as the human life.

As a conveyance of souls to the hereafter, the boat of Charon is a particularly well-known figure in Greek and Roman literature. He seems to have been unknown to the early Greeks as neither Homer nor Hesiod mentions him. However, in Homer the stage is set for his appearance, as the dead must cross the Ocean to reach the Elysian Fields![19] Thus the introduction of the figure of a ferryman could have been quite spontaneous. It appears as early as the sixth century B.C. to have been fixed even in many of the details characteristic of later Greek literature.[20] Whether the notion of such a ferryman was a native development, or whether it was imported from Egypt after that country was opened to the Greeks in the seventh century, is difficult to determine.[21] It seems plausible that it may have arisen on Greek soil.

The second main theme with which the ship is connected in Greek literature is that of the voyage of human life.[22] A people inti-

---

[18] See above, n. 15.
[19] Homer, *Odyssey*, XXIV, 2, 10f. Cf. F. Gisinger, "Okeanos," Paully-Wissowa, *Real-Encyclopädie*, XVII : 2, 2314.
[20] F. Cumont, *After Life in Roman Paganism* (1922), p. 75.
[21] Diodorus (n. 3), I, 96; Piper (n. 4), I : 1, 220; J. Ambrosch, *De Charonte etrusco* (1837), pp. 23-44; O. Gruppe, *Griechische Mythologie* (1906), I, 404f.
[22] In this portrayal of the development of the basic theme of the ship of life we have followed J. Kahlmeyer, *Seesturm und Schiffbruch* (1934), p. 39. H. Rahner,

mately associated with the sea, as were the Greeks, easily saw parallels between a sea voyage and the vicissitudes of life. Such a basic comparison appears repeatedly in Greek literature.[23] Thus Euripides portrays Hecuba, queen of Troy, lamenting the disaster fallen upon her country and family:

> Breast not with thy prow the surges of life, who on
> Waves of disaster, alas! art tost.[24]

Such passages aid in interpreting certain Greek funerary inscriptions. One Attic grave bears the words, "Saved from the seas, I have this harbor; may everyone who sails be saved unto his homeland."[25] Although this may refer to the deceased person's having survived an actual shipwreck, yet the "harbor," and the "homeland," are clearly symbolic of death or the hereafter. Accordingly the "seas" are probably the storms of life, and "everyone who sails," a general reference to mankind on the voyage of life.

A development of this basic theme is the comparison of the common fate of persons bound by ties of affection or family to the common fate of persons in a ship.[26] Sophocles has Ismene

---

"Antenna Crucis III," *Zeitschr f. kath. Theol.*, 66 (1942), pp. 210ff., presents a similar, but not altogether identical, development.

In speaking of developments in symbolism, we do not mean that symbolisms of the ship can be shown to have undergone such developments historically, in any *chronological* sequence. The universality of these figures, together with their closeness to the basic facts of everyday life, suggests that they were more or less concurrently present in ancient Greek thought and literature. The idea of "development" is rather an attempt to portray their interrelationships as ideas.

[23] The detail to which this might be expanded is illustrated by the catalogue of meanings attached to the ship, as given by Artemidorus, the soothsayer (*Oneirokritika* II, 23, quoted by Rahner [n. 22], 66 [1942], p. 207): smooth journey = good; storm = danger; anchor and port = rest; mast = the Lord; shipwreck = death.

[24] Euripides, *The Daughters of Troy*, 103f. (Loeb ed., I [1930], 365); cf. Plato, *Laws* VII, 803; Plutarch, *Moralia*, 476 A, "On Tranquility of Mind."

[25] σωθείς ἐκ πελάγους τοῦτον ἔχω λιμέναν σωζέσθω ἰς πατρίδαν πᾶς ὁ πλοϊζόμενος, Kaufman (n. 11), pp. 179f., quoted from Koumanoudes, Ἀττικῆς ἐπιγρ., 1613; also quoted by C. Bonner, "Desired Haven," *Harv. Theol. Rev.*, 34 (1941), p. 67. Cf. the grave stela of Kallineikos at Istanbul, A. Salač, *Bull. de corr. hellén.*, 44 (1920), pp. 354-357, Bonner (n. 3), 85 (1941), p. 90; E. R. Goodenough, *Jewish Symbols*, VIII (1958), 159f.; Fig. 143; cf. Fig. 148.

[26] How current this notion of the unity of persons sailing together in a ship was, is illustrated by a number of passages that refer to the presence of pious fellow shipmates as a good omen, and the reticence of people to sail in the same ship with

express her desire to die with her condemned sister Antigone by declaring:

> But now thy bark is stranded, I am bold
> To claim my share as partner in the loss.[27]

The comparison of the common fate of persons in the same social unit with the fate of men aboard the same ship, implies that the social unit itself is represented by the ship. This is explicit in a large number of passages where the ship is a **symbol of the state**.[28] The earliest occurrence of this figure is probably in a fragment of Alcaeus.[29] Thereafter the ship as the state appears in a large number of passages from the lyricists,[30] dramatists,[31] philosophers,[32] orators,[33] and historians.[34] In a particularly striking example, Plato describes at length a ship with a faulty captain and an ignorant and unruly crew. Then he declares: "... the condition we have described is the exact counterpart of the relation of the state to the true philosophers."[35]

The chronological range and variety of literature in which the ship as the state appears show how widely recognized was this particular symbolism. In many of these passages, the ship is portrayed in a

---

men of evil reputation: Euripides, *Electra*, 1355; Xenophon, *Cyropaedia* VIII, 1, 25; Antiphon, *On the Murder of Herod*, 82f. Cf. Jonah 1 : 7-15.

[27] Sophocles, *Antigone*, 540f. (Loeb ed., I [1932], 357). Cf. Euripides, *The Madness of Hercules*, 1225.

[28] Thus Kahlmeyer (n. 22), p. 39, sees the symbolism of the state as a ship to be a "Sonderfall des Motivs 'Schiffsgemeinschaft = Lebensgemeinschaft.'" See also Rahner (n. 22), 66 (1942), pp. 209-214, who discusses this figure and its relation to the symbolism ship = church.

[29] Fragment Z 2, Edgar Lobel and Denys Page, eds., *Poetarum Lesbiorum Fragmenta* (1955), p. 265. Heraclitus (*Allegoriae Homericae* [ed. E. Mehler, 1851,] p. 7), thus interprets this fragment. For the modern debate over his correctness, see Kahlmeyer (n. 22), pp. 39f. Cf. also Fragment 6, and T. Reinach and A. Puech, *Alcée Sapho* (1937), p. 62, n. 2.

[30] Theognis 855f. Cf. lines 671-682; Pindar, *Pythian Odes* X, 71f.; Bacchylides, *Carmen* XII [XIII].

[31] Aeschylus, *Seven Against Thebes*, 760f.; 1080ff. (Loeb ed., I [1930], pp. 384f.); Sophocles, *Oedipus the King*, 22-24; 692-695; 922f. Euripides, *Suppliants*, 473-475; 879; *Rhesus*, 322f.; Aristophanes, *The Wasps*, 29; *The Knights*, 361, 432ff., 703ff.

[32] Plato, *Republic* VI, 488; *The Statesman*, 302; *Alcibiades*, I, 135; *Laws*, VI, 758.

[33] Lysias, *Against Andocides*, 49; Isocartes, *Areopagiticus*, 18; Demosthenes, *Philippics* III, 128 (69f.); Aeschines, *Against Ctesiphon*, 158.

[34] Polybius, *The Histories* VI, 44, 3; Plutarch, *Phocion* I; *Solon* XIX; *Caius Marcius Coriolanus* XXXII; Dio Cassius, *Roman History* LII, 16, 3.

[35] Plato, *Republic* VI, 488 (Loeb ed. [1925] p. 161).

storm to represent the state beset by danger. This may be significant for the interpretation of the ship in the New Testament.

A further expansion of the idea of life as a voyaging ship is the notion of the world as a ship, with a god as pilot.[36] Thus Lucian has Zeus declare of himself, "like the master of a ship, I stand by myself high up on the stern with the tiller in my hands."[37]

The idea of divine guidance in the voyage of life may have its backgrounds in legends of actual ships being piloted through dangerous waters by a god.[38] Closely related to this notion was the special connection between the rudder of a ship and certain gods who were thought to exercise special watchcare over the rudder, and in this way, over the entire ship and its occupants.[39]

Other nautical symbols closely related to the ship appear in Greek literature. The anchor is a figure of hope, and particularly of hope centered upon a person. Euripides has Hecuba, wife of Priam, cry,

> Gods of the Underworld, save ye my son,
> Mine house's anchor, its only one.[40]

The harbor is a symbol for death or the after-life.[41]

As the voyaging ship represents the course of life, so the foundering of a ship represents the ruin of a life. Thus Plato uses the figure of shipwreck to describe the misfortune of a man destroyed by political misadventure.[42]

Just as the ship also symbolized the state, so shipwreck could represent national disaster. Polybius likens the Athenian populace, grown self-confident and unmanageable after successfully withstanding a period of danger, to a ship's company: "Often after

---

[36] Rahner (n. 22), 66 (1942), pp. 219f., presents a strong case for a relation between the ship as the soul and the ship as the world, connected by the logos as pilot of both. Mach (n. 17), pp. 228f. relates the concepts ship = world and ship = state inasmuch as ancient writers conceived the world as a political entity. But see also Bonner (n. 25), p. 49, n. 2.

[37] Lucian, *The Double Indictment*, 2 (Loeb ed., III [1st ed., 1921], 89); cf. *Zeus Rants*, 46; Plato, *The Statesman*, 272E, 273E, 273C, and *Critias*, 109C.

[38] Homer (n. 19), IX, 142f.; Aeschylus, *Agamemnon*, 664-666; Libanius, *Oratio* XXI, 17. Cf. Bonner (n. 25), pp. 64-66; (n. 3), p. 88.

[39] S. Eitrem, "De Servatore Mundi Navis Gubernatore," *Coniect. Neotest.*, 4 (1940), pp. 5-7.

[40] Euripides, *Hecuba*, 79f. (Loeb ed., I [1930], 253, 255). Cf. *Helen*, 277ff.; Epictetus, fr. 30 (89); Helidorus VII, 25.

[41] See further references in Rahner (n. 22), 66 (1942), p. 94, nn. 48f.; Kahlmeyer (n. 22), pp. 34f.

[42] Plato, *Republic* VIII, 553; cf. Polybius (n. 34) IV, 48, 11; XVIII, 55, 7.

escaping from the perils of the widest seas and fiercest storms they are shipwrecked in harbour and when close to the shore."[43]

In summary we may say that the first main theme in Greek literature presents the ship as a conveyance of souls after death, with death as a passage through waters to the hereafter under the guidance of a ferryman.

The second main theme, the ship as a human life, involves a number of amplifications. Moving from the simple notion of the voyage of a ship as the course of human life, Greek writers emphasized the interdependence and common fate of men sailing in the same ship. Thus the ship was conceived as representing a social unit, particularly the state, or in some instances, the world, with God as pilot. The theme of the state as a ship appears with special frequency in Greek literature and seems to present a particularly important analogy to early Christian usage.

The ship as a symbol in Roman literature and art

In Roman literature and art, the figure of the ship follows the same pattern of ideological development as among the Greeks. Only a few new emphases are apparent.

The Roman Charon and his ship present the same dour picture as do their Greek counterparts, but often with an intensification of the gloomier aspects, due probably to the influence of the Etruscan figure Charun, a hateful demon thought to accompany the dead and watch over their graves.[44]

This delineation is counterbalanced to some extent, however, by a happier development in the figure of the ship of the dead, for, as in Egypt, it also becomes a means of transport for the fortunate to the Elysian Fields. Thus Propertius has several ships convey the dead, each to a different abode:

> Two mansions are there allotted beside the foul stream of Hell; and all the dead must ply the oar this way or that. One bark bears the adultery of Clytemnestra, another the monstrous timber of the feigned Cretan cow;

---

[43] Polybius (n. 34) VI, 44, 7 (Loeb ed., III, 371); cf. Dio Cassius (n. 34) LII, 16,4.
[44] *Hercules Furens*, 764-777; Juvenal, *Satire* III, 266f.; Apuleius, *The Golden Ass* VI, 18. Waser, "Charon," Paully-Wissowa (n. 19), III : 2, 2177f.; W. H. Roscher, "Charon," *Ausführliches Lexikon der griechischen und römischen Mythologie*, I : 1 (1884-86), 886. Cf. Michelangelo's portrayal of Charon, derived from Dante, in "The Last Judgment," above the altar in the Sistine Chapel; Virgil, *Aeneid* VI, 298-304.

but lo! yet others are swept away in a wreathed boat, where blessed airs fan the roses of Elysium...[45]

This development appears to be important for the figure of the ship in Christian grave inscriptions, where it stands in marked contrast to the ship of Charon and represents the arrival of the soul in Paradise.

A further development of this motif, during the imperial period, was the idea that the Fortunate Isles were located in the **sun and moon**. Such an idea has already been seen in Egypt, and it also finds parallels in Hindu and Manichaean teaching. The removal of paradise to the sky meant that Charon now transported souls across a celestial river.[46]

As with the Greeks, the second main theme with which the ship is connected in Latin literature is that of **human life**. The vicissitudes of life are likened to those of a sea voyage, its trials especially being compared to storms,[47] while shipwreck represents personal disaster.[48] Closely related to this theme is that of the **pilot**, representing forces that bring human life to a happy or an unfortunate end.[49] At the same time the figure of the ship is expanded to represent the world, with God as its pilot.[50]

With Roman writers, as with Greek, the ship also represents the corporate life of men united in a **political body**.[51]

Thus Cicero refers to the "ship of state,"[52] and defending himself to L. Papirius Paetus for desiring to retire from public office, he says picturesquely, "I was seated on the poop, and held the tiller, but now there is hardly room for me where the bilge-water is."[53]

---

[45] Propertius, *Elegies* IV, 7, 55f., 59f. (Loeb ed. [1929], p. 311).
[46] Cumont (n. 20), pp. 93, k 155.
[47] Horace, *Epistles* II, 2, 199ff.; *Odes* I, 34; II, 10, 1-4.
[48] Seneca, *To Marcia on Consolation* VI, 3; *Epistle* CVIII, 37; Horace, *Odes* IV, 15; Propertius (n. 45), III, 9; Cicero, *In Catilinam* II, 11, 24; *Letter to His Friends* IV, 13, 2; *Philippic* XII, 8, 19; Cicero in Quintilian, *Institutio oratoria* VIII, 6, 47. (Mach [n. 17], p. 231, points out a close parallel in a Midrash of R. Simeon, *Lev. R.* IV, 6, 7e). Cf. Ovid, *Tristes* I, 5, 36.
[49] Terence, *Phormio*, 688f.; Seneca, *Epistle* XVI, 3. These themes also appear in Roman art; see F. J. Dölger, IXΘYΣ, V (1932-43), 133f., 475f.; Eitrem (n. 39), p. 8; cf. Petronius, *Satyricon*, 71.
[50] Apuleius, *De mundo*, 35.
[51] Cf. the double meaning of the word *gubernator:* "a helmsman," and "a ruler," "a governor."
[52] Cicero, *Against Piso*, 20; cf. *The Republic* I, 40, 63; *Epistulae ad Familiares* XII, 25a, 5; *Letters to Atticus* II, 7; IV, 19 [18]; *De Oratore* I, 11, 46; *Pro Sexto Roscio Amerina* XVIII, 51.
[53] Cicero, *Epistulae ad Familiares* IX, 15, 3 (Loeb ed., II [1928], 235).

Probably the best-known example of the ship as the state is the ode of Horace where the figure is fully developed together with the stormy sea as a world of trouble threatening the Roman state:

> O ship, new billows threaten to bear thee out to sea again. Beware! Haste valiantly to reach the haven! Seest thou not how thy bulwarks are bereft of oars, how thy shattered mast and yards are creaking in the driving gale, and how thy hull without a girding-rope can scarce withstand the over-mastering sea? . . ."[54]

Quintilian cites this poem as an example of allegory, explaining it as "the ode, in which Horace represents the state under the semblance of a ship, the civil wars as tempests, and peace and good-will as the haven."[55]

The anchor is a familiar figure on early Christian tombs, where in many cases it is doubtless a symbol of hope (cf. Hebrews 6 : 19). Dölger has given five instances of its presence on apparently pagan graves.[56] If the symbolism there can be related to the notion of the ship as the course of life, the anchor could imply the successful and peaceful completion of life's journey and arrival in the desired haven of the hereafter.

In almost every development of the ship as a symbol, Roman literature and art copied the Greeks. This demonstrates the vitality, popularity, and widespread use of that figure to represent the two basic ideas of the voyage of the soul to the hereafter and the course of human life, with its corollary of the ship of state. All of these notions appear to be important for the interpretation of the ship in early Christian literature and art.

---

[54] Horace (n. 48), I, 14 (Loeb ed. I [10th ed., 1934], 43); cf. Livy, *Ab urbe condita* XXIV, 7, 12.
[55] Quintilian (n. 48), VIII, 6, 44 (Loeb ed., III [1921], 327).
[56] Dölger (n. 49), II, 399-401; III, Pl XXXIX, 3.

CHAPTER III

HEBREW AND JEWISH BACKGROUNDS

The ship as a figure in the Old Testament

Nautical symbolism is rare in the Old Testament. When it appears, virtually never does it follow patterns familiar to Egyptian, Mesopotamian, and classical literature and art. Israel was essentially a people of the land. Its traditions were those of the desert and the hill-country. Palestine had no waterways – the Old Testament never speaks of a boat on the Jordan –, and the sea was a foreign element. The Israelite was at home only when his feet were on dry ground.[1] When the ship does appear as a figure, it is usually connected with foreign, and often unfriendly powers.

The earliest instance of such an implication is in the Song of Deborah (Judges 5 : 17). Recounting the activities of the various tribes during the battle with Sisera, the poet asks, "And Dan, why did he abide (יגור) with the ships?" Here a land-locked tribe (Northern Dan, as associated with Asher, Zebulon, and Naphtali, vs. 17f.) is specifically characterized by ships. Budde, following Studer, points out that the verb גור means basically, "to sojourn," and suggests that the passage refers to Danites' having taken employment on Phoenician ships.[2] Such economic dependence on Phoenicia could have made them reticent to join the other tribes against the Canaanites. If this interpretation is correct, the ship represents a foreign element in Israel's life, which hindered a part of her people from performing their duty to the nation.

A similar theme appears in connection with the "ships of Tarshish."[3] Jehoshaphat's unsuccessful attempt to revive Solomon's

---

[1] In referring to the various miraculous passages of Israelites through water, it is almost always stated specifically that they passed through on *dry ground* (חרבה: Ex. 14: 21; Josh. 3 : 17; 2 Kings 2 : 8; יבשה: Ex. 14: 16, 22, 29; 15 : 19; Josh. 4 : 22; Neh. 9 : 11; Ps. 66 : 6; cf. Heb. 11 : 29).

[2] K. Budde, *Das Buch der Richter* (1897), p. 46.

[3] The term תרשיש (אניות or) אני, "Tarshish-ships," seems to refer to a ship engaged in the metal trade, rather than to vessels that necessarily always went to the port of Tarshish; Albright, "New Light on Early History of Phoenician Colonization," *Bull. Am. Sch. Or. Res.*, 83 (Oct., 1941), pp. 21f.

trade on the Red Sea by building "Tarshish-ships" is merely recorded in 1 Kings 22 : 48f. in connection with the statement that Edom (and so the port of Ezion-geber) was now a dependency of Judah, but 2 Chronicles 20 : 35-37 interprets the foundering of the fleet as a divine judgment because the project was undertaken in partnership with Ahaziah of Israel, "who did wickedly."[4] Here the ship is a figure of unholy partnership with Yahweh's enemy, and its destruction signalizes his displeasure with such an alliance. Ps. 48 : 7, where Yahweh destroys "Tarshish-ships" by the east wind, may also be an allusion from a similar point of view to the destruction of Jehoshaphat's fleet.

Speaking probably toward the end of Uzziah's reign, when Judah had become wealthy through the re-establishment of the copper trade from the gulf of Aqabah (Elath, 2 Kings 14 : 22; 2 Chr. 26 : 2),[5] Isaiah announces that because, among other acts of wickedness, the people of Judah "strike hands with foreigners" (2 : 6),[6] Yahweh has rejected them. Then he continues (vs. 12, 16): "For the Lord of hosts has a day... against all the ships of Tarshish." Similarly, when Jonah desires to flee "from the presence of the Lord" (Jonah 1 : 3), he boards "a ship going to Tarshish."

The "Oracle concerning Tyre" in Isa. 23 begins with the words, "Wail, O ships of Tarshish." As one of the most characteristic features of Phoenician civilization, the "Tarshish-ship" stands here almost as a figure for that civilization itself, against which Yahweh's judgments are levelled. Similarly in Eze. 27 : 4-9a, 25b-36, the figure of a Phoenician merchant ship is specifically applied to Tyre. Here the ship symbol is more fully elaborated than anywhere else in the Old Testament. The international character of Tyrian trade is indicated by the materials of which the ship is constructed. The wreck of the ship symbolizes the destruction of Tyre. Although here the ship represents a city-state, this symbolism can scarcely be connected with the similar figure in Greek literature. The latter is related to the companionship of sailors, whereas the figure here derives from the fact

---

[4] For differing views on the relationships between the stories in Kings and Chronicles, see I. Benzinger, *Die Bücher der Könige* (1899), p. 126; W. Rudolph, *Die Chronikbücher* (1955), p. 263.

[5] N. Glueck, *Bull. Am. Sch. Or. Res.*, 72 (Dec., 1938), pp. 6-8; 79 (Oct., 1940), pp. 12f.

[6] Reading, as Kittel suggests, ובידי נכרים ישפיקו for MT ובילדי נכרים ישפיקו.

that the merchant ship was a particular characteristic of Tyrian economy and culture.[7]

In Isaiah 60 : 9 "Tarshish-ships" are the vehicles by which Israel is to be gathered to restored and glorified Jerusalem. The whole picture of the returning dispersion is condensed in the figure of these ships with their people and cargo.[8] Elsewhere a symbol of Gentile prosperity by which Israel might easily be ensnared, here "Tarshish-ships" are a figure of that same wealth as it flows into the coffers of the Chosen People (vs. 11, 16).

In other passages the ship is placed in an eschatological setting, representing punishment and oppression at the hands of enemies. Thus in Isa. 33 : 21, future peace and freedom from foreign oppression are symbolized by the absence of galleys and other foreign ships.[9]

Similarly, among the catastrophes to overtake Israel if she is disobedient, is that "the Lord will bring you back in ships to Egypt," (Deut. 28 : 68). Ships here seem specifically to be vehicles of captivity. Israel had not left Egypt by ship, and the threat that she might return by that means implies that she would not go of her own will, but would be transported by foreigners.[10]

In the same vein are references to the "ships of Kittim" (Num. 24 : 24; Dan. 11 : 30). Since in 1 Macc. 1 : 1; 8 : 5; Jubilees 24 : 28-29, the Kittim are the Macedonians, their mention in Numbers, where their ships "shall afflict Asshur and Eber," probably points to the conquest of the Persian Empire by Alexander.[11] In Dan. 11 : 30,

---

[7] Cf. the figure of a ship on ancient Phoenician and modern Lebanese coins (for a general discussion of the ship on ancient coins, see K. Regling in Fr. Frhr. von Schröter, *Wörterbuch der Münzkunde* [1930], pp. 595f.; and the ivory relief of a ship with Isis as a symbol of Alexandria on the ambo of Henry II in the cathedral at Aix-la-Chapelle (cited by H. Rahner, "Antenna Crucis III," *Zeitschr. f. kath. Theol.*, 66 [1942], p. 214, n. 70).

[8] P. Volz, *Jesaia II* (1932), p. 246.

[9] צי (elsewhere only in Num. 24 : 24; Eze. 30 : 9; Dan. 11 : 30; always of foreign ships; cf. Egyptian $ḏ3i$, "to ferry across") probably sharpens the implication that the ships in question are foreign.

[10] Eze. 30 : 9 and Isa. 43 : 14 may also present the ship as a figure of terror and captivity (cf. J. Herrmann, *Ezekiel* [1924], p. 189; Volz [n. 8], p. 42), but in both cases the text is uncertain.

[11] In Ezra 6 : 22, אשור is Persia; J. A. Montgomery, *The Book of Daniel* (1950), p. 455, and R. H. Pfeiffer, *Introduction to the Old Testament* (1948), pp. 277f. suggest that עבר may be עבר הנהר, "beyond the river," i.e., the country west of the Euphrates (Neh. 2 : 7); thus the two terms would represent the limits of the Persian Empire.

however, the "ships of Kittim" are clearly the Romans, who in the person of C. Popilius Laenas halted Antiochus Epiphanes, the "king of the north," in his campaign against Egypt in 168 B.C. In both instances these ships (צִיִּים, foreign ships [9]) connote invading peoples from across the Mediterranean, whose action is significant for sacred history.

The lyric and wisdom literature employs the figure of the ship quite differently from other Old Testament passages. Here, in harmony with the literary forms involved, the ship is seen as an object in nature. This provides the basis for its figurative use.

In Ps. 104 : 26, the ship is conceived as a creature of God and a denizen of the deep, testifying to his wisdom as creator: "There go the ships, and Leviathan which thou didst form to sport in it."[12] A similar feeling of awe and mystery attaches to the ship in one of the "numerical" proverbs of "Agur the son of Jakeh" (Prov. 30 : 19; cf. Wisdom 14 : 1-7). Of the natural phenomena he does not understand, one is "the way of a ship on the high seas." Here the association of the ship on a parallel basis with natural creatures is similar to Ps. 104 : 26. Such an attitude may be associated with the widespread custom of shaping a ship's prow in the form of an animal.

In Ps. 107 : 23f. the sea itself, rather than the ship, excites wonder: "Some went down to the sea in ships, ... they saw the deeds of the Lord, his wondrous works in the deep." In the succeeding verses (25-32) this thought is developed through the picture of storm, in which the sailors "reeled and staggered like drunken men," and yet after the hurricane are brought "to their desired haven." In all this is revealed the steadfast love of Yahweh. Here are a number of themes associated with the ship especially in Greek literature: seafaring as an experience combining great danger with awesome adventure,[13] the divine protection of ships, and the "desired haven" as the successful end of the voyage.[14] The present context emphasizes the theme of divine protection, for the sailors are one in a series of groups who

---

[12] A number of emendations have been proposed for אֳנִיּוֹת, "ships," in this passage, perhaps because a ship is hardly a creature of God. However, the poet is concerned with the wonders of the sea as seen in its inhabitants, and, poetically, he classes the ship as one of these along with the Leviathan.

[13] Rahner (n. 7), 66 (1942), pp. 206-210, sees this theme as "die Urform nautischer Symbolik," and derives from it the symbolisms, ship = state, ship = soul, ship = world.

[14] On this theme in classical and patristic literature, see especially C. Bonner, "Desired Haven," *Harv. Theol. Rev.*, 34 (1941), pp. 49-67.

have been delivered from danger by Yahweh (cf. vs. 4-22).[15] However, the nautical themes found here are not necessarily drawn from other literatures, but may be simply the reaction of any pious person to the experience of a storm at sea.

Two other figurative uses of the ship appear in the Proverbs. In ch. 23 : 34, a drunken man is like a man aboard ship tossed by the waves of the sea.[16] In ch. 31 : 14, the efficient housewife, like a merchant ship, is ready to travel far and wide to obtain necessities for her family.[17]

The figure of the pilot seems to lie behind the word תחבלות "guidance, direction, counsel," which appears in the Old Testament only in the wisdom literature (Job 37: 12; Prov. 1 : 5; 11 : 14; 12 : 5; 20 : 18; 24 : 6). Probably derived from חבל, "to bind," and related to חֶבֶל, "a rope," חֹבֵל "a sailor" (i.e., one who handles the rope), and חִבֵּל, probably "a mast," this word seems originally to have referred to rope-pulling in steering a ship.[18] Of the three times that the LXX translate it as κυβέρνησις (Prov. 1 : 5; 11 : 14; 24 : 6), two are concerned with the governing of a nation. Prov. 11 : 14a reads, "Where there is no guidance (תחבלות), a people falls," and Prov. 24 : 6a declares, "For by wise guidance (תחבלות) you can wage your war." It cannot be insisted that the figure ship = nation was consciously in the writer's mind here, for this word was clearly used for "guidance," without regard for its derivation, just as "governing" today rarely brings up the picture of a pilot, with which it originally was connected. Nevertheless, these two verses constitute analogies to numerous passages in Greek literature in which the head of a state is referred to as a κυβερνήτης.

Finally, in Job 9 : 25f., the ship illustrates the passage of human life: "My days are swifter than a runner... They go by like skiffs of reed." In the similar classical figure, the ship is life because it portrays life's varying fortunes; but here the simile derives from

---

[15] H. Schmidt, *Die Psalmen* (1934), p. 197.
[16] B. Gemser, *Sprüche Salomos* (1937), p. 68.
[17] G. Wildeboer, *Die Sprüche* (1897), p. 91. Cf. a Midrash on Gen. 20 : 17 cited by R. Mach, *Der Zaddik* (1957), pp. 240f. from *Pesiqta de-Rab Kahana* XLII, 177a, in which Sarah and the wife of Abimelech, who were barren, are compared to ships taken from their owners and commandeered for the king's service.
[18] W. Zimmerli, "Zur Struktur der alttestamentlichen Weisheit," *Zeitschr. f. at. Wiss.*, 51 (1933), p. 183, n. 2.

the swiftness of the "skiffs of reed," representing the rapidity with which life passes.[19]

The ship as a figure in Jewish-Hellenism

In Jewish-Hellenistic literature and art, the themes connected with the ship are not those typical of the Old Testament. Instead we have characteristic classical symbolism, overlayed with Jewish piety. Thus Sirach 33 : 2 presents the storm-tossed ship as the soul unfaithful to the Law. *The Letter of Aristeas*, 251, employs the classical figures of the ship as life, the port as the hereafter, and the pilot as God. Similarly, in Wisdom 5 : 10, 13, the sailing ship is the course of human life.

A variation on this theme appears in *4 Macc.* 7 : 1-3, where the steadfast soul, sailing in the ship of religion, through storms of emotion, reaches the desired haven of immortality. Here the rudder also is a symbol of religion, for from the standpoint of the pilot, the rudder is equivalent to the ship.

Philo frequently uses the figure of the ship as the human life, with minor variations to emphasize his characteristic principle that life must be dominated by reason. He declares:

> A ship, again, keeps to her straight course, when the helmsman grasping the tiller steers accordingly, but capsizes when a contrary wind has sprung up over the sea, and the surge has settled in it. Just so, when Mind, the charioteer or helmsman of the soul, rules the whole living being as a governor does a city, the life holds a straight course, but when irrational sense gains the chief place, a terrible confusion overtakes it.[20]

Here the ship is the "soul" (ψυχή), the "whole living being" (ζῷον ὅλον), and the "life" (βίος).[21] The use of ἄλογος to describe the "irrational sense" implies that the "helmsman," defined here as the "mind"

---

[19] B. Duhm, *Das Buch Hiob* (1897), p. 55. The LXX base the comparison on the fact that ships leave no track in the sea, which may be nearer to the classical figure (cf. Wisdom 5 : 10, 13).

[20] Philo, *Allegorical Interpretation* III, 224 (Loeb ed., I [1929], 453).

[21] E. R. Goodenough, *Jewish Symbols*, VIII (1958), 160-163, discusses the related figure of Noah's ark and finds that for Philo it symbolizes the human body (*Allegorical Interpretation of Genesis* II, 1-7, 19, 25, 34, 46). He shows that in one passage particularly (*On Dreams* II, 225) the voyage of Noah represents the achievement of "justice" (δικαιοσύνη) in which "God gives to the man the man's own true nature" (p. 161).

(νοῦς), is also the logos. In several other passages Philo uses the figure of the pilot explicitly for the logos, in this sense of the faculty by which man is able to conceive the divine Logos.[22] This latter aspect of Logos, the agency by which the absolutely transcendent God moves upon the world, is referred to by Philo as "the Word which the Helmsman of the Universe grasps as a rudder to guide all things on their course."[23] Here, as in pagan Greek literature, the ship that elsewhere in Philo is the individual life becomes the universe. In another instance, the ship is the empire; speaking of the emperor, he says: "Having taken in hand the rudders, he pilots the common ship of mankind safely."[24]

Josephus also likens God to a pilot directing the ship of the universe. Taking issue with the Epicureans for refusing to believe that the universe is governed (κυβερνᾶσθαι) by God, he argues, "If it were leaderless in this fashion, it would be shattered... just as we see ships go down when they lose their helmsmen."[25]

The *Syriac Apocalypse of Baruch* 85 : 10f., originally a Jewish-Greek document probably from the close of the first Christian century, applies the figure of the ship nearing its port both to the individual soul reaching the end of life, and to the world nearing its consummation. This double symbolism demonstrates the close association of these two ideas.

The comparison of a human being to a ship, and his tribulations and enemies to a storm also appears in the Thanksgiving Psalms from Qumran. The Psalmist complains,

> ... the hordes of the wicked rage against me;
> like ocean gales they storm [26]
> ....
> ... [men] render my life like a ship storm tossed on the deep,

---

[22] Philo, *The Unchangeableness of God*, 129; (n. 20), III, 80, 118; *The Special Laws* IV, 95. Rahner (n. 7), p. 218, points out that Chrysippus the Stoic (in Arnim, *Stoicorum veterum fragmenta*, III, 95, lines 10-12) had already likened the (Stoic) Logos to a pilot.
[23] Philo, *The Migration of Abraham*, 6 (Loeb ed., IV [1932], 135); cf. *On the Cherubim*, 36; *Who is the Heir of Divine Things*, 301.
[24] Philo, *Legation to Gaius*, 50 (Gr. text, Bonner ([n. 14], p. 49, n. 2).
[25] Josephus, *Jewish Antiquities* X, 278f. (Loeb ed., VI [rev. ed., 1951], 312); cf. 3 *Macc.* 6 : 2. As the identical figure in classical literature was found to have a literal parallel in the idea of a god guiding an actual ship, so a similar literal parallel appears in Wisdom 14 : 3, 6.
[26] 1 QH ii, 12, in T. H. Gaster, *The Dead Sea Scriptures* (1956), p. 129.

or like a bastion city beleagured by the [foe].
Yea, I am in distress....[27]

The foregoing passages from Jewish literature suggest interpretations for some of the ships that appear on Hellenized Jewish graves in Palestine and the Diaspora, as cited by Goodenough.

At Marisa, southwest of Jerusalem on the road toward Gaza, a number of Jewish tombs have been found from the period ca. 150 B.C. to ca. A.D. 150. In Tomb I on a door jamb are scratched an eagle, an unfinished deer, the prow of a ship, two unidentified objects, and what are apparently the Seal of Solomon and the Star of David. On the opposite door jamb is a Cerberus and a Greek inscription in four lines, the meaning of which is not clear.[28] This is obviously a highly Hellenized grave. The ship had become such a universally recognized figure for the course of life and its ultimate culmination in the world beyond that the Hellenized Jew could adopt it to represent his own hope in the afterlife without feeling any paganization of his Jewish faith.[29] At the same time, the Cerberus suggests that this ship may be a conveyance of souls to the hereafter, if not indeed Charon's bark. These two symbolisms stand rather distinctly apart in classical literature. Here however, they may blend into the generalized notion of the ship of life bearing the soul through the seas of existence to the haven of the hereafter.

Several ships appear on Jewish graves at Sheikh Ibreiq in western Galilee southeast of Haifa. This is probably Beth She'arim, the central burying place for Jews in Palestine from ca. A.D. 100-ca. 350. In one tomb were found small inlays apparently from a wooden box or coffin. On one of these was a ship, on another a dolphin.[30] The combination of ship and dolphin seems to have particular reference to the arrival of the soul in a fortunate afterlife, as the dolphin was thought to be an omen of good sailing and to carry shipwrecked seamen to land.[31]

From the standpoint of New Testament interpretation, perhaps

---

[27] 1 QH iii, 6ff., in Gaster (n. 26), p. 135.
[28] Goodenough (n. 21), I (1953), 66, 68.
[29] Goodenough (n. 21), II (1953), 43f.
[30] Goodenough (n. 21), I, 167; III (1953), figs. 980, 981; cf. figs. 67, 77, 78.
[31] Other examples of the ship in connection with Jewish graves: 1 Macc. 13 : 27-29; Goodenough (n. 21), I, 155; II, 43, 64; III, 304-306, 836; VIII, 157-159; cf. E. W. Beyer and H. Lietzmann, *Die jüdische Katakombe der Villa Torlonia in Rom* (1930), Pl. 18 d. C. Bonner, "The Ship of the Soul," *Proc. of the Am. Phil. Soc.*, 85 (1941), 90.

the most important instance of the ship symbol in Jewish literature appears in the *Testament of Naphtali*. In the passage in question (ch. 6 : 1-8 : 2), Naphtali recounts a vision regarding the future of Israel:

> VI. And again, after seven days, I saw our father Jacob standing by the sea of Jamnia, and we were with him. 2. And, behold, there came a ship sailing by, without sailors or pilot; and there was written upon the ship, The ship of Jacob. 3. And our father saith to us: Come let us embark on our ship. 4. And when we had gone on board, there arose a vehement storm, and a mighty tempest of wind; and our father, who was holding the helm, departed from us. 5. And we, being tost with the tempest, were borne along over the sea; and the ship was filled with water, (and was) pounded by mighty waves, until it was broken up. 6. And Joseph fled away upon a little boat, and we all were divided upon nine planks, and Levi and Judah were together. 7. And we were all scattered unto the ends of the earth. 8. Then Levi, girt about with sackcloth, prayed for us all unto the Lord. 9. And when the storm ceased, the ship reached the land, as it were in peace. 10. And, lo, our father came, and we all rejoiced with one accord.
>
> VII. These two dreams I told to my father; and he said to me: These things must be fulfilled in their season, after that Israel hath endured many things.
> 2. Then my father saith unto me: I believe God that Joseph liveth, for I see always that the Lord numbereth him with you. 3. And he said, weeping: Ahme, my son, Joseph, thou livest, though I behold thee not, and thou seest not Jacob that begat thee. 4. He caused me also, therefore, to weep by these words, and I burned in my heart to declare that Joseph had been sold, but I feared my brethern.
>
> VIII. And lo! my children, I have shown unto you the last times, how everything shall come to pass in Israel. 2. Do ye also, therefore, charge your children that they be united to Levi and to Judah;
> For through them shall salvation arise unto Israel,
> And in them shall Jacob be blessed.[32]

Here the main symbols are clear. The ship is identified as "the ship of Jacob," which can only mean that it represents the Israelite (and/or Jewish) nation.[33] The great storm must be a time of trouble for the nation, and the break-up of the ship, national disaster. These figures are familiar in classical literature. The words "we were all

---

[32] R. H. Charles, *The Testaments of the Twelve Patriarchs Translated* (1908), pp. 144-146.
[33] P. Riessler, *Altjüdisches Schrifttum ausserhalb der Bibel* (1928), p. 1337; E. Peterson, "Das Schiff als Symbol der Kirche," *Theol. Zeitschr.*, 6 (1950), p. 78; Goodenough (n. 21), VIII, p. 164.

scattered unto the ends of the earth" indicate the dispersion of Israel. Though broken up at sea, in 6 : 9 the ship is again afloat and reaches land in peace. This, together with the return of Jacob and the reunion of the brothers, represents the final gathering of Israel. In view of 7 : 1 and 8 : 1, at least the climax of the vision has eschatological import.

The Testaments of the Twelve Patriarchs have been assigned widely varying dates, ranging from the end of the third century B.C.[34] to the latter second century after Christ.[35] There is no general agreement regarding the relation of their Jewish and Christian elements. In 1953 M. de Jonge saw them as a Jewish-Christian composition based on Jewish materials and traditions.[36] Subsequently he has modified his position, suggesting that the Christian writer(s) "may have been only the last of a series of collectors and redactors of Testament material,"[37] and that while the Testaments may not have been composed by a Christian author, they "underwent at any rate a thoroughgoing Christian redaction."[38] A. S. van der Woude identifies them as originally a Jewish document that has been rewritten and abbreviated, probably by a Jew and then interpolated by a Christian.[39] F. M. Braun holds that they were written originally by a Jew on the basis of diverse Jewish documents and traditions, and were edited later by a Christian.[40] Quite differently, M. Philonenko attributes them almost entirely to the Qumran sect.[41]

[34] E. Meyer, *Ursprung des Christentums*, II (1925), 44, recognizes that they contain Christian additions, "but the kernel goes back into pre-Seleucid times, since the additions, which, in contrast to the original tendency, speak of the sin of the priests, stem from this particular time."

[35] M. de Jonge, "The Testaments of the Twelve Patriarchs and the New Testament," in K. Aland et al., eds., *Studia Evangelica* (1959), p. 556. For surveys of the history of the criticism of the Testaments, see E. Kautzsch, *Die Apokryphen und Pseudepigraphen* (1900), II, 458-460; Charles (n. 32), pp. xxxviii-xli; G. Resch, "Das hebraische Testamentum Naphtali," *Stud. und Krit.* (1899), pp. 207f. De Jonge, *The Testaments of the Twelve Patriarchs* (1953).

[36] M. de Jonge, *The Testaments of the Twelve Patriarchs* (1953). This was seconded by J. T. Milik in *Rev. Bibl.*, 62 (1955), p. 298.

[37] M. de Jonge, "The Testaments of the Twelve Patriarchs and the New Testament" (n. 35), p. 550.

[38] M. de Jonge, "Christian Influence in the Testaments of the Twelve Patriarchs," *Nov. Test.* 4 (1960), p. 197.

[39] A. S. van der Woude, *Die messianischen Vorstellungen der Gemeinde von Qumran* (1957), pp. 190-216.

[40] F. M. Braun, "Les Testaments des XII Patriarches et le problème de leur origine," *Rev. Bibl.*, 67 (1960), pp. 516-549.

[41] M. Philonenko, *Les interpolations chrétiennes des Testaments des Douze Patri-*

Regardless of these differing views, it is now possible to show that the vision in *T. Naph.* 6 belongs to the Jewish, rather than to the Christian elements in the Testaments. In 1894, M. Gaster published a Hebrew text of *T. Naph.* found in the *Chronicle of Jerachme'el*, a medieval composition containing a number of older Jewish legends.[42] This Hebrew testament shows a number of parallels with the Greek *T. Naph.* Gaster held the Hebrew to be the original, and the Greek to be a recension of it. With the exception of Resch,[43] no other scholar has accepted this view.[44] But neither can the Hebrew text be thought to rest directly on the Greek, for there is little verbal agreement between the two, and each contains much material not found in the other.[45] Consequently it is necessary to postulate the existence of an original document upon which the authors of each text drew for general framework and some materials.[46]

The problem stood at this point when in 1956 J. T. Milik announced the discovery at Qumran of a well-preserved fragment from Cave IV of a *T. Naph.* in Hebrew.[47] This document has no relationship to the Hebrew *T. Naph.* published by Gaster. The text contained on the Qumran fragment recounts the genealogy of Bilha, corresponding to the Greek *T. Naph.* 1 : 6-12. The new Hebrew text, however, is much longer.

Although it is impossible at present to reach final conclusions on the relationship of the Qumran *T. Naph.* to the Greek and the previously discovered Hebrew texts, the new text may represent the *Vorlage* of the other two, or at least may lie somewhere in their literary

---

arches et les manuscrits de Qoumrân (Cahiers de la Rev. d'Hist. et de Phil. Rel., No. 35 [1960]). This view was first proposed by A. Dupont-Sommer, *Aperçus préliminaires sur les manuscrits de la mer Morte* (1950), p. 116.

[42] The Hebrew text is found in R. H. Charles, *The Greek Versions of the Testaments of the Twelve Patriarchs* (1908), App. II, pp. 239ff.; English translation in *Apocrypha and Pseudepigrapha*, II, 361-363.

[43] Resch (n. 35), pp. 206-236.

[44] Charles (n. 32), pp. lxviif.

[45] De Jonge (n. 36), p. 53.

[46] Peterson (n. 33), pp. 77-79, thinks of a Jewish apocalyptic book in which the salvation of the ship of Israel is accomplished by the prayers of the saints, as lying behind *T. Naph.* 6; Tertullian, *On Baptism*, 12; Clement of Alex., *Who is the Rich Man that Is Saved?* 34, 3; and Pseudo-Clement, *Epistle to James*, 314f.

[47] J. T. Milik, "Prière de 'Nabonide' et autres écrits d'un cycle de Daniel," *Rev. Bibl.*, 63 (1956), p. 407, n. 1; cf. idem, *Dix ans de découvertes dans le désert de Juda* (1957), p. 32. This fragment was acquired in 1955. Three little pieces of the same work had already been obtained in 1952. None of these has yet been published.

ancestry.[48] Although the fragment recently discovered apparently does not contain the vision with which we are concerned, it does prove the existence of an undeniably Jewish *T. Naph.* in Palestine at least as early as the first century of the Christian era. The fact that both the Greek and the Hebrew Testaments contain this vision makes virtually certain that their common Jewish ancestor also included it. Therefore it seems reasonably sure that this vision of the ship of Israel beset by storm was known in Palestinian Jewish circles at the time of the writing of the New Testament, and possibly much earlier.

But what does the figure of Joseph represent, who in the midst of the storm flees away in a little boat? In the Testaments as they now stand, no one interpretation of Joseph throughout is possible.[49] Often he is held forth as a model of chastity and brotherly kindness, and in some of these instances he may represent nothing more than this. Elsewhere, in passages that are either Christian interpolations or transformations, he is a figure of Christ.[50] But neither of these alternatives offers a possible interpretation of Joseph in *T. Naph.* Here, in both visions, he represents a part of Israel that separates from the main body: in the first vision he mounts a bull and ascends into the sky; in the second, he takes to a little boat and leaves his brethren in the storm. At the end Jacob declares his conviction that Joseph still lives and that God counts him with the children of Israel. Reicke has suggested that the figure of Joseph may be explained as

---

[48] Other evidence for Semitic documents lying behind the Greek Testaments was provided by the discovery among the Cairo Genizah documents now in the Cambridge University Library of two Aramaic fragments that parallel parts of *T. Levi* (published by H. L. Pass and J. Arendzen, "Fragment of an Aramaic Text of the Testament of Levi," *Jewish Quart. Rev.*, 12 [1900], pp. 651-661; cf. de Jonge [n. 36], pp. 129-131). Further fragments of this Aramaic testament have been discovered in Caves I and IV at Qumran, (D. Barthélemy and J. T. Milik, *Discoveries in the Judean Desert I, Qumran Cave I* [1955], pp. 87-91; Milik, "Le Testament de Lévi en Araméen," *Rev. Bibl.* 62 [1955], pp. 398-406). Milik concludes that the *Testament of Levi* and *Naphtali* found at Qumran were used by a Christian author as sources and as models for the composition of the other Testaments as they exist in the Greek text (ibid., 62 [1955], p. 406; 63 [1956], p. 407, n. 1); cf. de Jonge [n. 36], p. 118; [n. 37], p. 552).
[49] De Jonge (n. 36), pp. 55-57; idem (n. 38), pp. 196f.; Philonenko (n. 41), pp. 55-58.
[50] *T. Zeb.* 3 : 2; 4 : 4, 10; *T. Gad* 2 : 3; *T. Benj.* 3 : 8; *T. Jos.* 17 : 8; cf. De Jonge (n. 36), pp. 98ff.; B. Reicke, *Glaube und Leben der Urgemeinde* (1957), p. 141, points out that this theme is found also in Tertullian, *Adv. Marc.*, III, 18; Ambrose, *De Jos. patr.*, 14.

representing Hellenistic Judaism.[51] Joseph is connected inevitably with Egypt,[52] the center of Jewish Hellenism. Stephen, a leader of the Hellenists in the early church at Jerusalem, in his defense before the Sanhedrin emphasizes the story of Joseph and refers to the patriarchs' showing jealousy toward him (ζηλώσαντες τόν 'Ιωσήφ, Acts 7 : 9). This seems to reflect the hatred of the Zealots for Hellenistic Jews in general, and in particular, the uprising of Jews especially zealous for the Temple and Mosaic traditions, against the Hellenist Stephen. The fact that Joseph fed his brethren may also be connected with the special concern of the Hellenists in the Jerusalem church for the material welfare of the group, as evidenced by the Seven. In a number of passages in the Testaments Joseph seems to typify Christ. This symbolism probably derives from Alexandrian Judaism, where the figure of Wisdom is associated with Joseph (Wisdom 10 : 13f.). Some of these apparently Christological passages (*T. Zeb.* 4, 5; *T. Jos.* 1-17; possibly also *T. Sim.* 4 : 2-5; 8 : 3-4; *T. Levi* 13 : 9; *T. Gad* 1 : 4-9), in a possible pre-Christian form of the Testaments may have implied Hellenistic Judaism as characterized by Wisdom. So understood, the Testaments would present an apology for Hellenism, in the sense of a syncretistic Judaism that stood apart from the official religion. This would be quite in harmony with the close relations that exist between the Testaments and the Qumran literature, and the evidence, as Cullmann has shown, of a connection between the milieu represented by Qumran (and the Testaments) and the Hellenists of the early church.[53] If these identifications and connections are valid, the little boat in which Joseph escapes from the wreckage of "the ship of Jacob" would seem to represent a **religious movement** derived from but not entirely parallel with the official religion of the Jewish nation.

This vision of the ship in *T. Naph.* appears to be of particular significance for our study, since the ship in storm as a symbol for Israel in the tribulation of the "last times" seems to have had direct contacts with a milieu that had much in common with the circles in which the New Testament arose.[54]

---

[51] Reicke (n. 50), pp. 141f.
[52] Cf. *T. Jos.* 20 : 6 (Charles, *Apocrypha and Pseudepigrapha*, II, 354): "For he [Joseph] felt even for the Egyptians as though a member (of their nation)."
[53] O. Cullmann, "The Significance of the Qumran Texts for Research into the Beginnings of Christianity," *Journ. of Bibl. Lit.*, 74 (1955), pp. 213-226.
[54] Goodenough (n. 21), VIII, 164, while concerned with Christian ship symbolism in patristic literature rather than in the New Testament, says of T. Naph. 6:

The ship stands for the Jewish nation also in *4 Ezra* 12 : 42, where the people are portrayed as saying to Ezra:

> For of all the prophets thou alone art left to us,
> as a cluster out of the vintage,
> as a lamp in a dark place,
> as a haven of safety for a ship in a storm.[55]

Most of the meanings of the ship symbol that we have noted thus far in Jewish literature reappear in the Talmud and the Midrash. A number of examples have been collected by Mach:[56] the voyaging of a ship is used as an illustration of the fate that attends the course of human life, with its safe return to its home port as man's departure from this world;[57] the concentration and skill of a successful pilot is an example of the deliberation required of a man to overcome temptation;[58] the ship is employed repeatedly as a figure for Israel;[59] the ship is a symbol of the nations of the Gentiles: as it is built of many kinds of wood, so the Gentiles are composed of many peoples;[60] finally, the ship is a symbol of the world.[61]

These rabbinical uses illustrate how the various implications of the ship symbol known to Judaism before the end of the first Christian century lived on in classical Jewish literature. In this sense they provide a parallel to the history of the same symbol in early Christianity.

"It seems highly probable that in this dream we have the Jewish original of the Christian ship which was the Church."
[55] Charles (n. 52), II, 615. The Latin text of 12 : 42 is obviously corrupt: "sicut portus navis salvatae a tempestate." Charles' emendation of *navis* to *navi* is based on the Syriac and first Arabic versions.
[56] Mach (n. 17), pp. 223-241.
[57] *Midrash Tanhuma* (S. Buber, ed.,), *Wayyahel* 1 (Mach [n. 17], p. 236); cf. *Ex. R.* XLVIII, 1, 78a; *Eccl. R.* VII, 1, 18a, (Mach, *op. cit.*, pp. 235, n. 7; 236; Goodenough [n. 21], VIII, 164).
[58] *Pesiqta de-Rab Kahana* XXVII, 176a; *Lev. R.* XXI, 5, 30a (Mach [n. 17], p. 235).
[59] Mach (n. 17), pp. 230f. cites a number of instances in which this figure appears: *Deut. R.* XI, 3, 118d; *Yalqut Deut.* 33, sec. 951; *Pesiqta Rabbathi* XLVII, 191a; *Siphre Deut.*, sec. 346; *Num. R.* XV, 18, 676; *Midrash Tanhuma behaaloteha* 11. See also Goodenough (n. 21), VIII, 164f.
[60] *Midrash ha-Gadol Genesis* 36, 39, (similar, but shorter, *Rab.* LXXXIII, 996f.) quoted by Mach (n. 17), p. 231, n. 3.
[61] *Babylonian Talmud, Baba Bathra* 91 a-b, (Mach [n. 17], p. 225). See also *Gen. R.* XII, 12, 110f., where God's creation of the world is compared to the building of a ship (Mach [n. 17], pp. 226f.).

CHAPTER IV

SUMMARY OF BACKGROUNDS:
THE SHIP AS A FIGURE IN THE HELLENISTIC WORLD

Recognizing the artificiality of the subject divisions – Greek, Latin, Jewish – that we have employed, we shall now summarize the evidence for the symbolism of the ship in the Mediterranean world from the fourth century B.C. onward. Every use made of the ship symbol by classical writers and orators was taken up and echoed by Hellenistic authors, so that in surveying the use of our symbol by the latter, we are in fact summarizing it for the whole of Graeco-Roman literature.

The evidence for the ship symbol in Palestine is not abundant, yet every one of the leading motifs connected with it in Graeco-Roman literature and art appears in Palestinian Judaism before or contemporary with the writing of the New Testament. The ship as a human life or soul is used in Sirach 33 : 2, in the second century B.C. The closely related figure of the ship nearing its port as both life and world nearing their end appears in the *Syriac Apocalypse of Baruch* 85 : 10f., perhaps of Palestinian origin and probably from the first century of the Christian era. What is perhaps a combination of this figure with the ship of Charon, representing the arrival of the soul in the hereafter, is found on a grave at Marisa from a date between the middle of the second century B.C. and the second Christian century. From sometime before A.D. 70, and perhaps much earlier, the *Testament of Naphtali* 6 : 1-8 : 2 presents a strikingly developed example of the ship in storm as the Jewish nation in the eschatological time of trouble. The passage in which this occurs was probably current in Palestinian circles not unrelated to those from which the earliest Christian literature sprang. A further testimony to the ship as a symbol for the Jewish nation is provided by *4 Ezra* 12 : 42, probably from the first Christian century and possibly from Palestine.

Thus in Palestinian Jewish literature and art from the second century B.C. through the first century of our era, the themes of ship = life, ship = nation, ship = world, and the ship as a conveyance to the hereafter probably all appear.

Alexandrian Judaism provides a number of instances of the ship symbol. In the *Letter of Aristeas*, 251, probably from the second century B.C., the ship represents human life, the port is the hereafter, and the pilot is God. Sometime within the next two centuries the Wisdom of Solomon 5 : 10, employs the figure of the ship in the same way. For Philo, a contemporary of Jesus, the ship was soul and life, the pilot was mind and Logos: he also applied the ship symbol to the empire and the universe. *Fourth Maccabees* 7 : 1-3, probably from the first Christian century and assigned variously to Alexandria, Jerusalem, and Antioch,[1] makes a typically Jewish application of the ship symbol as the pious soul, while the port is immortality.

Also in Egypt the old ideas of the ship in connection with the dead continued to live, as witnessed by Diodorus' reference to the use of a ship in funeral ceremonies. How far the ship was still associated with the afterlife in terms of the sun-ship is difficult to determine; while something like this seems to have survived in Hellenistic syncretism, it appears to have had little or no influence on Jewish literature.[2]

In the pagan literature of the Graeco-Roman world, the typical classical usages of our symbol appear in widely separated places. In the second century of our era, Lucian of Samosata in upper Mesopotamia and Apuleius at Carthage give almost identical pictures of Charon and of God (Zeus) guiding the world as a pilot does a ship; while at the beginning of the previous century, Ovid, exiled to Pontus near the mouth of the Danube, had written of the shipwreck of his life.

For the most part, however, our examples of the ship symbol during this period come from Greece and Rome. In the second century B.C., Polybius, in Achaea, used the idea of shipwreck to represent both personal disaster and the downfall of the state. Early in the second century after Christ, Plutarch, in Chaeronea, employed similar figures, with the ship as the body, which might be abandoned, and the harbor as the hereafter; he also refers to the state as a ship.

Rome is the source of our largest group of examples of the ship as a symbol. In the second pre-Christian century, Terence referred to personal disaster as shipwreck. In the following century Cicero used the same figure; Horace spoke of life as a voyage, and they both employed the figure of the ship as the state. At the turn of the era Livy wrote of the state as a ship with the pilot as its ruler. Later in the

---

[1] M. Hadas, *The Third and Fourth Books of Maccabees* (Dropsie College ed., 1953), pp. 95-100, 109-113.
[2] E. R. Goodenough, *Jewish Symbols*, II (1953), 275.

first century Seneca employed the familiar figure of shipwreck to personal disaster, and referred to philosophy as a pilot. The ship of the dead, commanded by Charon, is described in succeeding centuries by Virgil, Seneca, and Juvenal, and in the first century B.C. Propertius presented a happier kind of ship of the dead that bore its passengers to the Elysian Fields.

Thus in the chief literary centers of the Graeco-Roman world – Rome, Greece, and Alexandria – the characteristic motifs connected with the ship symbol were well represented. These all made their impact sooner or later on the Christian symbol of the ship as the church: the church as the bearer of the soul through the storms of life and to the harbor of Paradise, the church in contrast to the ship of state, and the church as comprehending the whole world. But for the New Testament, the appearances of this symbol in Palestine are of particular importance, both because of close historical relationships and because the Jewish figure of the ship most nearly coincides with the earliest Christian symbolism.

In the table that follows are brought together some writers of the Hellenistic period who use the ship symbol, together with the various applications they make. This table is not exhaustive, but rather illustrative of the geographic and semantic spread of our symbol.

DISTRIBUTION AND MEANINGS OF THE SHIP SYMBOL IN THE GRAECO-ROMAN WORLD

Symbolism	Palestine	Egypt	Greece	Rome	Other
Ship as transport to afterlife	Grave inscriptions at Marisa	Diodorus (?)		Virgil Propertius Seneca Juvenal	Lucian (Mesop.) Apuleius (N.Afr.)
Ship as life or soul	Sirach *Hodayoth* *Apoc. Bar.*	*Aristeas* Wisdom Philo	Polybius Plutarch	Terence Cicero Horace Seneca	Ovid (Pontus)
Ship as state or nation	*T. Naphtali* *4 Ezra*	Philo	Polybius Plutarch	Cicero Horace Livy	
Ship as world or universe	*Apoc. Bar.*	Philo		Josephus	Lucian (Mesop.) Apuleius (N.Afr.)

EXCURSUS

THE SYMBOLISM OF THE SEA IN PRE-CHRISTIAN LITERATURE

The figure of the sea is particularly important in interpreting the ship symbol in early Christianity. It has often been studied in detail;[1] here we can trace only its general outlines.

Basic to an understanding of the sea in ancient thought is the notion that the world has arisen from it. A classic expression of this is the Babylonian Creation Epic, where Tiâmat, the mother-godess, represents the sea. When she seeks to destroy the gods, their leader, Marduk, kills her and then proceeds to create heaven, earth, and mankind.[2] Here the sea is at once an element inimical to the forces of creation and order, and yet the element from which all else is derived. These two notions, **evil element** and **primal element**, are the leading motifs in virtually all ancient symbolism of the sea.[3]

In our discussion of the ship in the Old Testament, we have already referred to the characteristic antipathy of the Hebrew toward the sea. Gunkel's thesis that the myth of a struggle between Yahweh and a sea monster is implicit in many Old Testament figures of speech[4] has been clearly demonstrated by the texts discovered at Ugarit.[5]

---

[1] See especially P. Reymond, *L'eau, sa vie, et sa signification dans l'Ancien Testament* (Suppl. to *Vet. Test.*, Vol. VI [1958]); O. Kaiser, *Die mythische Bedeutung des Meeres in Ägypten, Ugarit und Israel* (Beih. zur Zeitschr. *f.d.at. Wiss.* 78 [1959]); also above, ch. I, nn. 6, 7.

[2] "The Creation Epic," Tablets I-VI, J. B. Pritchard, *Ancient Near Eastern Texts* (1950), pp. 60-69.

[3] H. Rahner, "Antenna Crucis," *Zeitschr. f. kath. Theol.*, 66 (1942), pp. 90f., from classical and patristic sources interprets the sea as a symbol of the world; distinguishing under this two sharply defined motifs: the sea as life ("the bitter sea"), and as the seat of demonic powers ("the evil sea").

[4] H. Gunkel, *Schöpfung und Chaos* (2d ed., 1921), pp. 82-88.

[5] E.g., III AB, A in *Syria*, 16 (1935), pp. 29-45; G. Virolleaud, *La Déesse 'Anat* (1938), V AB, D 35-44, pp. 50f.; W. F. Albright, *Bull. Am. Sch. Or. Res.*, 84 (Dec., 1941), p. 16; A. Lods, "Quelques remarques sur les poèmes mythologiques de Ras Chamra et leur rapports avec l'Ancien Testament," *Rev. d'Hist. et de Phil. Rel.*, 16 (1936), pp. 114f.; Reymond (n. 1), pp. 186-194; Kaiser (n. 1), pp. 44-77.

This myth is never recounted explicitly in the Old Testament. The closest Old Testament parallel to its Ugaritic form is Isa. 27 : 1: "In that day the Lord with his hard and great and strong sword will punish Leviathan the fleeing serpent, Leviathan the twisting serpent, and he will slay the dragon that is in the sea." This and related passages (e.g. Job 3 : 8; 7 : 12; 26 : 12; Ps. 74 : 13f.; Isa. 51 : 9; Eze. 29 : 3) contain a number of obvious parallels with Ugaritic texts. These show that the Old Testament figures of Leviathan, Rahab, the dragon, and the fleeing, twisting, multi-headed serpent all reflect the old Semitic idea of a primeval sea monster conquered in combat with a god. In the Old Testament this myth expresses the triumph of Yahweh over powers of evil. There, as at Ugarit, the dragon figure is intimately associated with the sea.[6] At times the dragon is in the sea (Isa. 27 : 1; Eze. 32 : 2; Amos 9 : 3), but more often the sea is identified with the dragon as the enemy over whom Yahweh is victorious (Job 7 : 12; 26 : 12; Ps. 74 : 13f.; 89 : 9f.; 148 : 7; Isa. 51 : 9f). Still elsewhere the sea is mentioned as subdued by Yahweh without reference to the dragon, but in such a way that the Yahweh-dragon myth must be presupposed (Job 38 : 8-11; Ps. 93 : 3f.; Isa. 44 : 27; Jer. 51 : 36; Hab. 3 : 13-15). Thus the sea is an element essentially hostile to Yahweh, but one which he has conquered and now holds in submission.

This myth finds less distinct analogies in the Creation Story. Whether or not תהום, "the deep" (Gen. 1 : 2) derives from Tiâmat,[7] it is associated with the figure of the dragon in Ps. 148 : 7 (perhaps also Gen. 49 : 25; Deut. 33 : 13; Ps. 77 : 16). If the Yahweh-dragon myth was known to the writer of Gen. 1, it is clear that he has "broken" the old mythology of a struggle, and has presented God as all-powerfully creating everything, even the dragons (Gen. 1 : 21).[8] Similarly in Prov. 8 : 29, while the viewpoint of Gen. 1 is maintained, the wording suggests a possible connection with the myth. Such a re-

---

[6] For more extensive discussions see H. G. May, "Some Cosmic Connotations of Mayim Rabbîm," *Journ. of Bibl. Lit.*, 74 (1955), pp. 9-21; Raymond (n. 1), pp. 189ff.; Kaiser (n. 1), pp. 140-152.

[7] Pro: J. Hempel, "Drache," *Rel. Gesch. u. Gegenw.*, 2d ed., I (1927), 1998; L. Köhler and W. Baumgartner, *Lex. in Vet. Test. Libr.* (1953), sub voce; Reymond (n. 1), p. 187; contra: A. Heidel, *The Babylonian Genesis* (1951), p. 100.

[8] So Hempel (n. 7), loc. cit.; G. Lindeskog in A. Fridrichsen et al., *The Root of the Vine* (1953), p. 3. May (n. 6), pp. 11f., 14, n. 19, sees a conflict at creation ("when Yahweh's wind blew over the watery abyss") which the writer has largely camouflaged so that his monotheism is not threatened by a dualism (ibid., p. 12, n. 14); cf. Reymond (n. 1), pp. 187f.; Kaiser (n. 1), pp. 114-120.

lation is even clearer in Ps. 104 : 6f., 9. In these passages, if the sea is not hostile to Yahweh, at least it is an element over which he must maintain strict control.

In Hellenistic-Jewish literature the Yahweh-dragon myth may lie behind Sirach 43 : 23, "By his counsel he hath stilled the deep,"[9] and *1 Enoch* 60 : 16, where God is said to hold the sea a captive. It is clearly involved in the *Syriac Apocalypse of Baruch* 29 : 4 and *4 Ezra* 6 : 51, where at the last day the sea-dragon is to be killed and given to the redeemed to eat. This is reminiscent of Ps. 74 : 14, which is also given an eschatological turn in *T. Asher* 7 : 3: when the Messiah comes, he will break "the head of the dragon in the water."[10]

In Egypt, although the Nile was deified as an unmitigated blessing, the sea was a figure of evil. Kaiser has shown that with the possible exception of a reference in the "Instruction for Merikare," (1. 131) from the First Intermediate Period, this idea appears at the earliest during the Middle Kingdom, and principally from the imperial period onward. He sees it as largely an importation from Phoenicia.[11] At a much later time, Plutarch reports that the worshippers of Osiris and Isis identified the sea with the evil Egyptian god Typhon.[12] H. Rahner has shown that Typhon, as the sea, was connected with the Greek Ophioneus, who, defeated in a conflict with Kronos, was thrown into the sea. Because of his name, in Hellenistic speculation he was identified with the ὄφις, the primeval serpent who ruled the sea. Similarly in Latin mythology, he was identified with Oceanus.[13] The Mandaean literature also reflects the idea of the sea as an element of evil, in that the sea is the world of earthly existence from which the soul is to be saved.[14]

Closely related to the idea of the sea as evil and demonic was its connection with death and the underworld. This may derive also

---

[9] R. H. Charles, *Apocrypha and Pseudepigrapha* (1913), I, 477.
[10] Charles (n. 9), II, 345.
[11] Kaiser (n. 1), pp. 36-39, 78-91. G. Posener, "La légende égyptienne de la mer insatiable," in *Mélanges Isidore Lévy* (Ann. de l'Inst. de Philol. et d'Hist. Or. et Slaves, XIII [1953]), pp. 461-478, places greater emphasis on the "Instruction for Merikare'" and discounts the idea of this theme having been borrowed.
[12] Plutarch, *De Iside et Osiride*, 7, 32; cf. Reymond (n. 1), p. 192, who notes the Syrian origin of the myth of Typhon.
[13] Rahner (n. 3), 66 (1942), pp. 97-102.
[14] P. Lundberg, *La typologie baptismale dans l'ancienne église* (1942), pp. 92f., 96 cites M. Lidzbarski, *Ginzā* (1925), (Rechter Teil) 3, p. 103: 5; 11, p. 265: 28; (Linker Teil) 1 : 2, p. 433; 2 : 3, p. 457: 30f.; idem, *Mandäische Liturgien* (1920), p. 47.

from the sea as the primeval deep and the original element of evil.[15] It finds analogies in the Babylonian "waters of death" and in the classical figure of Ocean. Thus in Deut. 30 : 12f., the idea seems to be that the opposite of heaven is the underworld, and that it is located "beyond the sea."[16] Paul, quoting this passage loosely (Rom. 10 : 6f.), changes "beyond the sea" to "into the abyss" and immediately identifies it as the place of the dead.

Psalm 18 : 5f., 16f. (par. 2 Sam. 22 : 5f., 16f.), as Gunkel has pointed out, contains two motifs: the descent of the psalmist to the underworld, and the appearance of Yahweh in a storm, who so arouses the sea that it surges back and lays bare the underworld. At this Yahweh reaches down and snatches away the psalmist.[17] Here the "waves of death" (2 Sam. 22 : 5) are parallel with "the cords of Sheol" (v. 6) and the underworld is in the bottom of the sea "at the foundations of the world" (v. 16). Ps. 69 : 2f., 15f., presents similar imagery.

In Ezek. 26 : 19f. Yahweh declares that in destroying Tyre, he will bring the "deep" and "the great waters" over her, which clearly refers to the primeval sea. Then he threatens: "... I will thrust you down with those who descend into the Pit, to the people of old, and I will make you to dwell in the netherworld...." This netherworld, then, is in the depths of the sea. Much the same thought is expressed by Job 38 : 16f.

In classical literature at an early date, the figure of Ocean was connected with the dead. For the Greek the sun entered the underworld by dropping into the sea, and its very waters were thought of as deadly.[18] H. Rahner has collected a large number of passages from both Greek and Latin literature to show that the classical view of the sea is that of an unfriendly, fierce, and treacherous element that by its very nature is the enemy of man. Only by skill and daring can he overcome it.[19]

The second basic theme in the symbolism of the sea is that of primal element. Thus the sea is a symbol of the world. Individu-

---

[15] May (n. 6), p. 14, n. 18.
[16] Cf. "Epic of Gilgamesh," X, ii, 18-27 (Assyrian Vers.).
[17] Gunkel, *Die Psalmen* (1926), p. 64; cf. p. 62; H. Schmidt, *Die Psalmen* (1934), p. 28.
[18] Heraclitus, quoted by Hippolytus, *Elenchos* IX, 10, 5; cf. F. J. Dölger, ΙΧΘΥΣ, II (1922), 59f.; H. Herter, "Okeanos," Paully-Wissowa, *Real-Encyclopädie*, XVII: 2, 2357; Rahner (n. 3), 66 (1942), p. 98, n. 77; p. 99.
[19] Rahner (n. 3), 66 (1942), pp. 91-94.

alized, it becomes the world across which each man must make his life's voyage. The passages already noted in which the voyaging ship is the course of human life, a storm-tossed ship is a man or a state beset by troubles, and a shipwrecked vessel is a ruined person or state, all imply this symbolism. A somewhat similar motif also appears frequently in Greek literature from Homer on, in which the sea represents an army or a nation, winds are influences that distrub it, and the storming sea is therefore a host or a nation in uproar.[20] All these figures also were popular with Latin writers.[21]

Similarly in the Old Testament waters represent belligerent nations. In Isa 8 : 7, the rising, overflowing waters of the Euphrates represent invading Assyrians. This passage is echoed in Jer. 47 : 2, where "waters... rising out of the north" represent an army descending upon the Philistines (cf. ch. 46 : 7f., representing the armies of Necho II). In Isa. 17 : 12f. the simile is expanded to that of the sea, representing not one army or nation, but "many peoples" (cf. Eze. 26 : 3, 19). May has pointed out analogies between this passage and the Ugaritic text describing Baal's conflict with the sea and river. Thus the primeval cosmic struggle continues in the conflicts between Yahweh and the heathen nations.[22]

The two basic motifs of primal element and evil element combine in Jewish and early Christian apocalyptic literature. In Dan. 7 : 1-11, the Yahweh-dragon myth merges with the symbolism of the sea as the nations of the world. Here four beasts rise out of the "great sea", which as Montgomery notes, is the primeval ocean.[23] The burning of the dragon-like fourth beast (v. 11) reflects the triumph of Yahweh over the sea-dragon, recast eschatologically.[24] But in v. 17 the beasts are specifically interpreted as four kings, and the sea is the earth (the peoples of the earth, cf. Isa. 17 : 12f.), from whom these kings (or kingdoms) are derived. The portrayal of these "kings" as arising from the "great sea" implies that they are essentially hostile to God, and even more, that the whole world is at enmity with him and "the saints of the Most High" (cf. Dan. 7 : 25).

The *Syriac Apocalypse of Baruch* 53-71 provides an enlightening

---

[20] E.g., Homer, *Iliad* II, 142-146; Polybius, *Histories* XI, 29, 8-11; further references: J. Kahlmeyer, *Seesturm und Schiffbruch* (1934), pp. 8-10, 13.
[21] E.g., Livy, *Ab Urbe Condita* XXXVIII, 10, 4-6.
[22] May (n. 6), pp. 11f.; cf. Ps. 144: 7: "many waters ... the hand of aliens."
[23] J. A. Montgomery, *A Critical and Exegetical Commentary on the Book of Daniel* (1950), p. 285; cf. Isa. 51: 10; Amos 7: 4; Rev. 17: 8.
[24] Hempel (n. 7), *loc. cit.*

example of this apocalyptic symbolism. There a cloud full of black, white, and multicolored waters rises from "a very great sea," and covers "all the earth." Then it pours down its waters, alternately black and white (or bright), twelve times. The final rain is the blackest of all and is mingled with fire; wherever it falls, it works "devastation and destruction." In the interpretation (chs. 56-71) the cloud is "the duration of the world." The black and the bright waters represent successive periods in sacred history characterized by transgression and reformation. The last, darkest, waters "belong to the whole world" (ch. 69 : 1) and signify the eschatological time of trouble.

That the waters in this vision signify "the duration of the world" is particularly important. They represent the world from the standpoint of all that occurs in it during its time of existence. Here the ideas of world, time, and history are comprehended in the symbol of waters, much as they are united in the Hebrew concept of 'olam.[25] The successive outpourings have special significance for the history of the Chosen People, and culminate eschatologically.

Two passages in *4 Ezra* seem to make much the same use of waters. In chs. 11f., an eagle (= Daniel's fourth beast = Rome, ch. 12 : 11f.) arises out of the sea. A lion (= the Messiah) then appears and conquers him. In *4 Ezra* 13 the Messiah (cf. vs. 25f.) in the form of a man arises from the sea.[26] In each of these passages the sea represents the world in the sense of events transpiring in it which have eschatological significance. Thus the Messiah's arising from the sea may be his appearance within the course of history. A cosmic notion also seems to be associated with the sea in *Jubilees* 8 : 22 and *Sibylline Oracles* 5 : 530f.

In the Revelation all the motifs that we have seen connected with the sea appear to combine. In ch. 12 : 12 (cf. v. 9), the dragon, "that ancient serpent," is thrown into the "earth and sea." Elsewhere in the Revelation the combined figures of earth and sea represent the whole world (ch. 7 : 1f; 10 : 2, 5; cf. Ex. 20 : 4, 11; Ps. 69 : 34). The fact that the dragon is involved suggests the added thought that here the sea may also be his special habitat, in the sense of the abyss (ch. 11 : 7; cf. ch. 12 : 17; 13 : 1). Thus the sea in chs. 12f. seems to re-

---

[25] E. Jenni, *Das Wort 'ōlām im Alten Testament* (1953), pp. 50, 86f., has shown that throughout the Old Testament (except Eccl. 1 : 10; 3 : 11), '*ōlām* has the basic meaning of "most remote time" ("fernste Zeit"), but that in the Jewish apocalyptic literature of the first Christian century it means "the world."
[26] Cf. J. Klausner, *The Messianic Idea in Israel* (1956), pp. 358-361.

present the world as the stronghold of the demonic powers symbolized by the dragon and the beast,[27] and the terms "earth" and "sea" may be complementary rather than antithetical.

In Revelation 8 : 7-11; 16 : 2-7, the objects of divine wrath are the earth, the sea, and the rivers. The appearance of rivers with the sea is not surprising when we remember that in the Old Testament (as in the Ugaritic literature)[28] rivers are coupled with the sea as the enemy of God (Hab. 3 : 8, 13-15). Thus the earth, sea, and rivers may represent not only the totality of the physical world, but also the nations in rebellion against God.

The figure of the sea as nations is explicit in Revelation 17. There the "great harlot" is seated "upon many waters" (v. 1), and these are defined as "peoples and multitudes and nations and tongues" (v. 15). Similarly in ch. 18 : 21, to symbolize the fall of "Babylon," an angel throws "a stone like a great millstone" into the sea. Anticipating the fall of Rome, the writer probably thinks of it as sinking beneath the other nations of the world.

In all these instances in the Revelation, the sea may also be considered from the point of view noted in the *Syriac Apocalypse of Baruch* 53-71, where the factors of time, historical content, and eschatological significance combine. Thus the nations as the sea are at the same time strongholds of demonic power, and significant factors in the eschatological drama.

In Revelation 20 : 13, the "sea" and "death and Hades" (one concept, cf. ch. 1 : 18; 6 : 8; 20 : 14), both give up the dead at the Great Resurrection. Since the expression "death and Hades" is as applicable to those lost at sea as to those buried in a tomb, it appears probable that it is really an explanation and intensification of the term "sea", rather than a contrast to it. Similarly in v. 14 only "death and Hades" are thrown into the lake of fire, for they comprehend what is implied by the "sea." If this is correct, v. 13 provides another instance of the sea as the abode of the dead. The casting of "death and Hades" into the lake of fire is then equivalent to the declaration in ch. 21 : 1, "the sea was no more" (cf. *Sib. Or.* 5 : 158f.; *Ass. Mos.* 10 : 6). This would signify not only the end of death, but also the end of the world and of history.

---

[27] Cf. H. B. Swete, *The Apocalypse of St. John* (3d ed., 1951), p. 161.
[28] May (n. 6), p. 10.

PART II

THE NEW TESTAMENT

CHAPTER V

THE PROBLEM OF SYMBOLISM IN THE GOSPELS

In the foregoing pages we have seen that almost universally in the ancient world, the ship was a common figure both in literature and art. Turning now to the New Testament, and particularly to the Gospels, we may ask whether any of the repeated references to ships there may also have symbolic significance. In attempting to answer this, we must first consider two subsidiary questions: (1) whether a symbolic interpretation is possible of passages that were written apparently as sober narrative; and (2), if so, whether the ship in these passages may be assigned figurative meaning.

The question of symbolic interpretation of narrative in the synoptic Gospels, must be considered in the light of their purpose and standpoint. Over a half century ago, J. Weiss pointed out that the purpose of Mark was not to write a formal biography of Jesus, but, as declared by his title, "the beginning of the gospel of Jesus Christ, the Son of God" (ch. 1 : 1), to give utterance to the proclamation of the apostolic church. Weiss emphasized that Mark's purpose was practical instruction, and that he illustrated the basic idea of the early Christian proclamation by pictures from the life of Jesus.[1]

The earliest tradition regarding Mark's activity bears out this view. Eusebius' well-known quotation from Papias declares on the authority of John the Presbyter that Mark

> ... followed Peter, who used to give teaching (διδασκαλίας) as necessity demanded but not making, as it were, an arrangement of the Lord's oracles, so that Mark did nothing wrong in thus writing down single points as he remembered them.[2]

This probably reliable tradition reveals the matrix in which the Gospel of Mark was formed: the demands of the daily life of the church in its

---

[1] J. Weiss, *Das älteste Evangelium* (1903), pp. 22-24, 103.
[2] Eusebius, *Ecclesiastical History* III, 39, 15 (Loeb ed., I [1953], 297).

inner development and outward expansion called forth the materials from which the evangelist composed his Gospel. Thus Mark's account may be seen as grounded in apostolic "teaching" (διδασκαλία).

Dibelius has emphasized the same point of view also in regard to Matthew and Luke. Seeking the motive for the formation of the gospel tradition, he directs attention to the Lucan Prologue, where "eyewitnesses and ministers of the word" (Lk. 1 : 2) are declared to be those by whom the earliest gospel tradition was transmitted. From this he concludes that preaching, motivated by the Christian mission, was the means by which the memories of Jesus' disciples were disseminated. This preaching he sees as including all that is implied by the words, "the things of which you have been informed" (Lk. 1 : 4): missionary proclamation, exhortation of believers, and instruction of catechumens. Thus the first Christian preachers were not concerned primarily just to recount the life of Jesus, but rather to proclaim salvation in Christ. To provide foundation and confirmation for this, they presented the words and deeds of their Master. Hence Dibelius, followed by form critics in general, has seen the process by which the gospel tradition took shape as one of filling out the framework of the kerygma (as portrayed, for example, in the typical kerygmatic sermons in Acts) with traditions regarding Jesus.[3] The evangelists, with the avowed purpose of proclamation, drew upon these kerygmatic materials and gave them literary form.[4]

---

[3] M. Dibelius, *Die Formgeschichte des Evangeliums* (2d ed., 1933), pp. 12, 14-16; H. Conzelmann, *The Theology of St Luke* (1960), pp. 10-12. R. Morgenthaler, *Die lukanische Geschichtsschreibung als Zeugnis* (1949), Part 2, pp. 7-24, concludes that various figures and constructions, characterizing Luke's literary style are intended as *witness*. On the basic historicity of the outline of Jesus' career as given in the apostolic preaching, see B. Reicke, *Glaube und Leben der Urgemeinde* (1957), pp. 39-41; cf. pp. 17f.; T. W. Manson, "Present-day Research in the Life of Jesus," *The Background of the New Testament and its Eschatology* (1956), p. 214; H. Riesenfeld, *The Gospel Tradition and its Beginnings* (1957), pp. 10-30, who sees the Gospel traditions as springing from Jesus himself and being preserved with great care by a small group of disciples, rather than as originating in the early Christian proclamation.

[4] In attributing the formation of Gospel tradition to Christian proclamation, Dibelius specifically excepts the category of "novels" (Novellen), which includes the nature miracles with which we are concerned in this chapter. These he sees as the work of story-tellers ([n. 4], pp. 66ff.). However, while Dibelius is interested primarily in the development of these stories before the evangelists wrote, we are concerned with them as they constitute a part of the Gospels, where they appear to partake of the general purpose of the evangelists, which was proclamation.

This conclusion implies that the Synoptists see Jesus as he was understood by the church.[5] Hoskyns and Davey have emphasized that nowhere in these Gospels do we find a purely "historical" Jesus presented un-theologically: the evangelists write with the purpose of showing that Jesus' life and death fulfilled divine promises through the prophets and psalmists. These authors see this also as grounded in Jesus' own self-consciousness, which gave form and color both to his words and actions and to the evangelists' presentation of them.[6] Thus in the figure of Jesus, history and theology combine.

Accordingly, as Reicke has pointed out, the Synoptists present a double picture of our Lord: Jesus as his contemporaries saw and understood him during his lifetime, and Jesus as he was understood by the church after the resurrection and Pentecost.[7] This is not the common distinction between "the Jesus of history" and "the Christ of faith." The question of a "historical Jesus" cannot rightly be raised here. The distinction is rather between a Jesus not fully understood even by his closest disciples, and a Jesus seen in the full light of revelation. For the evangelists, the latter was more important, and even more historical, because they were convinced that it represented Jesus' own concept of himself. This two-fold view of the Synoptics suggests that the evangelists at times may have presented their stories in such a way as to imply symbolically deeper understandings of Jesus' life.

A particularly important evidence of double meanings in the synoptic narratives appears in certain aspects of their vocabulary. Cullmann has demonstrated that in the Fourth Gospel various significant words are used with double meanings to refer both to facts in

---

[5] On evidence indicating that the narratives and sayings by which they portray him have a basis in his life, see Fr. Büchsel, *Die Hauptfragen der Synoptikerkritik* (1939), pp. 77-94; H. Riesenfeld, "Tradition und Redaktion im Markusevangelium," *Neutestamentliche Studien für Rudolf Bultmann* (1954), p. 158; idem (n. 3), pp. 16-30.

[6] E. Hoskyns and N. Davey, *The Riddle of the New Testament* (1931), pp. 60ff.

[7] B. Reicke, "Einheitlichkeit oder verschiedene 'Lehrbegriffe' in der neutestamentlichen Theologie?" *Theol. Zeitschr.*, 9 (1953), pp. 409f.; see also J. Schniewind, *Das Evangelium nach Markus and das Evangelium nach Lukas* (1937), p. 200; E. Percy, *Die Botschaft Jesu* (1953), p. 299. From another standpoint, Conzelmann (n. 3), pp. 13ff., has noted in Luke the strong sense of difference between the time of Jesus' earthly life and the time of the church in which the Gospel was written. J. M. Robinson, *The Problem of History in Mark* (1957), pp. 63-85, discusses the life of Jesus seen from the standpoint of the church, in Mark.

Jesus' life and to later facts of salvation-history.⁸ Similarly in the synoptic Gospels a number of words may be shown to have double meanings, one referring to the life and words of Jesus as experienced by his contemporaries, the other implying a deeper understanding of them in view of the resurrection and Pentecost. Thus the Baptist's announcement of Jesus as one who would baptize with "a holy wind and fire" (ἐν πνεύματι ἁγίῳ καὶ πυρί, Mt. 3 : 11; Lk. 3 : 16) achieves its post-resurrection significance with the "rush of a mighty wind" and the "tongues as of fire" at the reception of the Holy Spirit at Pentecost (Acts 2 : 2-3; cf. John 20 : 22).⁹ K. L. Schmidt has drawn attention to the double significance of the verbs προάγειν and ἀκολουθεῖν in Mk. 10 : 32. On the one hand they describe Jesus' journey to Jerusalem with his disciples; on the other, they imply that Jesus precedes his disciples in self-sacrifice and martyrdom and that they must follow his example (cf. Mk. 14 : 28 = Mt. 26 : 32; Mk. 16 : 7 = Mt. 28 : 7)¹⁰ On the basis of Mk. 8 : 27ff., E. Schweizer has pointed out that only those who follow Jesus in this way can see through the messianic secret and know who he really is. Schweizer also has shown the close connection between this concept of "following" and the idea of abasement and exaltation.¹¹ Since the logion ending "whoever humbles himself will be exalted" appears in three different contexts in the Synoptics (Mt. 23 : 12; Lk. 14 : 11; 18 : 14), it may have circulated in the early church somewhat independently of any one specific setting in Jesus' life. This suggests that Paul may have seen it as more than simply an ethical maxim, and may have applied it consciously to Christ in Phil. 2 : 8f. Although we cannot read a christological meaning into this logion in the Synoptics, the early church may have attached such a significance to it in other contexts.¹²

⁸ O. Cullmann, "Der johanneische Gebrauch doppeldeutiger Ausdrücke als Schlüssel zum Verständnis des vierten Evangeliums," *Theol. Zeitschr.*, 4 (1948), pp. 360-372; idem, *Early Christian Worship* (1953), pp. 50-57; beginnings in this direction were made by H. J. Holtzmann, *Lehrbuch der neutestamentlichen Theologie* (2d ed., 1911), II, 421.
⁹ This is not to say that πνεῦμα ἅγιον was understood only as "a holy wind" before Pentecost; cf.the term "holy spirit" in the Qumran literature (e.g., 1QS iv, 18-21; 1QH vii, 7; ix, 32), but its association with "fire" in the statement attributed to John emphasizes the naturalistic meaning.
¹⁰ K. L. Schmidt, "Προάγω", *Theol. Wörterb. z. N.T.*, I (1933), 130.
¹¹ E. Schweizer, *Erniedrigung und Erhöhung bei Jesus und seinen Nachfolgern* (1955), pp. 17-19.
¹² Another instance in which the idea of "following" may have a double meaning – though we suggest this with caution – is ἄνωθεν in Luke 1 : 3: "for sometime past" and "from above."

Reicke has drawn attention to the probability that ἀνάλημψις in Lk. 9 : 51 has a double meaning.[13] Like the Hebrew מַעֲלָה it would seem to signify either "pilgrimage" or "ascension." Here then, it may refer both to Luke's major theme of Jesus' pilgrimage to Jerusalem and also to his ascension, (cf. Acts 1 : 2, 22). All three reports of Jesus' conversation with the blind man (men) of Jericho (Mk. 10 : 51f.; Mt. 20 : 32-34; Lk. 18 : 41-43) suggest double meanings. The man asks that he may "see again" (ἀναβλέπειν), and when he is healed he ἀνέβλεψεν καὶ ἠκολούθει, which may mean that he "saw again and followed" or that he "looked upward and followed." The Marcan and Lucan accounts also contain the declaration, familiar in other contexts of healing, "Your faith has made you well (σέσωκεν)." Here a soteriological overtone is unmistakable.

In connection with the passion story, a number of words appear to be used with double meanings. In Lk. 12 : 50, Jesus refers to his passion as a "baptism." The verb βαπτίζειν, in its primary sense of immersing, overwhelming, follows a well-attested usage here in the sense of one's being immersed in, or overwhelmed by, trouble or pain.[14] Jesus looks forward to his passion as a wave of adversity. From a later perspective, however, the reference to the passion as a baptism has a deeper meaning. Cullmann has pointed out that in the baptismal story, Jesus is clearly recognized as the Suffering Servant of Isa. 42 : 1 (cf. Mt. 3 : 17); 53 : 3-9.[15] Thus the baptism pointed to his suffering and death, a fact which Paul had already seen before the Synoptists wrote (Rom. 6 : 3f.). Similarly Jesus' reply to John's protest, "It is fitting for us to fulfil all righteousness" (Mt. 3 : 15) is understandable only in the light of Christ's making possible the righteousness of sinners through his death. In view of all this, the reference to the passion as a baptism gains a theological significance understandable only from a later point of view.

The words regarding the passion that immediately follow in Lk. 12 : 50, "How I am constrained until it is accomplished!" (τελεσθῇ) may mean also, "How I am constrained until it is made perfect!" Here, as in John 19 : 28, 30, the historical accomplishment of Jesus' suffering is shown also to be the perfect culmination of his mission – a fact which no one before the resurrection was able to appreciate, as Luke shows (ch. 24 : 10-21; cf. in the present context, ch. 12 : 56).

---

[13] B. Reicke, "Instruction and Discussion in the Travel Narrative," in K. Aland et al., *Studia Evangelica* (1959), p. 211.
[14] Isa. 21 : 4 (LXX); Josephus, *Jewish War* IV, 137.
[15] O. Cullmann, *Baptism in the New Testament* (1951), pp. 16-21.

The verb παραδοῦναι is used with a double sense in the Synoptics, as Karl Barth has shown.[16] Often it refers to Jesus' being "delivered" to his enemies (Mt. 17 : 22; Mk. 9 : 31; Lk. 9 : 44, to men; Mt. 20 : 18, Mk. 10 : 33, to high priests; Mt. 20 : 19; Mk. 10 : 33; Lk. 18 : 32, to Gentiles; Mt. 26 : 2, to be crucified; Mt. 26 : 45; Mk. 14 : 41; Lk. 24 : 7, into the hands of sinful men; Mt. 27 : 2; Mk. 15 : 1, to Pilate). But Luke (ch. 1 : 2) uses it also in its other sense of passing down a tradition, and in this case, specifically of the tradition regarding the life of Jesus (cf. ch. 10 : 22). That the early church recognized a relationship between these two concepts as connected with Jesus is suggested by Paul's use of them together: "For I received from the Lord what I also deliv˙red (παρέδωκα) to you, that the Lord Jesus on the night when he was betrayed (παρεδίδοτο) took bread" (1 Cor. 11 : 23). In view of this it seems significant that Jesus' admonition to the disciples that "they will deliver you up (παραδώσουσιν) to councils" (Mt. 10 : 17-19; Mk. 13 : 9-11; Lk. 21 : 12-15) is in direct connection with their witnessing "before governors and kings for my sake, to bear testimony before them." This witness is not to be premeditated, but given under immediate inspiration of the Holy Spirit. Thus the "delivery" (παράδοσις) of the disciples to their enemies results in their witnessing to that which is delivered (παράδοσις) concerning Christ, and this latter delivery involves inspired, post-resurrection insights. In this the disciples are followers of their Master, for his delivery by Judas to the Jews and by them to the Gentiles made possible the παράδοσις of the gospel by the disciples first to the Jews and then to the Gentiles. In view of παράδοσις in this sense of witness, the various passages noted above in which Jesus is said to be delivered to men, the high priests, Gentiles, and to Pilate, may have also a deeper meaning, relating not only to historical events of his passion, but also to their essential significance in the proclamation of the church. When all this is viewed from the standpoint that God "gave" (ἔδωκεν) his Son (John 3 : 16), the intrinsic relationship between the divine act of giving, Judas' act of delivering Jesus, and his followers' act of delivering the Gospel proclamation becomes apparent.

Finally, in connection with the earthquake at the crucifixion, Mt. 27 : 52 tells of the raising of "many bodies of the saints who had fallen asleep" (κεκοιμημένων). In the following verse this is associated with Jesus' resurrection by the statement that after that event they came out of their tombs and went into "the holy city." As Cullmann has shown in connection with John 11 : 11,[17] so here the verb κοιμᾶσθαι has a double sense, the derived meaning, "to die," being the more obvious. But the connection with the resurrection suggests that its basic meaning, "to fall asleep," also is intended. The evangelist seems to imply that in view of the timeless significance of the resurrection

---

[16] K. Barth, *Church Dogmatics*, II, 2 (1957), 480-506.
[17] O. Cullmann, *Early Christian Worship* (1953), p. 55, n. 1.

of Christ, these "saints" had not really been dead in the ultimate sense of the term.

Similarly the statement that they went "out of the tombs" and "into the holy city" after Christ's resurrection (Mt. 27:53) suggests more than just an entrance into Jerusalem. The expression "the holy city" appears in the Gospels only in scenes involging the supernatural: here and at Mt. 4 : 5 in connection with Jesus' temptation by Satan. Furthermore, it stands here in contrast to "the tombs." As the place to which the resurrected saints (ἅγιοι) go, "the holy city" (ἡ ἁγία πόλις) would seem to be *their* city, not only the literal Jerusalem, but also by implication, "the Jerusalem above" (Gal. 4 : 26; cf. Rev. 21 : 2, 10).

These aspects of the synoptic vocabulary seem to bear out the idea that the Gospels were written from a double point of view: Jesus as he was only partially comprehended by the eyewitnesses, and Jesus as he later was understood by those same eyewitnesses and the rest of the church in view of the resurrection and Pentecost.

Closely related to this point of view is the question of the messianic secret. This problem was first brought into prominence at the beginning of the twentieth century by W. Wrede.[18] Seeking to determine the point in early Christian history at which Jesus became known as the Messiah, Wrede maintained that during his lifetime Jesus had neither claimed to be nor was recognized as such. On the basis of Peter's declaration at Pentecost that "God has made him both Lord and Christ, this Jesus whom you crucified" (Acts 2 : 36), he concluded that the Messiahship of Jesus was first seen as the result of the resurrection. Gradually this concept was projected by the church back into his earthly life, particularly through a reinterpretation of the meaning of events such as his supernatural birth, his reception of the spirit, his miracles, and especially his death. (Wrede did not exclude the possibility that some of these factors may have led to a suspicion and hope that Jesus was the Messiah even during his ministry.)[19] This development produced a tension between the recognition, on the one hand, of evidences of Messiahship in the current concept of Jesus' life, and the earlier belief, on the other hand, that his messiahship began with the resurrection. This tension was resolved, according to Wrede, when the church propounded the idea of the messianic secret: that Jesus consciously was the Messiah during

---

[18] W. Wrede, *Das Messiasgeheimnis in den Evangelien* (1901).
[19] Wrede (n. 18), p. 214.

his lifetime, but that he did not wish it to be known, and consequently forbad repeatedly that it be proclaimed. Wrede saw Mark as having written his Gospel from this point of view and as having contributed to the development of this solution of the problem.[20]

Wrede's theory has enjoyed wide discussion and in recent years has been popularized by Bultman's acceptance.[21] Regardless of whether Jesus was unconscious of messiahship, Wrede is correct in seeing the Gospels as having been written from the standpoint of the church after the resurrection.[22] Only on this basis can the obvious presence of a messianic secret in the Gospels be explained, particularly if this secret is held to be historical in the life of Jesus. In view of his repeated commands not to reveal his messiahship, the evangelists would have been obliged to say nothing that might show Jesus the prophet and teacher as also the Christ, if they had written only from a standpoint contemporary with his life. Instead, as Wrede declares, their predominant interest was a view of his life in which the resurrection constituted the focal point, and from which all else was understood and evaluated.[23] Thus the Synoptists' revelation of the messianic secret involved a double view of Jesus.

Repeatedly it has been pointed out that the **nature miracles** are presented by the Synoptists with the particular intention of revealing the messianic secret to the understanding reader.[24] It seems of particular importance for our problem, that the three major appearances of the ship in the synoptic Gospels – in the stories of the storm on the sea, Jesus' walking on the water, and the miraculous draft of fish – occur in connection with such miracles. These, to use Dibelius' term, are "secret epiphanies,"[25] that is, they reveal Jesus as divine,

---

[20] Wrede (n. 18), pp. 145f., and especially pp. 214-229.
[21] R. Bultmann, *Geschichte der synoptischen Tradition* (3d ed., 1957), p. 1. Serious objections to Wrede's hypothesis have been raised by Fr. Büchsel (n. 5), pp. 11-17; E. Percy (n. 7), pp. 279-299; E. Sjöberg, *Der verborgene Menschensohn in den Evangelien* (1955), pp. 104-108; O. Cullmann, *The State in the New Testament* (1956), pp. 26ff.
[22] Wrede (n. 18), pp. 283f., notes that G. Volkmar, *Die Evangelien oder Marcus und die Synopsis der kanonischen und ausserkanonischen Evangelien* (1870), had preceded him in this insight.
[23] Wrede (n. 18), p. 228; cf. Percy (n. 7), pp. 294f.
[24] Wrede (n. 18), pp. 218, 236f.; Dibelius (n. 3), pp. 91f.; Bultmann (n. 21), pp. 370f.; Reicke (n. 7), pp. 408f.; Hoskyns and Davey (n. 6), p. 123. Contra, V. Taylor, *The Formation of the Gospel Tradition* (1949), pp. 131-134, 143; idem, *The Gospel according to St. Mark* (1952), p. 143.
[25] Dibelius (n. 3), p. 232.

but only to a small, select, inner circle of disciples. Here also the double view of Jesus prevails, for Mark is at pains to show that the disciples did not understand the significance of these miracles (ch. 4 : 41; 6 : 52). Only after the resurrection do they really betray the messianic secret. Thus in these miracle stories lies a deeper meaning than merely that of a supernatural act. If this double point of view is indicated by many individual words and by the messianic secret and its revelation through the nature miracles, it would seem possible to seek a deeper, symbolic meaning in these miracles prefiguring subsequent moments in the history of salvation.

Turning to the Fourth Gospel, we may inquire next whether its purpose and standpoint suggest the possibility of symbolic interpretation.

The purpose of this Gospel is set forth in ch. 20 : 31: "But these things are written that you may believe that Jesus is the Christ, the Son of God, and that believing you may have life in his name" (cf. ch. 19 : 35). This evangelist's purpose, even more clearly and frankly than the Synoptists', is proclamation; hence he looks upon Jesus not only as contemporaries saw him, but especially as the church of the latter first century understood and proclaimed him. This is particularly apparent when he points out that the disciples did not comprehend the real meaning of Jesus' words until after the resurrection, when they "remembered" and understood (ch. 2 : 22; 12 : 16; cf. ch. 2 : 17; 8 : 27f.; 11 : 49-52; 21 : 19). As Cullmann has emphasized, the evangelist looks upon this remembering as a revelation due directly to the coming of the Spirit, who "will guide you into all the truth," and "will glorify me" (ch. 16 : 13, 14; cf. 7 : 39). This revelation is vouchsafed both to the evangelist and to the reader, who thereby is able to see deeper perspectives not only where the evangelist has pointed them out, but also in many other narratives and sayings of Jesus. Cullmann has demonstrated this by a comparison of ch. 3 : 14 with 12 : 32f. In the former instance the figure of Moses' lifting up the serpent as applied to the Son of Man is left unexplained, but in the latter passage the lifting up of Christ is interpreted as his crucifixion. This insight shows the deeper meaning of ch. 3 : 14, though it is derived from quite another context. Thus the evangelist has provided one instance of a logion involving a deeper perspective from the standpoint of salvation-history, in which that perspective is not specifically stated.[26]

---

[26] Cullmann (n. 17), pp. 48-52.

Another evidence of double meanings in the Fourth Gospel is the large number of words in its vocabulary that are employed in a double sense. Cullmann has studied these in detail.[27] In John they are even more frequent and striking than in the Synoptics, and demonstrate clearly the author's dual perspective regarding the life and words of Jesus. They also constitute evidence that this double point of view is to be sought not only in passages where the evangelist is concerned to point it out, but also in instances where he is not.

At this point an important difference may be noted between the double perspective of the Synoptics and that of the Fourth Gospel. The deeper insight of the former, as we have seen, is that of the church as it understood Christ in view of the resurrection, as it came to see the meaning of his earthly life for the history of salvation. The Gospel of John shares this insight, but its perspective is yet broader and deeper, for, as Reicke has said, we have here a double view of our Lord himself: "The prophet of Nazareth is also even here upon earth *the Lord* of a kingdom that is not of this world, *the church*."[28] This appears evident both from the discourse on the shepherd and his sheep (ch. 10 : 1-30) and from the allegory of the vine and branches (ch. 15 : 1-11), as well as from the direct statement of Jesus to Pilate in ch. 18 : 16.

The double view of Jesus in the Fourth Gospel is not two views, but one. Here Jesus is at once earthly and heavenly, the prophet of Nazareth and the Lord of the church. For the evangelist this perspective is the only true one, for it alone sees the Lord as he was understood by "the disciple whom Jesus loved," the disciple upon whose authority the Fourth Gospel rests (John 21 : 24). This disciple is presented as having had special claims to intimacy with Jesus and knowledge of him that often exceeded even those of Peter (ch. 1 : 40f.; 13 : 23f.; 18 : 15f.; 20 : 2, 4; 21 : 7, 20-23). This intimacy and understanding are the basis of the Fourth Evangelist's conviction that his view is the only complete, and consequently the only truly historical picture of Jesus.

That this view of Christ is one of the major preoccupations of the Fourth Evangelist has been maintained by Cullmann. He sees its author as concerned in a large number of places to show a direct connection between events in the life of Jesus and the sacraments.[29]

---

[27] See n. 8; cf. C. F. D. Moule, *An Idiom Book of New Testament Greek* (1953), p. 197.
[28] Reicke (n. 7), p. 142; cf. Dibelius (n. 3), p. 286; Schniewind (n. 7), *loc. cit.*
[29] Cullmann (n. 17).

It is precisely the sacraments that set forth most concretely the presence of Christ in his church. Thus again the Fourth Gospel may be seen to portray the figure of Jesus as at once earthly and heavenly, and present in his church.

This double prospect in the Gospel of John suggests that here, even more clearly than in the Synoptics, we may expect to find deeper meanings in narratives regarding Jesus. As these meanings appear to exist both in vocabulary and in figurative references to the sacraments, it may not be impossible that they also may be found in figures that refer to other aspects of Christ's relationship to his church.

The nature of symbolic interpretation

At this point we shall define more precisely what is meant by symbolic interpretation of the Gospels by comparing it with two other important hermeneutical methods, allegorizing and demythologizing. It is not our purpose to attempt an evaluation of these methods, but simply to compare and contrast the symbolic approach with them.

Allegory in the widest sense may be defined as "a figurative representation conveying a meaning *other* than and in addition to the literal".[30] So defined, it includes symbol, fable and parable. Quintillian explains it similarly:

> *Allegory*, which is translated in Latin by *inversio*, either presents one thing in words and another in meaning, or else something absolutely opposed to the meaning of the words. The first type is generally produced by a series of metaphors.[31]

He gives as an example of the first type Horace's famous ode (I, 14) in which the Roman state is elaborately portrayed as a ship. Here allegory is, in fact, an extended symbolism.

From the standpoint of Biblical exegesis, however, the term "allegory" may also be defined more narrowly.[32] We mean by it the method of exegesis that characterized the Alexandrian School, and

---

[30] "Allegory," *Encyclopaedia Britannica* (11th ed., 1910-11), I, 689.
[31] Quintilian, *Institutio Oratoria* VIII, 6, 44 (Loeb ed., III [1921], 327). R. P. C. Hanson, *Allegory and Event* (1959), pp. 37-40 sketches the use of the term "allegory" in ancient literature.
[32] However this is not always done; cf. F. von Hügel, "Gospel of St John," *Encyclopaedia Britannica* (11th ed., 1910-11), XV, 454-455, and J. H. Bernard, *The Gospel according to John* (1948), I, lxxxiii, who speak of allegory as composed of symbols. For other definitions, see Hanson (n. 31), p. 7; A. Jülicher, *Die Gleichnisreden Jesu* (2d ed., 1899), p. 58; T. W. Manson in Major, Manson, Wright, *The Mission and Message of Jesus* (1946), p. 327.

indeed dominated much of Biblical interpretation well into the Middle Ages. Historical events recorded in Scripture were considered at best as of only subsidiary importance, and often as completely without significance; that which was really of value was their "spiritual" meaning. This "spiritual" significance was to be discerned by allegorical interpretation. Origen, the classical representative of Christian allegorizing declared that literal exegesis often leads to error.[33] A second principle of the allegorical method was the insistence that every passage of Scripture is susceptible to this kind of interpretation.[34] This led easily to great extremes in exegesis.[35]

These features of allegorical exegesis – depreciation or complete rejection of literal interpretation, and application universally to Scripture – constitute two earmarks of the method that distinguish it from the symbolic interpretation we are suggesting.

While the allegorical method is largely rejected today, another approach which has some features in common with it has become popular. This is the program of demythologizing initiated by Rudolf Bultmann. He sets out from the conviction that the old-world view of the universe in which the supernatural impinges on the natural, orderly process of cause and effect is untenable for a scientific mind. Bultmann sees such elements in the New Testament as myths.[36] "Myth" he defines as "the report of a happening or event, in which supernatural, superhuman powers or persons are operative."[37] "Mythology is the use of imagery to express the other wordly in terms of this world and the divine in terms of human life, the other side in

[33] Origen, *De principiis* IV, 1, 11-20; for a full discussion of the allegorical method in the early church, see Hanson (n. 31).

[34] Origen (n. 33), IV, 3, 5, states this at least in theory. In actual practice, however he declares a few times that certain biblical passages are not to be allegorized: e.g. *Comm. in Matt.* XV, 15, 25; cf. Hanson (n. 31), p. 238.

[35] As, for instance, Clement of Alexandria's exegesis of the jot and tittle (Mt. 5 : 18) as representing the "right and good" (the straight iota) and the "crooked and unjust" (the curved tittle) (Catena on Lk. 16 : 17, *The Ante-Nicene Fathers*, II [1885], 578), or Augustine's elaborate interpretation of the story of the Good Samaritan (*Questiones evangeliorum* II, 19, cited by C. H. Dodd, *The Parables of the Kingdom* [1950], pp. 11f.).

[36] R. Bultmann in H. W. Bartsch, *Kerygma and Myth* (1957), pp. 1-8; *Kerygma und Mythos*, II (1952), 181; cf. G. Miegge, *Gospel and Myth in the Thought of Rudolf Bultmann* (1960), pp. 1-15.

[37] Bultmann (n. 36), II, 180. A similar definition is given by Dibelius (n. 3), p. 265, who argues that the story of Jesus cannot be of mythical origin, because the paradigmatic material in the Gospels, which he considers to be oldest, does not contain mythical elements.

terms of this side. For instance, divine transcendence is expressed as spacial distance."[38] The purpose of such expression is to emphasize that man is dependent upon powers he cannot control. Hence for modern, scientific man, these mythological elements in the New Testament must be interpreted existentially, in terms of man's situation as man, that is, demythologized. Indeed, Bultmann sees the New Testament itself as inviting and initiating such interpretation, the Fourth Gospel providing a demythologization of the eschatology represented in the Synoptics. He proposes that a similar program be carried out for the rest of the New Testament.[39]

Demythologizing moves in an almost opposite direction from allegorizing. While the latter seeks to derive the "spiritual" from the literal meaning of Scripture, demythologizing attempts to distill that which is existentially significant from that which from the beginning has been intended as myth. Precisely because from the beginning this myth was intended to have existential import, this distillation is the real, and in this sense, the literal, meaning.[40] Hence while allegorizing works from literal to "spiritual," demythologizing moves from mythical to what, from its own standpoint, is literal. However, both methods have this in common, that they result in a devaluation of the importance of the event, and lay emphasis instead on its meaning. At this standpoint symbolic interpretation differs from both allegorizing and demythologizing, for it seeks a unity between the event and its theological significance which maintains the importance of both.

In applying the term "symbolic" to this point of view, we use it in a more limited sense than has been done by such scholars as Loisy and Holtzmann, who, in emphasizing symbolic exegesis of the Gospels, have relegated the narratives to the status of legends.[41] Loisy, for instance, cites more than thirty stories in Luke as symbolic and declares that "the legend of Jesus and the teaching attributed to him are almost entirely a product of Christian tradition." In terms of the definitions we are using such an approach would appear to be allegorical rather than strictly symbolic. We should prefer the categories

---

[38] Bultmann, *Kerygma and Myth* (1957), p. 10, n. 2 (Ger. ed., I, 23, n. 2).
[39] Bultmann (n. 36), I, 23ff. (Eng. trans. [n. 36], pp. 11ff.); cf. Miegge (n. 36), pp. 16-61.
[40] M. Barth, "Introduction to Demythologizing," *Journ. of Rel.*, 37 (1957), p. 153.
[41] H. J. Holtzmann, *Lehrbuch der neutestamentlichen Theologie* (2d ed., 1911), II, 41ff.; A. Loisy, *L'évangile selon Luc* (1924), p. 23.

suggested by Lagrange, who, in contrast to myth and allegory, uses "symbol" to describe the way in which an author recounts history, the events of which suggest, and indeed, possess, further meaning.[42]

This is not to insist that the events recorded of Jesus' life should necessarily be proved historically. There are cases where this never will be possible. The concern of the New Testament exegete should not be primarily with historical proof of events narrated, but rather with the explication of what the evangelists understood to be the significance of the events about which they wrote. As we have pointed out in the preceding pages, the purpose of the Gospels is proclamation rather than simply biography. In dealing with them we are looking through the eyes of the evangelists from a post-resurrection point of view. Hence it would seem that the Gospels should be interpreted in the first instance from the situation of the evangelists themselves, who looked with eyes of faith back through Easter morning to the events of Jesus' life.

To say this, however, is not to underestimate the importance of the events that they narrated. Precisely because the evangelists took these events seriously as actual happenings, so the exegete, if he is to do full justice to his documents and their authors, must also take them seriously. As Kümmel has pointed out, the New Testament is concerned not only with the event of salvation in a timeless sense, but also with the history of salvation; and a history is a record of facts.[43]

This essential unity between the events of Jesus' life and their significance for subsequent moments in the history of salvation is portrayed, as we have seen, by words and phrases in the Gospels that have double meaning. As Cullmann states in this connection, we do not have here a relationship of figure and reality, but a co-ordination, both parts of which are meaningful and important. Nor are

---

[42] M. J. Lagrange, *L'évangile selon St. Jean* (7th ed., 1948), pp. XC-XCII; cf. E. Hoskyns, *The Fourth Gospel* (2d ed., 1948), p. 26; J. H. Bernard (n. 32), I, lxxxvi; Cullmann, "Der joh. Gebr. doppeldeut. Ausdr." (n. 8), p. 361; P. Niewalda, *Sakramentssymbolik im Johannesevangelium?* (1958), pp. 33f. The symbolic interpretation with which we are concerned, however, is to be distinguished from the *sensus plenior* of Roman Catholic exegesis. As defined by R. E. Brown, *The Sensus Plenior of Sacred Scripture* (1955), p. 92, it is a deeper meaning which, though intended by God, was not clearly intended by the writer, but is perceived through further revelation or as the result of developed understanding of revelation. Our concern throughout is with the original intention of the author.

[43] W. G. Kümmel, "Mythos im Neuen Testament," *Theol. Zeitschr.*, 6 (1950), pp. 321-337.

we confronted with "historical" and "symbolic" interpretations as alternatives, for this co-ordination unites the two in a single narrative.[44] Nor yet is the relationship that of a Platonic "participation" of the event in its spiritual or "ideal" meaning.[45] Rather, to use Cullmann's phrase, we have in these Gospel narratives an *interpretatio ex eventu*.[46]

The limits of symbolic interpretation

If, as we have tried to show, certain Gospel narratives may admit of symbolic interpretation, it must be recognized also that in attempting such interpretation we are undertaking a procedure that may easily run out of bounds. What norms are there for the exegesis of New Testament symbols? Here are some suggestions.

1. To be recognized as a valid symbol, a figure should be a *live* symbol.[47] There must be clear evidence either in its own context or in contemporary art or literature that it was recognized as having symbolic meaning. This means that at times we may not recognize some symbols because contemporary witness to them as such no longer exists. Nevertheless the interpreter cannot safely ignore this rule.

2. It should be demonstrable that the passage under consideration was intended as symbolism by its author. The neglect of this rule produced one of the excesses of the old allegorical method. But if a figure that is live as a symbol appears in a passage intended as symbolic, we may be reasonably safe in interpreting that figure symbolically.

3. Theological conclusions drawn from symbolism should go no further than can be derived by exegesis of literal passages of Scripture.[48]

---

[44] Cullmann (n. 42), p. 363; idem (n. 17), p. 56. A. N. Wilder, "Scholars, Theologians, and Ancient Rhetoric," *Journ. of Bibl. Lit.*, 75 (1956), p. 11, arguing from a different point of view, has also noted the impossibility of "our modern alternatives of literal versus symbolic. They [New Testament symbols] were meant neither literally nor symbolically, but naively... These meanings and associations had a very concrete social-cultural reference, something quite different from what we mean by a philological or theological context."
[45] Wilder (n. 44), pp. 7f.
[46] Cullmann (n. 42), p. 362.
[47] E. R. Goodenough, *Jewish Symbols*, IV (1954), 36, 43.
[48] This principle was recognized by Thomas Aquinas (*Summa*, Quaestio 9, cited by E. C. Blackman, "The Task of Exegesis," in the *Background of the New Testament and its Eschatology* [1956], p. 14). In 1941 the Pontifical Biblical Commission issued a similar decision (AAS 33, 466, quoted by F. Mitzka,

The ship in the New Testament and its backgrounds

Thus far we have sought to demonstrate the possibility that narratives in the Gospels, in principle at least, may admit of deeper meanings associated with the history of salvation which may be elucidated through symbolic interpretation. We now must address ourselves to the second question raised at the beginning of this chapter: is it possible that the ship in these Gospel narratives may have symbolic significance?

In a previous paragraph we set forth as one of the norms for determining a symbol that it must be a live symbol, current at the time of its use. Part I of our study has shown that the ship was a thoroughly live symbol in Greek, Roman, and Jewish literature and art at the time of the writing of the New Testament. Its chief significances were human life or the soul, the state, the world, the conveyance to the next world, and in Jewish literature (from a milieu particularly close to that of the New Testament), the Jewish nation. In Christian literature and art from the second century onward, the ship is a recurring symbol of the church. This suggests the possibility that in the New Testament such a symbolism also may have been intended.

But do the occurrences of the ship symbol in the first-century Roman world provide a basis for suggesting that in the New Testament the ship represents the church? Of the meanings we have seen attached to the figure of the ship, those of the Jewish nation and the state seem most significant in this connection. The probability that the *Testament of Naphtali*, in which the ship is the Jewish nation, was known and used in the Qumran community makes it possible that this symbolism was also known to writers of the New Testament. The thought that the church constitutes the new Israel (Rom. 4 : 11ff; Gal. 3 : 28f.) could provide a basis for transferring a symbol of Israel to the church. That such a transfer occurred in the case of the vine and its branches appears clear from a comparison of Old Testament passages (Ps. 80 : 8-16; Isa. 5 : 1-7; 27 : 2, 3; Jer. 2 : 21, 12 : 10) where the vine represents Israel, with John 15 : 1ff. where the vine and its branches represent Christ and his church.[49] Similarly at a later

"Symbolismus als theol. Methode," *Zeitschr. f. kath. Theol.*, 67 ([1943], pp. 27f.), limiting the interpretation of Biblical typology to that which can be proved literally by the usage of Christ, the apostles, inspired writers, or the traditional usage of the Fathers and the church, especially in the liturgy.

[49] Also like the ship symbol, the vine has pagan as well as Jewish backgrounds: among the Dionysiacs and Orphics it represented Dionysius (Goodenough [n. 47], IV, 37).

period almost the whole gamut of meanings attached to the ship symbol in ancient literature and art were brought over into Christianity and adapted to the Christian context.

Goodenough has demonstrated that such transfer and adaptation of live symbols was typical in the Hellenistic-Roman world. He has shown that the Jews repeatedly took pagan religious symbols, assigned them Jewish religious meanings, and employed them in synagogues and on graves. For example, the figure of Helios driving his chariot through the zodiac appears on the floors of three Palestinian synagogues, representing in this context not a pagan deity but the supreme God of the Jews.[50] If such a transfer of symbol could take place between as radically antithetical religions as the old sunworship and Judaism, a similar migration of the ship symbol might have occurred between Judaism and Christianity.[51] If this occurred, the originality of the New Testament is seen in that it assigned the symbol new meaning, and yet one entirely comprehensible in terms of its backgrounds in the Jewish-Hellenistic world.

The ship as a symbol of the church fulfills two characteristics of a good symbol set forth by Wilder and Goodenough. On the basis of a study of symbolism in secular literature, Wilder has emphasized that "a symbol draws its meaning from its concrete social context." Its power derives from "the dynamics of group life."[52] To be properly understood, then, it must be taken in the historical and social context of those who used it, and comprehended as referring to that context. This is demonstrated in the case of the ship symbol by the fact that it was a common figure for the state. Goldammer has emphasized its socio-political aspects as a background for the patristic figure of ship = church. The ideas of responsibility, striving, and discipline, the notions of leadership, and of crew and passengers and their mutual co-operation, all found in the figure ship = state, are equally applicable to the church. He also suggests that in conceiving of the church as a

---

[50] Goodenough (n. 47), IV, 41.
[51] Goodenough (n. 47), VIII (1958) p. 164, and E. Peterson, "Das Schiff der Kirche," *Theol. Zeitschr.*, 6 (1950), p. 78, see the figure ship = House of Jacob (as in *T. Naph.*) as the origin of the Christian figure ship = church. H. Rahner, "Antenna Crucis," *Zeitschr. f. kath. Theol.*, 75 (1953), p. 145, n. 5, recognizes this view as "wohl anzunehmend." K. Goldammer, "Das Schiff der Kirche," *Theol. Zeitschr.*, 6 (1950), p. 233, holds that the ship in *T. Naph.* is "not precise and meaningful enough" to provide a basis for interpreting New Testament narratives, and looks rather to the political-social symbolism of ship = state as the origin of the symbol in patristic literature.
[52] Wilder (n. 44), p. 9.

ship, early Christians subtly set it over against the Roman state and cult.[53] H. Rahner has also pointed out this socio-political background of the symbol, but sees it as only one aspect, along with the motifs ship = soul and ship = world, that contributed to the patristic figure of the ship as the church.[54] Along with these motifs of pagan origin, he also places the figures of Noah's ark and the ship of Peter as important sources for the patristic symbol.[55] Similarly Kahlmeyer sees in patristic usage a combination of the themes of ship = state, Noah's ark, and the disciples' boat on Galilee.[56] All of these writers have been concerned with the origin of the ship symbol as used by the Church Fathers, rather than in the New Testament. It is clear that with the development of Christianity the problem of its relations with the Roman state and society became more acute and that with the passage of time patristic ship-symbols grew more elaborate. However, there would seem to be nothing essential in the above socio-political notions connected with the ship that might not already have been associated with it in the minds of New Testament writers. There appears to be no compelling reason for setting up any one background of our symbol in Jewish or pagan usage as its exclusive origin. The figure of ship = Israel in the Testament of Naphtali probably lies closest to the New Testament ship in both milieu and thought, yet in the minds of New Testament authors, overtones from other sources also may have had their influence.[57]

A second characteristic of a good symbol, as pointed out by Goodenough, is that it unites in itself paradoxes of human nature and human fate.[58] Thus the cross unites agony and death with peace and victory, and represents the paradox of life through death. This also is demonstrated by the ship in the New Testament. It sets forth

---

[53] Goldammer (n. 5), p. 236.
[54] Rahner (n. 51), 66 (1942), pp. 210-227.
[55] Rahner (n. 51), 65 (1941), p. 124.
[56] J. Kahlmeyer, *Seesturm und Schiffbruch* (1934), p. 47; cf. C. Bonner, "Desired Haven," *Harv. Theol. Rev.*, 34 (1941), pp. 59, 64, 66; H. W. Beyer, "κυβέρνησις", *Theol. Wörterb. z. N.T.*, III (1938), 1036; P. Lundberg, *La typologie baptismale* (1942), pp. 75f., however, denies pagan influence and feels that the typology of the ark provides sufficient explanation.
[57] Rahner (n. 51), 67 (1942), pp. 216f., gives a number of references from classical authors in which the ship = the human body, and suggests a relation between this and the Pauline concept of the church as the body. To the references given by Rahner may be added *Corpus Hermet.* 7, 1b (quoted by Bonner [n. 56], p. 58) and Menander, 1100 (quoted by R. Mach, *Der Zaddik* [1957], p. 235).
[58] Goodenough (n. 47), IV, 37.

an entity which, though frail in itself, yet bears the Lord and his disciples through the storms of the sea. In the midst of the waves, it constitutes a refuge for Peter when he fails to walk on the water. H. Rahner finds this paradox of fearfulness and daring, of "gloriously bold, mortal danger" to be the basic motif of all nautical symbolism.[59] This is expressed vividly in the figure of the church sailing safely through the storms of the world.

In principle then, it appears that the ship in the Gospel narratives may admit of figurative meaning in some instances. This raises the question as to the presence of such meanings in the three sea narratives contained in the Gospels. In the following pages we shall undertake an investigation of these stories with this possibility in view. However, we must emphasize at the outset the experimental nature of our study. Resting on inferences and tenuous associations of ideas, such symbolic interpretation cannot claim finality, and in many instances can only be suggestive.

[59] Rahner (n. 51), 67 (1942), pp. 206-210.

CHAPTER VI

THE STORY OF THE STORM ON THE SEA
AND THE HEALING OF THE DEMONIAC

Mark 4 : 35 - 5 : 21.

Mark, when compared with the other Gospels, exhibits certain special theological interests and characteristics. Particularly important among these are the Messianic secret and its gradual revelation. Although Matthew and Luke both preserve passages that reflect this theme (Mt. 8 : 4; 16 : 20; 17 : 9; Lk. 4 : 41; 9 : 21), in Mark it is more frequent (in Mark 3 : 12; 5 : 43; 7 : 36, it occurs with no Synoptic parallels), and, more importantly, only in Mark does the Messianic secret have programmatic significance for the structure and theology of the Gospel. Thus in this Gospel Jesus' messiahship is first revealed at his baptism when he receives the Holy Spirit and enters upon a new relationship with the spiritual world. Thereafter supernatural beings (Satan, the angels, ch. 1 : 13; unclean spirits, ch. 1 : 23f.) are parties to the secret (in the Capernaum synagogue while the demon recognizes him as the "Holy One of God," the people speak only of "a new teaching" [ch. 1 : 27]). Only after extended experience of Jesus do the disciples recognize who he is. This experience consists, on the one hand, of Jesus' gradually defining himself in contrast to his environment (from John the Baptist, ch. 2 : 18ff.; from his family, ch. 3 : 33; from his home town, ch. 6 : 1ff; from the Pharisees, ch. 7 : 1-13; 8 : 11-13) and concentrating on his followers (as seen in his use of parables, ch. 4 : 2ff., 33f.); and on the other, of his providing his disciples with a series of impressive hints as to who he really is (e.g., forgiveness of sins, ch. 2 : 9; raising the dead, ch. 5 : 41ff.; miraculous feedings, chs. 6 : 35ff., 8 : 1ff.). All of this finally climaxes in Peter's confession at Caesarea Philippi (ch. 8 : 27ff.), when his messiahship is no longer a secret to the disciples.

The point of Mark's story of the storm is summarized in the words, "who then is this, that even wind and sea obey him?" (ch. 4 : 41). Accordingly this story appears to belong among the miracles that prepare for the revelation of the messianic secret. Thus it plays an important part in the programmatic development of Jesus' ministry as presented by Mark. As this development is a theological one, the story of the storm may be seen as having an essential *theological* significance in the Gospel of Mark. Loisy and Lohmeyer have analyzed its literary structure and find it to be poetic, or at least rhythmical, of the type, as Loisy says, intended "to be read publicly, declamed, sung as an expression and stimulant of faith."[1] Thus this passage may have been used also in Christian worship in recognition of the messiahship and divinity of Christ.

The setting of our narrative begins at ch. 4 : 1: "Again he began to teach beside the sea." Verses 2-33 contain a series of parables together with a parenthetical explanation of the parable of the sower. Then, when our narrative opens (v. 35), there is a clear reference back to v. 1: "On that day, when evening had come, he said to them, 'Let us go across to the other side!" Whether this connection between v. 1 and v. 35 is the work of the evangelist has been debated.[2]

The word "again" refers to ch. 3 : 7-9, where Jesus is beside the sea with a crowd of people on a previous occasion. His instruction there to the disciples "to have a boat ready for him because of the crowd" would seem to have a direct connection with his now taking to a boat because of another crowd. Aside from indicating the press of people about him, these repeated and specific references to a boat give the impression that for the author it is a significant feature of the story.

"And a very large crowd gathered about him, so that he got into a boat and sat in it on the sea" (4 : 1b). The close association of the ideas of crowd, boat, and sea suggests the later fact that, as Jesus' followers multiplied (the crowd), the boat of the church with Christ in its midst set forth upon the sea of the word. That the sea represents the world here may be inferred not only from its often having this meaning, but also from the parable of the net (Mt. 13 : 47ff.) and from the declaration that the apostles were to be "fishers of men" (Mk. 1 : 17; Mt. 4 : 19). In view of these sayings, H. Rahner suggests that Jesus must certainly have thought, and perhaps declared, "the

---

[1] A. Loisy, *L'évangile selon Luc* (1924), pp. 67f., divides the passage into six couplets of four lines each (the fourth with five lines and the fifth with three), each couplet beginning with καί; E. Lohmeyer, *Das Evangelium des Markus* (1937), p. 89.

[2] J. Wellhausen, *Das Evangelium Marci* (1903), pp. 38f.; M. Dibelius, *Die Formgeschichte des Evangeliums* (2d ed., 1933), p. 71; Lohmeyer (n. 1), p. 90, all see this connection as artifical. K. L. Schmidt, *Der Rahmen der Geschichte Jesu* (1919), pp. 135, 138; E. Klostermann, *Das Markus Evangelium* (2d ed., 1926), p. 52, think it possible that this connection was already a part of the tradition before Mark wrote.

sea is the world."[3] The fact that it is the Jews here whom he teaches harmonizes with the Marcan thought that the kingdom is essentially a new order of Israel. His teaching them on the sea may reflect the fact that even before the Gentile mission (see below on v. 35), the church took the gospel to the Diaspora.

The following verses (4 : 2-34) contain three parables of the kingdom, together with an extended and detailed interpretation, on a *figurative* basis, of one of them. The presence within the general context of our narrative of these parables of "the kingdom of God," together with the method of interpretation demonstrated may be an indication that the sea story connected with them is also significant for the doctrine of the church.[4] There are also repeated references to a deeper meaning in Jesus' words (vs. 11, 24f., 33f.).

"On that day, when evening had come" (4 : 35). Lightfoot has suggested connecting the thought of "evening" here with 1 Cor. 10 : 11b, "[We] upon whom the end of the ages has come," to imply a later time when the gospel began to be taken to the Gentiles, "across to the other side," which here, literally, was Gentile territory.[5]

"And leaving the crowd" (4 : 36a). This may represent the turning of the emphasis of the early Christian mission from the Jews to the Gentiles (cf. Acts 18 : 6). Lightfoot points out that the similar crowd in ch. 3 : 7ff., which Jesus also teaches from a boat, is said to come from those parts of Palestine inhabited by Jews, but that Samaria and Syria are omitted. Hence he suggests that this multitude may

---

[3] H. Rahner, "Antenna Crucis," *Zeitschr. f. kath. Theol.*, 66 (1942), p. 104. He also suggests that the following implications connected with the "world" in the New Testament may be associated with the figure of the sea: darkness, John 1 : 5; 9 : 4, 5; 12 : 46; Eph. 5 : 8; Acts 26. : 18; 2 Cor. 4 : 6; Phil. 2 : 15; 1 John 2 : 8; nothingness: 1 John 2 : 17; a possession of the enemy: John 12 : 31; 1 Cor. 2 : 6, 8; 2 Cor. 4 : 4; 1 John 5 : 19; but already conquered: John 16 : 33; 1 Cor. 11 : 32; 1 John 5 : 4.

[4] R. H. Lightfoot, *History and Interpretatoin in the Gospels* (1935), p. 89, "with great reserve and a keen sense of the dangers inherent in this form of exposition" suggests, in view of the parable interpretation in vs. 10-25, that the evangelist "was alive to the possibility of the form of interpretation" we are following here. "On the other hand," he recognizes, "there is no hint in 4 : 35-5 : 20, as there is in 4 : 1-34, that he has this aim in view."

[5] Lightfoot (n. 4), *loc. cit.*; J. Weiss, *Das älteste Evangelium* (1903), pp. 83-88, thinks Mark arranged and presented parts of his material particularly to emphasize the Gentile mission: the controversy over clean and unclean; the tour of Gentile territory; healing in the Decapolis; feeding the Four Thousand. Cf. also the centurion at the cross.

represent all Israel gathered to meet its Lord.⁶ This crowd taught by the sea from a ship is virtually identical with that in ch. 4 : 1ff.; it would seem that if one has a symbolic meaning, the other may also.

"They took him with them, just as he was, in the boat" (4 : 36b). Although in response to Jesus' command (cf. Mk. 13 : 10; Mt. 28 : 19f.) this is the action of the disciples: they take Jesus, not he, them.⁷ This may represent the apostolic leadership under which the ship of the church⁸ sets forth on the sea of the world, with its Lord in its midst, "just as he was." The word παραλαμβάνουσιν has been the object of considerable discussion because it seems to imply that Jesus only now was "received" into the ship by the disciples, whereas v. 1 indicates he was already there. Several scholars have seen this problem as evidence that vs. 1 and 36 are the result of an awkward combination by the evangelist of two originally unrelated traditions, a situation which he tried to smooth over by inserting the words, "as he was."⁹ However, if the evangelist was aware of a contradiction between vs. 1 and 36, he could as easily have substituted another word for παραλαμβάνουσιν to remove the difficulty, as to have inserted "as he was," unless he had a special purpose in retaining this particular word. Both in secular Koine and in the New Testament, παραλαμβάνειν is the correlative of παραδοῦναι (1 Cor. 11 : 23; 15 : 3; 2 Thess. 3 : 6; cf. Mk. 7 : 3f.; Gal. 1 : 9).¹⁰ The same double sense that attaches to the latter word may be found in παραλαμβάνειν: to receive a person or a thing literally, or to receive a tradition (cf. John 1 : 11), particularly for the purpose of passing it on. This second meaning may provide the reason for the evangelist's use (or retention) of παραλαμβάνουσιν in v. 36: as the church set forth into the world, it carried with it the tradition regarding Christ that the apostles had received (cf. 1 Cor. 11 : 23; 15 : 3; 2 Thess. 3 : 6).

---

⁶ R. H. Lightfoot, *Locality and Doctrine in the Gospels* (1938), pp. 118f.

⁷ Lightfoot (n. 4), *loc. cit.*

⁸ That the ship is the church in the present context has been suggested by several modern scholars (see Ch. I, n. 8). Among ancient and medieval writers who interpret the ship in the story of the storm as the church are Tertullian, *De baptismo*, 12; Augustine, *Sermo* 63, 1; Cyril of Alexandria, *Comment. in Lucam* VIII, 22; Peter Chrysologus, *Sermo* 20; *Sermo* 21; Bede, *In Matthaei evangelium expositio* II, 8; Walafrid Strabo [Ps. Jerome], *Expositio quatuor evangeliorum. Matthaeus* (Migne, *Patr. Lat.*, 30, 550); *Marcus*, (Migne 30, 561); ibid., *Comment. in evangelium sec. Marcum* IV; Remigius, *Homilia* IX.

⁹ See above, n. 2.

¹⁰ J. H. Moulton and G. Milligan, *The Vocabulary of The Greek Testament* (1949), p. 486.

"And other boats were with him" (4 : 36c). Lohmeyer finds καὶ ἄλλα δὲ "not impossible in the Koine, but unusual in such an unimportant (nebensächlich) sense."[11] Because of this and of the fact that no further mention is made of these other boats, he concludes that the original reading was ἄλλα δὲ πλοῖα οὐκ ἦν μετ' αὐτοῦ and that Mark removed οὐκ and inserted καὶ in order to provide a means of transportation for "those who were about him with the twelve" (v. 10). While καὶ ἄλλα δὲ is the *lectio difficilior*, the manuscript evidence for it (A C² D K syʰ) is less impressive than that for reading simply καὶ ἄλλα (ℵ B C* L Δ it syᵖ). In any event, Lohmeyer is doubtless right in connecting the "other boats" of v. 36 with "those who were about him with the twelve" in v. 10, so that, as J. Weiss notes, the presence of these additional boats implies the broadening of the circle of disciples.[12] That it is these additional disciples to whom the explanation of the parable of the sower is given, together with the words, "To you has been given the secret of the kingdom of God" (v. 11), seems to imply the growth of the church, especially when placed in the context of the "other boats." Allegorical explanations of these boats as representing Christians who succumb to tribulation and fail to reach heaven,[13] or heretics,[14] can hardly find support in the context of our story.

"And a great storm of wind arose" (4 : 37a). That the wind here is a figure of demonic powers is probable both in view of its general symbolism as such in folklore,[15] and also for more immediate reasons. The second word of Jesus' rebuke in v. 39, πεφίμωσο, appears in Mark elsewhere only at ch. 1 : 25, φιμώθητι, where it is Jesus' rebuke to an "unclean spirit" (cf. Lk. 4 : 35).[16] And indeed the term "unclean spirit" (πνεῦμα ἀκάθαρτον) admits also of the translation, "unclean wind."[17] In both cases Jesus is said "to rebuke" (ἐπιτιμεῖν) the spirit or the wind, implying a personification. Patristic exegesis frequently interprets the wind in this story as a demonic power.[18]

---

[11] Lohmeyer (n. 1), p. 90.
[12] Weiss (n. 5), p. 181.
[13] Bede, *In Marci evangelium expositio* II, 4.
[14] Walafrid Strabo [Ps. Jerome], *Expositio quatuor evangeliorum. Marcus* (Migne, *Patr. Lat.*, 30, 561).
[15] Klostermann (n. 2), p. 53; Rahner (n. 3), 66 (1942), p. 103.
[16] Cf. J. M. Robinson, *The Problem of History in Mark* (1957), pp. 40f.
[17] Cf. Wellhausen (n. 2), p. 39.
[18] Cyril Alex. (n. 8), *loc. cit.*; Bede (n. 8), *loc. cit.*; idem (n. 13) II, 4; idem, *In Lucam evangelium expositio* III, 8; Walafrid Strabo, *Comment. in evang. sec. Marcum* IV (Migne, *Patr. Lat.*, 30, 605); Remigius (n. 8), *loc. cit.*

"And the waves beat into the boat" (4 : 37b). The two main motifs connected with the sea, as evil and as the world, appear to combine and so to portray here the nations incited by demons to attack the church. This picture is eschatological (cf. Rev. 16 : 13-16).[19] The connection between such tribulation and the proclamation of the gospel to the Gentiles, which seems to be reflected in our story, is clear in Mk. 13 : 9f. (cf. Mt. 24 : 9-14, where the statements "you will be hated by all nations" [v. 9], "many false prophets will arise" [v. 11], and "this gospel of the kingdom will be preached throughout the whole world" [v. 14] are united in the same context).

"So that the boat was already filling" (4 : 37c). This may imply that in the midst of eschatological tribulation, the church is on the verge of going under; cf. Mk. 13 : 20, 22.

"But he was in the stern, asleep on the cushion" (4 : 38a). Such a position may have been that of the steersman,[20] or the place of honor.[21] The latter view seems more probable inasmuch as the steersman was not normally the commander, and Jesus was not a seaman, while the disciples were. Christ's position here in the ship may emphasize his **lordship in the church**.

"Asleep... and they woke him" (4 : 38b). Jesus' sleeping and arising from sleep to bring peace may suggest that when the church is beset by evil, it finds peace and victory through his **death and resurrection**.[22] But can the events of the Passion logically be inferred here immediately after references (v. 37) that seem to have a connection with Mk. 13? Lightfoot has exhibited a number of apparent relationships between Jesus' prophecy in Mk. 13 and the passion story in Mk. 14-15: παραδοῦναι used of the church in ch. 13 : 9, 11f., and of Jesus, chs. 14 : 10f., 18, 21, 41f., 44; 15 : 1, 10, 15; the "hour" in chs. 13 : 32 and 14 : 35, 41; 15 : 25; the coming of the Son of Man,

---

[19] E. Peterson, "Das Schiff der Kirche," *Theol. Zeitschr.*, 6 (1950), p. 79, notes the eschatological nature of this passage in connection with the vision of the ship in *T. Naph*. Walafrid Strabo (n. 14), *loc. cit.*, sees the storm as the persecution of the church by Antichrist, while Petrus Chrysologus, *Sermo* 21, interprets "that day" (v. 35) as the eschatological "day of the Lord."
[20] B. Weiss, *Das Marcusevangelium* (1872), p. 168.
[21] So Lagrange, *L'évangile selon St. Marc* (1947), p. 123, citing Virgil, *Aeneid* IV, 554; cf. V. Taylor, *The Gospel according to St. Mark* (1952), p. 275.
[22] Cf. J. Wilkens, *Der König Israels*, I (1934), 128. That Jesus' sleeping and waking may be associated with his death and resurrection was a common idea in the old exegesis: see Peter Chrysologus, *Sermo* 20; Bede (n.13), *loc. cit.*; idem, *In Lucae evengelium expositio* III, 8; Walafrid Strabo (n. 18), *loc. cit.*; Remigius (n. 8), *loc. cit.*

chs. 13 : 26 and 14 : 62.²³ Thus Mark may also imply references to both the prophecy and the Passion in the present context.

"'Teacher, do you not care if we perish?'" (4 : 38c). While there is no essential dependence of our narrative upon the vision of the ship in the *Testament of Naphtali*, a number of parallels exist: the ship, the twelve patriarchs or apostles, the eschatological storm, and prayer for salvation. With the last point, as Peterson has noted,²⁴ there is an important difference, for in the *Testament of Naphtali*, the prayer of Levi brings deliverance; but in the Gospel story, not the disciples' prayer, but the authority of the Messiah himself, present in his church, brings peace.

"And he awoke and rebuked the wind" (4 : 39a). The repetition of the thought that Jesus "awoke" and its association with his rebuking the wind (see above on. v. 37a) suggests that the resurrection involves a victory over demonic powers (Eph. 1 : 20-2: 7; Phil. 2 : 9-11; 1 Pet. 3 : 22).²⁵

"And said to the sea" (4 : 39b). The Western reading and that of Family 1, ἐπετίμησεν τῷ ἀνέμῳ καὶ τῇ θαλάσσῃ καὶ εἶπεν· (D 1, 118, 131, 209, bceff²q arm) seems to fit the context better.²⁶ The words "Peace! Be still!" are addressed more fittingly to the wind as a demon, and only secondarily to the sea as the object of its action. The following statement that "the wind ceased, and there was a great calm," also suggests this.

"'Peace! Be Still!'" (4 : 39c). The verb φιμοῦν, "to muzzle," suggests that the evil powers, here represented by the wind, are not yet finally destroyed, but are vanquished and bound.

"'Who then is this, that even wind and sea obey him?'" (4 : 41). Note the almost identical question at the casting out of the "unclean spirit," ch. 1 : 27. Here these words are addressed not only by the disciples to one another, but especially by the evangelist to the understanding reader. They imply that the story holds a deeper meaning, a revelation of who Jesus really is.²⁷ The story embodies a

---

²³ R. H. Lightfoot, *The Gospel Message of St. Mark* (1950), pp. 51-54.
²⁴ Peterson (n. 19), p. 79.
²⁵ Cf. Bede, *In Lucae evangelium expositio* III, 8 (Migne, *Patr. Lat.*, 92, 435): "Arising, he rebuked the wind, because with the celebration of the resurrection he laid low the haughtiness of the devil, while by death he destroyed him who had the power of death."
²⁶ Wellhausen (n. 2), p. 39.
²⁷ Dibelius (n. 2), pp. 91f. Cf. Gregory Nazianzen, *Carminum* I, 1, 28 (Migne, *Patr. Gr.*, 37, 507): "In this miracle those present perceived the nature of God."

"secret epiphany" for the revelation of the messianic secret. This final sentence sums up the whole point of the narrative:

1. It seems to imply a two-fold view of Christ: the exhausted, sleeping, human Jesus whom the disciples had had with them in the boat – the Jesus they knew; and the Lord who arose to command wind and wave – the Lord they did not yet know and could not understand.[28] Mark invites the reader to contemplate especially the latter aspect.

2. The wind is especially significant for the revelation of the messianic secret, for in Mark the demons are portrayed as being particularly aware of Jesus' identity and sensitive to him (Mk. 1 : 23-27; 3 : 11f.; 5 : 7; 9 : 20). In the presence of unbelievers, as in the synagogue at Capernaum, the command to silence is calculated to preserve the messianic secret, but in the presence of his disciples, a similar command to the demonic wind is intended to reveal it. Yet the real parallel between the two narratives is that for the reader who sees with eyes of faith, both incidents reveal who Jesus really is (cf. ch. 1 : 27 with ch. 4 : 41). This can be understood only in the light of the resurrection, for only there does Jesus' triumph over these powers become a conclusive fact.

3. Jesus' rebuking the sea reveals him to the discerning reader as divine, for in the Old Testament it is God who stills the sea (Ps. 65 : 7; 89 : 9; 106 : 9; cf. the Yahweh-dragon myth).[29] As Rahner has emphasized, the symbolism that portrays Christ here as triumphing over the demon-driven powers of the world (wind and sea) cannot be written off simply as an "echo of Hellenistic piety," even though its symbols may be demonstrated from that context.[30] These symbols are rooted in the Old Testament, and here they seem to convey the genuinely Christian consciousness that Christ has triumphed over the powers of evil.

4. A further significance of Jesus' triumph over the sea may be seen in connection with the mission of the church. In the Old Testament, God's conquest of the sea is repeatedly connected with his creation of the world. Similarly Jesus' triumph over the sea appears

---

[28] Lohmeyer (n. 1), pp. 92f.; cf. Bede (n. 73), *loc. cit.* (Migne, *Patr. Lat.*, 92, 173): "In this voyage, the Lord deigns to display each nature of his single person: while as man he sleeps in the ship, as God he quells by word the fury of the sea"; cf. Chrysostom, *Hom.* 28 *in Matt.*

[29] Weiss (n. 5), p. 182; Taylor (n. 21), p. 272; E. Hoskyns and N. Davey, *The Riddle of the New Testament* (1957), p. 123.

[30] Rahner (n. 3), 66 (1942), pp. 103f.

to be associated with his resurrection – the recreation of humanity (Eph. 2 : 4-6). Lindeskog has pointed out that just as the Israelites reached the conclusion that God's creative activity implied the salvation of the Gentiles, so also the early church was convinced that the recreation they had experienced in Christ called them forth to a world mission.[31] This relationship of the ideas of triumph over the sea, creation, and world mission is probably reflected in our narrative.

5. Lightfoot notes that "it is in the course of the transit [from Jewish to Gentile soil] that the problem of the nature and person of Jesus begins to make itself acutely felt."[32] This may reflect the appearance of Christological problems as the gospel was first presented to Gentile hearers.

6. The revelation of the messianic secret is the revelation of the Christ-event that lies at the midpoint of the history of salvation. The ensuing period between Pentecost and Parousia, which seems to be represented by our story, is rooted in that event. It should be no surprise then if all the motifs in our narrative reflect characteristics of this period of salvation-history. In fact, it is only in connection with the history of salvation that inner, co-ordinated relationships between them can be realized. Cullmann has emphasized that in foundation this period is the time of the reign of Christ, and in meaning for salvation-history it is the time of the preaching of the gospel to all peoples.[33] Both of these characteristics appear to be reflected in our narrative. Jesus' position in the ship suggests his lordship in the church, and this lordship is even more clearly demonstrated by his stilling the storm, which implies his triumph over supernatural powers. But the triumph expresses itself at this point only in a rebuke and a binding ($\varphi\iota\mu o\tilde{\upsilon}\nu$), not yet in a final destruction. This tension between "binding" and not yet accomplished annihilation is the tension that characterizes the present period in the history of salvation, which Cullmann has described as "the time between the decisive battle, which has already occurred, and the 'Victory Day'".[34] Here is "the only dialectic and the only dualism that is found in the New Testament."[35] The other characteristic of this period, the proclamation

---

[31] G. Lindeskog, "The Theology of Creation in the Old and New Testaments," in A. Fridrichsen et al., *The Root of the Vine* (1953), pp. 1-22.
[32] Lightfoot (n. 4), pp. 89f.
[33] Cullmann, *Christ and Time* (2d Eng. ed., 1950), p. 148; cf. p. 157.
[34] Cullmann (n. 33), p. 145.
[35] Cullmann (n. 33), p. 146; cf. Phil. 2 : 6ff.; 2 Tim. 1 : 10; 1 Pet. 3 : 22 with 1 Cor. 15 : 25; Heb. 10 : 13.

of the gospel, also appears to be a leading motif in our narrative. This gives the period its meaning in the history of salvation. It is the proclamation of the Christ-event lying at the center of that history, and of Christ's lordship in the church. At the same time it gives this period an eschatological character, for it is one of the signs of the end (Mk. 13 : 10; Mt. 24 : 14).[36] Another of these signs is the tribulations that come upon the church; hence it is understandable that our story should portray the ship of the church beset by winds and storm as it pursues its mission of proclamation. The various motifs in our story appear to find unification and co-ordination in terms of the history of salvation.

> At this point the objection may arise that we have been inconsistent in interpreting the storm at one time as the powers over whom Jesus is victor at his resurrection, and at another as evil powers attacking the church during the period after the resurrection, after these powers have already been bound. However, this two-fold application of the storm motif appears rather to illustrate the tension of which we have spoken: the victory over these powers is assured at the resurrection, but they are not yet wiped out and may still threaten (but not overwhelm) the church. Our story presents a symbolic picture, a mosaic of themes, in which the association of ideas is perhaps more important than their sequence. In this story the death and resurrection of Christ (his sleeping and awaking) occur at the mid-point of the voyage of the church, not because they happen at that point in the history of the church, but because they are the central fact both in the meaning of the story and in the history of salvation.

"The country of the Gerasenes" (5 : 1). Jesus and his disciples now were to deal with Gentiles. This may indicate that the events about to be narrated have meaning especially for the Gentile mission.[37]

"And when they had come out of the boat" (5 : 2a). The repeated mention of the boat here and in vs. 18 and 21, all in connection with the mission to Gentile territory, suggests that it may represent the Jewish-Christian church, particularly under the aspect of its mission to the Gentiles. Before the voyage begins, Jesus is already teaching Jews from it. While he most certainly leaves it upon regaining Jewish territory, Mark – who carefully notes both exit from and re-entry into it on Gentile soil – does not say so. Thus the present verse may

---

[36] Cullmann (n. 33), p. 158.
[37] Thus Bede (n. 13), *loc. cit.* (Migne, *Patr. Lat.*, 92, 176), remarks regarding the Gerasenes, "a nation of the Gentiles, which after the sleep of the passion and the glory of his resurrection, the Saviour deigned to visit by the preachers whom he sent forth."

imply that although the gospel was first carried to the Gentiles by the Jewish-Christian church, upon reaching the Gentile world it could no longer be contained within the limits of Jewish Christianity.

"A man with an unclean spirit" (5 : 2b). In the previous episode, demonic powers appear to be portrayed by the forces of nature. Now, as the gospel enters Gentile territory, humanity itself is shown as possessed. The various characteristics stated of this man reflect graphically the early Christian view of the Gentile world: he dwells among the dead, he is uncontrollable and completely wild (cf. Eph. 2 : 1-3).

"'Jesus, Son of the Most High God'" (5 : 7). In the other two instances in Mark in which demons declare Jesus' identity (ch. 1 : 24, 3 : 11) the words "Most High God" do not appear. This together with the fact that this sometimes syncretistic title occurs only here in Mark (but cf. ch. 11 : 10), may reflect the fact that it issues from the mouth of a Gentile (cf. Acts 16 : 17).

"'My name is Legion; for we are many'" (5 : 9). This seems to emphasize the multiplicity of demonic powers with which the heathen world is possessed; cf. 1 *Enoch* 6 : 6.

"The herd... were drowned in the sea" (5 : 13). That the demon-possessed swine immediately run for the sea seems to imply a connection between demons and the sea similar to that in the preceeding narrative of the storm. The fact that swine were considered unclean suggests the possibility that they may have been thought in some sense to belong to the underworld of the sea.[38]

"And as he was getting into the boat" (5 : 18). The former demoniac wishes to enter the ship with Jesus. If the ship here represents the Jewish-Christian church, the question of the man's entering the boat may reflect the problem of whether Gentile converts were to be incorporated into the Jewish-Christian community, as Lightfoot has proposed (cf. the man's desire, ἵνα μετ' αὐτοῦ ᾖ, with ch. 3 : 14, of the Twelve, ἵνα ὦσιν μετ' αὐτοῦ).[39]

---

[38] Similarly the reduction of the Prodigal Son (Lk. 15 : 11ff.) to feeding swine seems to suggest not merely social, but spiritual degredation. Cf. the *Hymn of the Pearl* in the *Acts of Thomas*, 108-113 (E. Hennecke, *Neutestamentliche Apokryphen* [2d ed., 1924], pp. 277-281), where the son is sent by his father to "Egypt" to take away the pearl "that is there in the midst of the sea which is surrounded by the devouring serpent." Arriving there, however, he is drugged by the Egyptians and forgets his mission until reminded by a letter. He then fulfills his task and returns home, where he is honored by his father. The parallels between these stories suggest that possibly the swine in the Lucan narrative were thought to have a chthonic or demonic implication.

"But he refused" (5 : 19a). Gentiles are not to join the Jewish-Christian church (cf. Acts 15 : 19f.; Gal. 5 : 2f.).

"'Go home to your friends'" (5 : 19b). Rather Gentiles are to further the mission for their own people.

"'Tell them how much the Lord has done for you'" (5 : 19b). This command for proclamation appears out of harmony with Jesus' repeated instruction to those whom he healed not to reveal his identity (ch. 1 : 44; 5 : 43; 7 : 36; 8 : 26). B. Weiss sees this as a command not to general proclamation, but only for the man to share his blessing with his own family.[40] H. J. Holtzmann and others have held that Jesus wished to keep his identity secret only among the Jews, and that here, on Gentile soil, he felt at liberty to command his followers to proclaim himself.[41] Wrede finds this explanation unsatisfactory in that it presupposes too glaring a contradiction for an evangelist imbued with the idea of the messianic secret. He sees Jesus' refusal to take the man with him back to Jewish territory as arising from fear on Jesus' part that the man would betray his identity. Therefore Jesus' words to him are really an injunction to preserve the secret: the man is to keep it within his own family circle (οἶκος, cf. ch. 8 :26), and at that he is only "to report" (ἀπαγγέλλειν) what "the Lord" has done for him, a report that would not necessarily involve an identification of Jesus. But the man disobeys and goes instead among the public in the Decapolis and begins "to proclaim" (κηρύσσειν) what *Jesus* had done for him.[42] Lightfoot objects to Wrede's view on the ground that if the man really disobeyed Jesus' command, we should expect at the beginning of v. 20 ὁ δέ (cf. ch. 1 : 45; 7 : 36) instead of καί (but may not καί have here an adversative sense?[43]). Consequently he understands the man's action to have been in obedience to Jesus' command: Jesus' instruction is that the man should make known to the Gentiles what Israel's God (ὁ κύριος) had done for them; his obedience to this injunction is carried out by proclaiming that these blessings are conferred through *Jesus* (cf. Rom. 15 : 8-12).[44]

From the double point of view we have suggested for the interpre-

---

[39] Lightfoot (n. 4), p. 90.
[40] Weiss (n. 20), p. 181.
[41] H. J. Holtzmann, *Die Synoptiker* (3d ed., 1901), p. 9.
[42] W. Wrede, *Das Messiasgeheimnis in den Evangelien* (1901), pp. 140f.
[43] Cf. J. H. Moulton, *A Grammar of New Testament Greek*, II (1919), 422f. While this is a particular characteristic of the Fourth Gospel, it also appears in classical Greek.
[44] Lightfoot (n. 4), pp. 89f.

tation of these stories, a further explanation of the present passage may be possible. The story of Jesus' stilling the storm contains the paradox of a "secret epiphany"; Jesus' identity is revealed to his inner circle, but even they scarcely understood (cf. ch. 6 : 52), and the real revelation is that intended for the Christian reader. Similarly, at the casting out of the unclean spirit, Jesus' identity is proclaimed, but this also seems to make little impact on the disciples' understanding, and is again, like the cleansing in ch. 1 : 23-27, a revelation primarily from a later point of view.

On the level of the immediate situation, the story may be explained as containing an injunction to keep the messianic secret. This is in harmony with Mark's otherwise consistent presentation of Jesus, on this level, as desiring to maintain secrecy. The distinctions between τὸν οἶκόν σου and τῇ Δεκαπόλει, ἀπάγγειλον and κηρύσσειν, ὁ κύριος and Ἰησοῦς are too distinct for us to ignore Wrede's conclusion that the secret is here in view. But, as in ch. 1 : 23ff., that which is intended as a secret at one level is also intended by the evangelist to be a revelation at another. From this second point of view, which we have attempted to elucidate symbolically, the messianic secret is no longer a secret; the events that occasioned Jesus' injunctions to secrecy have now become means of revealing his true identity. Mark may purposely have employed the ambiguous καὶ at v. 20 (rather than a decisive ὁ δὲ), because he intended the possibility of a double interpretation; from the standpoint of Jesus' life, the secret was to be maintained, and the man was disobedient; but from the standpoint of the mission of the church which seems to be reflected symbolically from ch. 4 : 1 onward, the man's proclamation of Jesus would represent the revelation of that secret to the Gentiles (cf. Eph. 3 : 1-3). The progression from ὁ κύριος to Ἰησοῦς may imply the proclamation to the Gentiles that Jesus is Lord (cf. Acts 10 : 36; 2 Cor. 4 : 5; Phil. 2 : 9-11; 1 Pet. 3 : 15).

Matthew 8 : 23-9 : 1.

The literary structure of this story from v. 23 to v. 27 is similar to that in Mark, if not more poetic,[45] suggesting that it may have been employed in some liturgical way.

The setting of this narrative differs from that in Mark. Jesus'

---

[45] E. Lohmeyer and W. Schmauch, *Das Evangelium des Matthäus* (2d ed., 1958), pp. 162f.; J. Wilkens (n. 22), I, 127f.; A. Loisy, *L'évangile selon Luc* (1924), p. 68.

getting into a ship to teach the crowds (Mk. 4 : 1) finds no parallel here, and he seems first to enter it just before departing for the eastern shore (Mt. 8 : 23; par. Mk. 4 : 35f.). To this extent Matthew has not preserved Mark's setting, but has followed rather a principle of organization determined by subject matter. Verses 18-22 are made up of two pronouncement stories dealing with the meaning of following Jesus. Matthew introduces our narrative by connecting it with the theme of these stories: "And when he got into the boat, his disciples followed him" (v. 23).[46] This is an inversion of the sense of Mark, where the apostles take Jesus. The presence at the beginning of our story of the verb "to follow" (ἀκολουθεῖν), which has a double significance, suggests that the evangelist saw a deeper meaning in this narrative than merely that of a miraculous deed. For him the point of the story seems to be this: the disciple is to follow his Lord into the ship, across the sea, through storm, to "the other side, to the country of the Gadarenes" (v. 28). In terms of the symbolism we have proposed in interpreting the story in Mark, this may mean that the believer will follow his Master into the church, and as a part of the mission of the church, out into the world, where he will meet and survive tribulation in proclaiming the gospel to the Gentiles. If this is correct, our story is a part of the evangelist's preparation for the speech in ch. 10 in which Jesus sends forth the Twelve.

"There arose a great storm on the sea" (8 : 24). Whereas Mark's term for the storm is λαῖλαψ ἀνέμου (ch. 4 : 37), "a tempest of wind," Matthew uses σεισμός, "an earthquake." This word appears again in Matthew in the contexts of Christ's death and resurrection (ch. 27 : 54; 28 : 2) and of the eschatological tribulation (ch. 24 : 7). As in the Marcan account, all of this seems to lie within the implications of our story. The first evangelist, in fact, goes farther than Mark in connecting eschatological events with the figures of a ship and a storm when he portrays Jesus as comparing "the coming of the Son of man" with "the days of Noah" (Mt. 24 : 37). There is, however, a significant difference between this figure and our narrative. In the former, salvation depends upon being in the ark; in the latter, the disciples are saved not because they are in the ship, but because Jesus is in their midst.

"'Save, Lord; we are perishing'" (8 : 25). As Dibelius notes, this cry has a more edifying tone than its parallel in Mark.[47] It may be

---

[46] Schmidt (n. 2), p. 138; cf. Wellhausen (n. 2), p. 39.
[47] Dibelius (n. 2), p. 74.

seen as the prayer of the church to its Lord, recognizing him as its Saviour ("save"), and confessing its human distress ("we are perishing").[48]

"And the men marvelled" (8 : 27). The specific reference to the disciples as "men" (ἄνθρωποι; contrast Mk. 4 : 41) suggests that in a deeper sense men in general are meant: the revelation of the messianic secret, implied in their question, is not to be restricted to the disciples.[49]

The healing of the demoniacs (ch. 8 : 28-9 : 1), as in Mark, follows the story of the storm, but here the ship is not in view (except at ch. 9 : 1). The evangelist does not appear to be concerned with the problem of the relation of Gentile converts to the Jewish-Christian church: he says nothing of Jesus' leaving the boat or of the demoniac's desire to enter it with him. His concentration is still on the mission to the Jews, and while the implications of our story for the Gentile mission cannot be missed (as also in ch. 2 : 1ff.; 3 : 7ff.; 8 : 5ff., 11ff.), he raises no issue here regarding it. Not until after Jesus' rejection (ch. 13 : 53-58) in "his own country" does the evangelist begin to show him as uttering words that point clearly to the necessity of the Gentile mission: ch. 15 : 21ff.; 22 : 2ff.; 25 : 14ff. But even these are cryptic indications, and a clear injunction to go to the Gentiles comes only after the resurrection at ch. 28 : 19f. It is not surprising then that our narrative, coming in the early part of the Gospel, does not reflect concern for the problems occasioned by the Gentile mission.

Luke 8 : 22-39.

The literary structure of the Lucan story of the storm (vs. 22-25) is metrical, like that in Mark and Matthew. Loisy has divided it into four couplets (vs. 22, 23, 24b, 25b).[50]

The setting of Luke's story differs from that in both Mark and Matthew. Like Matthew, Luke has no indication of Jesus' teaching the Jews from the boat before the voyage begins, as in Mark. But unlike Matthew, he has retained Mark's connection of the story with the parables of the kingdom (Lk. 8 : 4-18), though less closely. Between the parable section and the storm narrative, Luke has inserted the pronouncement story (vs. 19-21) regarding the true family

---

[48] Lohmeyer and Schmauch (n. 45), p. 163.
[49] Thus Basil of Seleucia, *Oratio* XIII (Migne, *Patr. Gr.*, 85, 269), concludes a sermon on our narrative with the words, "What sort of man is this? If of this ye inquire, this is the Son of the living God."
[50] Loisy (n. 45), pp. 66f.

of Jesus, which in this setting may indicate his universalism. The connection with the parable material is loosened even more by the change he makes in Mark's chronological setting. Whereas Mark places the voyage on the evening of the day in which Jesus had uttered the kingdom parables (Mk. 4 : 35), Luke breaks this chronological connection by beginning his story ἐγένετο δὲ ἐν μιᾷ τῶν ἡμερῶν (ch. 8 : 22), implying that the crossing took place at a later time. Taken together, these tendencies to disassociate the storm narrative from its immediate Marcan setting may reflect Luke's interest in the Gentile, rather than the Jewish, mission. The Marcan story seems to hold both Jewish and Gentile aspects of the Christian mission clearly in view; in Matthew the distinction between the two is scarcely apparent, while with Luke the story appears to focus on the Gentile mission.

"'Let us go across to the other side of the lake'" (8 : 22a). Conzelmann suggests that Luke uses "lake" (λίμνη) rather than "sea" (θάλασσα) as in Mark and Matthew, because to a Gentile writing from the perspective of the Mediterranean, "sea" would scarcely be appropriate for such a minor body of water.[51] For Luke the sea of Galilee is the boundary for Jesus' activity.[52] This is apparent in the present narrative (see vs. 22, 26, 37, 40); thus Jesus' crossing the sea probably gives emphasis to Luke's interest in the Gentile mission. Furthermore, for Luke the lake is a place of secret epiphanies. Only once does Jesus appear there publicly (ch. 5 : 1-3), and this is followed immediately by an epiphany, in which apparently none but his disciples is involved.[53] No other boats but those of the disciples are ever mentioned as being on the lake (cf. ch. 8 : 22 with Mk. 4 : 36). In the present story the lake is the scene of an epiphany, which seems to have a particular implication for the Gentile mission.

"So they set out" (8 : 22b). Luke's concept of the voyage of the church on its Gentile mission is best understood from his history of that enterprise in the Acts. Such a history indicates the importance in his mind of the period in the history of salvation following Pentecost, the period characterized by the Christian mission. Conzelmann points out that Luke's view of this period involves a clearer realization of its following a regularly developing plan than is apparent in either

---

[51] H. Conzelmann, *The Theology of St Luke* (1960), p. 42, n. 1.
[52] Conzelmann (n. 51), p. 39; cf. J. Wellhausen, *Das Evangelium Lucae* (1904), p. 38.
[53] Conzelmann (n. 51), p. 42.

Mark or Matthew.[54] During this period the expansion of the church and its persecution go together (cf. Acts 4 : 24ff.; 5 : 41f.; 9 : 16).[55] This tension seems to be reflected in our story by the storm that attacks the ship of the church on its voyage.

"Then they arrived at the country of the Gerasenes" (8 : 26). Whereas Mark and Matthew use simply ἔρχεσθαι, Luke describes the arrival in Gentile territory with the more colorful καταπλεῖν, "to sail down," i.e., into port. If our interpretation is correct, this would present a vivid picture of the ship of the church coming to port in the heathen world for the proclamation of the gospel.

"Sitting at the feet of Jesus" (8 : 35). This detail, not found in Mark and Matthew, seems to reflect Luke's greater concentration on the Gentile mission. Not only are Gentiles cleansed, as in Matthew; not only are they also to proclaim what God has done for them, as in Mark; but here they are depicted as receiving instruction after their cleansing, and before their commission to proclaim (v. 39). This agrees with Luke's more developed sense of the programmatic nature of the Christian mission (cf. the geographical program in Acts 1 : 8). It may also reflect problems encountered by the early church, in which Gentiles, once converted, were eager to proclaim before they had been sufficiently instructed. Reicke has shown that Luke is conscious of problems the church encountered in its growth, and that he often presents his material with a view of giving indications for their solution.[56]

"Begged that he might be with him" (8 : 38). While Matthew drops this episode, Luke preserves it, but makes no specific mention of the ship, either at this point (cf. Mk. 5 : 18) or when Jesus returns to the western shore (cf. Mk. 5 : 21). These differences may have arisen without particular intent. On the other hand, they may reflect the fact that for Luke the church is just as much Gentile as Jewish. Mark appears to consider the church a new order of Israel, focusing on the mission of the Jewish-Christian church to the Gentile world, as his specific references to Jesus' leaving and re-entering the ship suggest.

---

[54] Note Bede's sense of the programmatic nature of Luke's narrative of the stilling of the storm and the Gerasene demoniac (*In Lucae evangelium expositio* III, 8 [Migne, *Patr. Lat.*, 92, 440]): "When he had left the people of Judea, from whom he was descended in the flesh, and had gone through the tempest of his passion, he took care of the salvation of the Gentiles. This done, he returned to his own country, for 'blindness has come upon part of Israel, until the fulness of the Gentiles comes in, and so all Israel shall be saved.'"
[55] Conzelmann (n. 51), pp. 209-215.
[56] B. Reicke, *Glaube und Leben der Urgemeinde* (1957), pp. 17f., 120.

While Luke is highly conscious of the problems raised by the Gentile mission (cf. Acts 15), he considers it a normal development in the growth of an institution that is neither essentially Jewish nor Gentile, but transcends both.[57]

In summarizing our attempt to interpret these stories, we would emphasize once more the experimental and tentative nature of its results. In regard to none of the interpretations proposed can we say more than that they appear to indicate the things suggested. However, if the main outlines of our interpretation are correct, the meaning of this story may be summarized as follows.

In Mark the disciples' voyage with Jesus in the ship reflects the mission of the church, and perhaps particularly that of Jewish-Christianity. At first, as Jesus teaches Jews from near the shore, the church concentrates its mission upon Jews. Then as the ship sets forth across the sea, so the church turns to the broader perspective of the Gentile mission. This mission has eschatological significance, for it is a characteristic of the period between the cross and the Parousia. Consequently the church is attacked by demonic forces (the winds) which stir up the nations (the sea). But salvation lies in the fact of Jesus' death and resurrection (his sleeping and awakening), and in this he has conquered the demonic powers that dominate the world. Moreover he is present in his church as it faces the onslaughts of these same powers. When Jesus contacts Gentiles (arrives on the farther shore), the demonic power that holds them captive is broken, and they are set free (the cleansing of the demoniac). Then the question arises as to the relationship of converted Gentiles to the Jewish-Christian community (the man's desire to enter the ship), and they are told that they are not to join it, but are to go to their own people and proclaim what God has done for them.

The main differences that Matthew presents in contrast to Mark are that he does not seem to reflect the problem between Jews and Gentiles in the church, but rather lays emphasis on the thought of the disciples' following Jesus in the mission. Luke similarly does not betray concern for the Jewish-Gentile problem, but he seems to be more clearly conscious than Matthew that the mission portrayed here is specifically to the Gentiles. He also seems to exhibit particular concern for practical problems encountered by that mission.

---

[57] Significant in this connection is the place in his narrative to which Luke assigns Jesus' rejection at Nazareth; cf. Lightfoot (n. 4), p. 199.

Such interpretation of this story cannot be proved to have been in the minds of the evangelists. Yet when the motifs here are interpreted in the manner suggested, they present unity and coherence and are in harmony with the individual purpose and outlook of each of the synoptic Gospels. They seem to be reasonable possibilities.

CHAPTER VII

THE STORY OF JESUS' WALKING ON THE SEA

Mark 6 : 45-54.

This story is part of a complex of three narratives: the Feeding of the Five Thousand (vs. 30-44), the Walking on the Sea (vs. 45-52), and the Healing at Gennesaret (vs. 53-56). That the first two of these were connected in Christian tradition even before Mark is evident for several reasons. (1) The second narrative begins with a clear reference to the first in the statement that Jesus sent the disciples away "while he dismissed the crowd" (v. 45). (2) As we shall see below, Jesus' constraining the disciples to leave is probably best understood in the light of the aftermath of the Feeding. (3) At the end of the story, the reference to the disciples' failure to "understand about the loaves" (v. 52) ties the two narratives together not only in point of time, but especially in meaning.[1] (4) These two narratives are joined in John 6 : 1-21, which suggests a very old tradition.

In Mark this complex is placed in a broader and looser context of narratives that are also significant for the meaning of our story. The ch. 6 : 1-6 Jesus is rejected in his "own country" (πατρίς); this is followed (vs. 7-13) by the mission charge to the Twelve and their going forth; then comes (vs. 14-16) Herod's reaction to the mission and, as an explanatory appendage (vs. 17-29), the story of the Baptist's death. These loosely associated narratives form the backdrop for the two closely connected stories of the Feeding and the Walking on the Sea.[2] Lightfoot has suggested that Jesus' rejection by the people of Nazareth is a turning point in Mark's Gospel and symbolizes the rejection of Jesus by the Jews in general.[3] This rejection is further dramatized when the Baptist is executed by a Jewish ruler. In Mark's chronological scheme this had occurred earlier, but is not mentioned until now. The presentation of these events at this point suggests that Mark is consciously giving a basis for Jesus' having turned the focus of his ministry thereafter toward the Gentiles as illustrated by

[1] Taylor, *The Gospel according to St. Mark* (1942), p. 327.
[2] Taylor (n. 1), p. 95.
[3] R. H. Lightfoot, *History and Interpretation in the Gospels* (1935), pp. 189ff., 199.

the tour of Tyre and Sidon (ch. 7 : 24ff.) and the Feeding of the Four Thousand "in the desert" (ch. 8 : 1ff.).[4] With this may be compared also his dispute with the Pharisees (ch. 7 : 1ff.). A positive indication of the importance of the mission in our context is the fact that in Mark's portrayal, Jesus' next major action after rejection is to send forth the Twelve.

In view of this setting, we may suggest that one of the major motifs in the compound narrative of the Feeding and Jesus' Walking on the Sea is the Christian mission. This seems to be obvious in the Feeding of the Five Thousand. It is not so apparent in the sea story. Here the voyage is not to Gentile territory, but in the opposite direction. Nor can it be inferred as clearly from the figure of the sea as the nations, for here the sea seems to have primarily a different significance. Rather the implication of the mission derives chiefly from the intimate connection of our story with the Feeding of the Five Thousand, which precedes it, and the healing narrative that follows it, for the latter climaxes with the subtly universalistic statement that "as many as touched" the fringe of his garment "were made well" (ἐσώζοντο, ch. 6 : 56).[5]

"Immediately he made his disciples get into the boat and go before him" (6 : 45). Apart from an immediate situation in Jesus' life probably involving the popular movement to make him king,[6] a deeper implication may also be present here bearing on the subsequent period of salvation-history. Jesus' command that the disciples "go before" (προάγειν) him may imply the gospel commission (cf. Mt. 28 : 19f.; Acts 1 : 8). Just as the sending forth of the Twelve in Mk. 6 : 7ff. confides to their hands a ministry of preaching and healing which until that time they had observed Jesus performing (cf. ch.

---

[4] J. M. Robinson, *Das Geschichtsverständnis des Markusevangeliums* (1956), p. 98.
[5] B. Weiss, *Das Marcusevangelium* (1872), p. 236, n. 1; idem, *Die vier Evangelien* (1900), p. 210, denies any connection of our narrative with the Gentile mission. He holds that Mark has provided an artificial inner connection between the stories of the Feeding and the Walking on the Water by the insertion of v. 52 to show how necessary it was, in view of the disciples' lack of understanding, for Jesus to turn from public ministry to the private instruction of his inner circle. However, according to Mark's ordering of materials, after these two miracles Jesus turns first to the Gentiles before he concentrates upon the disciples (Mk. 8 : 27ff).. Our concern is to understand what Mark intends by these stories, rather than their significance before they entered his hands.
[6] Bede, *In Marci evangelium expositio*, II, 6; R. H. Lightfoot, "A Consideration of Three Passages in St. Mark's Gospel," *In Memoriam Ernst Lohmeyer* (1951), p. 113; cf. C. H. Dodd, *The Interpretation of the Fourth Gospel* (1953), p. 334.

1 : 14f., 21-28 with ch. 6 : 12f.), so now Jesus sends them forth "before him" after having given, as an indication and example for their mission, the miracle of feeding the Five Thousand. This insight, of course, is from the later perspective of the evangelist.

The theme of mission suggests that the boat here again may represent the church.[7] A relation between it and the mission is already suggested at v. 32, where it is introduced as the vehicle by which Jesus reaches the site of the Feeding. This may imply that the church goes forth presenting Christ in the eucharist.[8] The story of the Feeding, then, seems to follow a pattern: the setting implies the mission of the church and the chief event of the story represents a central truth proclaimed by that mission. The same pattern seems to be present in the sea narrative that follows. The setting of the disciples going before Jesus in the boat suggests the church going forth on its mission. The events of the voyage appear to be significant of its proclamation.[9]

"And after he had taken leave of them, he went into the hills to pray" (6 : 46). If the Feeding of the Five Thousand represents the eucharist, the events of the present narrative may be related to other events of the Passion. Jesus' dismissing the multitude may represent the close of his public ministry, and perhaps his turning to the hills to pray may reflect his prayer in the Garden.[10]

"They were distressed in rowing, for the wind was against them" (6 : 48a). Although no real storm is portrayed here, the elements of demonic powers (wind[11]) and death (sea) are shown as threatening the church in the prosecution of its mission.

"He came to them, walking on the sea" (6 : 48b). In the story of the Stilling of the Storm, both ideas of the sea, as the world and as evil and death, seem to be present, although greater stress probably

---

[7] In the old exegesis, the boat in the narrative of the storm was frequently interpreted as the church: e.g., Augustine, *Sermo* 75, 4; *In Joannis evang.*, XXV, 5; Cyril of Alex., *In Joannis evang.* III, 4; Bede (n. 6), II, 6; Anselm, *Homilia* III.

[8] That Mark has the eucharist in mind when describing the feeding of the Five Thousand seems probable in view of his emphasis on the loaves as having a deeper meaning comprehended only by those whose hearts are not "hardened" (v. 52). This appears to be the messianic secret in connection with bread, which is the mystery of the eucharist. Cf. M. Dibelius, *Die Formgeschichte des Evangeliums* (2d ed., 1933), pp. 73, 92.

[9] E. Lohmeyer, *Das Evangelium des Markus* (1937), p. 136, notes that Mk. 6 : 30-8 : 26 says cryptically of Jesus essentially what Jesus himself declares to his disciples in ch. 8 : 27-10 : 45 concerning the necessity of his passion, death, and resurrection.

[10] Cf. J. Wilkens, *Der König Israels*, I (1934), p. 199.

[11] Cf. Augustine, *Sermo* 75, 4.

is due the former. But in the present context the ship is not sailing toward Gentile country. There is little if any indication that the mission is specifically to the Gentiles; rather, it seems to be the Christian mission in general. Hence the sea probably is best interpreted as the waters of death.[12] Jesus' walking on them would proclaim at once his victory over evil and death and his divinity (cf. Job 9 : 8; Sirach 24 : 5f. [8]).[13] As in the Stilling of the Storm, this story seems to contain a "secret epiphany," a revelation of the messianic secret. Such an epiphany provides another inner connection between our narrative and the Feeding of the Five Thousand. As Dibelius points out, the latter story is also an epiphany to the Christian reader, for it reveals to him his Saviour bestowing the Eucharist (cf. Lk. 24 : 30f.).[14] Lohmeyer shows that the epiphany each one contains has the same theological point: the Feeding portrays Christ as the Giver of life (cf. v. 52; John 6); his walking on the sea shows him to be Victor over death. Here are the positive and negative sides of the central theme of Christian proclamation.[15]

"He meant to pass by them" (6 : 48c). Strauss and Wellhausen have understood this clause to indicate that Jesus wished to pass by unseen in order to surprise the disciples on the farther shore.[16] Dehn takes Jesus' walking on the sea to be divine ecstasy not intended for human eyes, but which the disciples see accidently.[17] Lightfoot suggests that Jesus did not wish to encounter the disciples because of his disappointment and discouragement over their lack of comprehension (cf.

---

[12] As suggested by R. Bultmann, *Geschichte der synoptischen Tradition* (3d ed., 1957), p. 252, n. 1; Dibelius (n. 8), p. 277; G. Dehn, *Der Gottessohn* (3d ed., 1932), p. 142; Lohmeyer (n. 9), p. 135; Taylor (n. 1), p. 326.

[13] Cf. *Midrash Rabbah* on Ex. 16 : 4 (Soncino ed. [1939], p. 306): "A man can carve out for himself a way on a road, but he is not able to do so on the sea, but God carves out for Himself a path in the midst of the sea." Cf. J. H. Bernard, *The Gospel according to John* (1948), I, 186; E. Hoskyns and N. Davey, *The Riddle of the New Testament* (1931), p. 123. In the 39th *Ode of Solomon* the faithful soul finds his way across mighty streams that separate this world from the next by following the footsteps of his Lord. This apparently Jewish-Christian hymn, probably from about the end of the first Christian century, reflects a very early recognition that the figure of Jesus' walking on the water is significant of his triumph over death. Cf. G. Bertram, "Le chemin sur les eaux considéré comme motif de salut dans la piété chrétienne primitive," *Rev. d'hist. et de phil. rel.*, 7 (1927), pp. 531ff.

[14] Dibelius (n. 8), p. 92.
[15] Lohmeyer (n. 9), pp. 135 f.
[16] See Lohmeyer (n. 9), p. 133, n. 5.
[17] Dehn (n. 12), p. 141.

ch.1 : 35-39; 14 : 35).[18] However it may be questioned whether any of these interpretations do full theological justice to the Marcan context, in which the story taken as a whole appears to be an epiphany. Riesenfeld has shown that θέλω in the aorist or the imperfect (as here) must express an intention, or at least a desire.[19] In view of this, Dibelius and Lohmeyer are probably correct in understanding the clause to mean that Jesus desired to pass by before the disciples that they might see his divinity (cf. Ex. 33 : 18-23; 1 Kings 19 : 11f.).[20] In terms of the proclamation of the church this passage may reflect the post-resurrection appearances of Christ. Several features in the next two verses suggest this possibility. Thus v. 49, "they thought it was a ghost" (φάντασμα), may be compared with Lk. 24 : 37, where the disciples, beholding the risen Lord, "supposed that they saw a spirit" (πνεῦμα; D, Marcion, Appelles φάντασμα[21]). In v. 50, "they all saw him" is comparable with Lk. 24 : 33, "the eleven... and those who were with them," and 1 Cor. 15 : 5-8, especially v. 7, "then to all the apostles." They "were terrified" is paralleled by Mk. 16 : 8; Lk. 24 : 37. "It is I" may be compared with Lk. 24 : 39, "it is I myself." These parallels also suggest the possibility that Mark's original conclusion may have contained a resurrection story drawn upon by Luke.

"And he got into the boat with them and the wind ceased" (6 : 51). The theme shifts back from Jesus' walking on the sea, to the wind which had impeded the disciples' rowing. Whether these two themes were combined in the pre-Marcan tradition is difficult to determine,[22] but it seems significant that in both the voyage of the ship is an important feature, suggesting that the inner unity of the narrative as it now stands is found in its portrayal of the mission and message of the church. The combination of these themes seems to reflect the difficulties experienced by the church in its proclamation, and at the same time the idea that all such difficulties are overcome by virtue of the presence of Christ. The storm theme appears to be concerned more with the external problems of the mission; the theme of Jesus' walking on the sea, with the content of the proclamation.

"They did not understand about the loaves" (6 : 52). This

---

[18] Lightfoot (n. 6), *loc. cit.*
[19] H. Riesenfeld, *Zum Gebrauch von* θέλω *im Neuen Testament, Arb. u. Mitteil. aus d. nt. Sem. zu Uppsala* (1935), pp. 13f.
[20] Dibelius (n. 8), p. 92; Lohmeyer (n. 9), pp. 133f.
[21] Tertullian, *Against Marcoin* IV, 43; Hippolytus, *Philosophoumena* VII, 38, 4.
[22] Cf. Bultmann (n. 12), p. 231; Lohmeyer (n. 9), pp. 130-132.

statement plays a role at the close of the present epiphany story similar to that of ch. 4 : 41 in its context: without explaining the meaning of the miracle, the evangelist gives his reader a clear hint that the story contains a significance deeper than that which lies on the surface.

It also indicates that Jesus' walking on the water is closely connected with his feeding the Five Thousand, for failure to understand one is failure to understand the other. To know Christ as "the bread of life" is to know him as Conqueror over death. That Mark ties these miracles together in meaning is a strong indication that he intended both to be understood in these symbolical senses.

Further insight into what the evangelist intends his reader to "understand about the loaves" may be gained from ch. 8 : 14-21, which, following the feeding of the Four Thousand, is a more extended counterpart to the present verse. A specific reference there to the Five Thousand (v. 19) indicates that the evangelist sees the point of both his feeding narratives to be the same. Like the narrative of ch. 6 : 45ff., this passage is set in "the boat". The disciples' concern is with the fact that they have "only one loaf with them in the boat" (v. 14). While Jesus is warning them against "the leaven of the Pharisees and the leaven of Herod", they continue to discuss their lack of food. Jesus reminds them of the miraculous feedings and how much was left over each time, implying that in his hands the one loaf they have brought is sufficient for all. Seen only from the standpoint of the disciples' need of food, this passage would make better sense without the warning against the leaven (v. 15), for on first sight this verse seems to have no real connection with the point of the narrative.[23] Yet the implication of the final question, "Do you not yet understand?" (v. 21) is that a deeper meaning is involved. This suggests that the evangelist has a definite purpose in including the seemingly extraneous warning against the leaven of the Pharisees and Herod. In ch. 12 : 13-17, the "hypocrisy" (v. 15) of the Pharisees and Herodians consists of their attempting to entrap Jesus on the issue of his loyalty to Ceasar, an issue that presupposes the question of his messiahship. That such an issue is also implied by "the leaven" of the Pharisees and Herod is suggested by the evidence that after the miraculous feeding, the disciples were involved in an attempt to make Jesus king. Thus they were in danger of fostering a situation similar to that by which the Pharisees and Herodians previously had sought to entrap him. In view of this, the following interpretation of ch. 8 : 14-21 may be possible: the apostles, in the context of the church, are warned against attempting to interpret Jesus in terms of the common Jewish concept of the Messiah as a temporal king. This, in turn, raises the question of who he really is; if Messiah, what kind of Messiah? The references to the miraculous feedings provide the answer: he is a Messiah

---

[23] That this logion circulated independently of the present context is apparent from its inclusion in a series of logia in the Lucan travel narrative (ch. 12 : 1).

who has come as a Life-giver, to give life abundantly (cf. John 10 : 10). This seems to be what the evangelist intends the reader to "understand" from ch. 8 : 14-21.[24] If our interpretation of this passage is correct, it provides evidence that the story of Jesus' walking on the sea is intended as a revelation to those in the church of who he really is: the divine Messiah who conquers death and brings life and peace.

Matthew 14 : 22-33.

The first evangelist's narrative of Jesus' walking on the sea differs in two main aspects from that of Mark: (1) it adds the story of Peter's walking on the sea, and (2) it handles differently the revelation of Jesus' identity. At the same time Matthew preserves the complex of stories which form the Marcan context of our narrative, so that here too the basic theme of the story appears to be the mission and proclamation of the church. The drama of the mission seems to be heightened here, for not only is the progress of the ship impeded by the wind as in Mark, but the ship is "many furlongs distant from the land,[25] beaten by the waves" (v. 24). Coming as it does after Jesus' rejection in "his own country" (ch. 13 : 53ff.), when hints of the Gentile mission begin to appear in this Gospel, the increased emphasis on the sea in our story may reflect a greater concentration on the specifically Gentile mission than was apparent in the Marcan form of this narrative.[26]

In vs. 28-31 is added the account of Peter's walking on the water. As the events of vs. 15-27 seem to parallel the events of the passion, so Peter's leaving the ship and sinking in the sea may symbolize his

---

[24] Cf. John 4 : 7-15, where essentially the same point is set forth under the figure of water rather than bread: Jesus is the Giver of life, but the Samaritan woman misunderstands the figure to refer to literal water, just as the disciples take the bread here to mean literal bread.

[25] So B (Θφ sy^cp bo); ℵ C K (D) lat sy^h read μέσον τῆς θαλάσσης ἦν.

[26] Cf. the intimate connection between the motifs of storm and mission in the following comment on our narrative (Ps. Augustine [= Eraclius?], *Sermo* 72 [Migne, *Patr. Lat.*, 39, 1885]): "Finally after that, this ship was built in Jerusalem, and then from there was sent out in the midst of this roaring sea; the whirlpools of the tossing waves and the blasts of the raging winds bore it about hither and thither, and drove it upon the shores of every nation; it brought foreign goods to whatever place it came. For what is as foreign on this earth as the remission of sins through repentance, and the kingdom of heaven? And yet 'it was needful for Christ to suffer and to rise from the dead on the third day and for repentance and remission of sins to be preached in his name throughout all nations, beginning from Jerusalem' (Lk. 24 : 46f.). For from this very port this first ship weighed anchor."

denial of Jesus,[27] his leaving the church and almost being swallowed by the waters of death. Then he is saved and brought back to the boat, reinstated in the church by him who has conquered death (cf. John 21 : 15ff.). Instead of the words, "when he saw the wind" (v. 30), we should expect "when he saw the waves" (cf. v. 24), for one does not see wind, but rather its effect on the waves. This unexpected mention of the wind suggests that Peter's loss of faith is occasioned by the onslaught of a demonic power, and may be compared with Jesus' words to Peter (and all the disciples) in Lk. 22 : 31, "Simon, Simon, behold, Satan demanded to have you (ὑμᾶς), that he might sift you like wheat."

In an extended sense, Peter here may represent all the disciples, as he frequently does (cf. Mk. 8 : 29 par.; 8 : 33; 10 : 28 par.; Mt. 17 : 24).[28] The probability of this is strengthened by the fact that the evangelist sees Peter's denial as typical of the attitude of all the disciples at Jesus' trial (ch. 26 : 31, "You will all fall away"; v. 35, "so said all the disciples"; cf. Lk. 22 : 31, Σίμων ... ὑμᾶς; John 21 : 3, where just before his reinstatement, Peter has led the other disciples back to their old way of life). Peter's salvation at the hand of him who walks on the sea, then, may parallel not only his reinstatement by the risen Lord, but also the renewal of the commission to all the disciples implied in John 21 : 4-14. This is also suggested by the fact that the first evangelist seems to see the commission at ch. 28 : 19f. not only as a universalization of the original commission in ch. 4 : 18ff., but also as a reinstatement of all the disciples after their defection: ch. 26 : 31f., "Then Jesus said to them, 'You will all fall away because of me this night; ... But after I am raised up, I will go before you to Galilee'", finds its fulfillment in ch. 28 : 16-20, where the disciples "went to Galilee" and received the commission. This association of ideas also emphasizes further the theme of the mission in our narrative.

"When they got into the boat, the wind ceased" (14 : 32). That the wind ceases when Jesus enters the boat, rather than when he first appears to the disciples, or even when he speaks to them (v. 27), would seem to give this act a certain climactic status as well as to place emphasis on the significance of the boat. It may imply that Christ's return to and presence in his church after the resurrection and Pentecost insure it against being overwhelmed by demonic powers.

"And those in the boat worshipped him, saying, 'Truly you are the Son of God'" (14 : 33). Whereas Mark at this point has a question,

[27] Wilkens (n. 10), p. 199.
[28] O. Cullmann, *Peter: Disciple, Apostle, Martyr* (1953), pp. 23f.

"Who then is this ...?" (ch. 4 : 41), inviting the reader to penetrate the messianic secret, Matthew chooses to show that this story contains an epiphany, by flatly stating a confession. Both climaxes indicate the same thought: the divinity of the One who walks upon the sea. But the Matthean form raises an internal problem in that the evangelist has placed this recognition of Jesus as "Son of God" before Peter's confession at Caesarea Philippi (ch. 16 : 16). This arrangement seems to rob the latter of the climactic place it otherwise occupies in this Gospel (cf. ch. 16 : 21).[29] Yet our author would seem to have had a conscious purpose in giving his form of the story a climax different from Mark's. Why does he do this? Two points seem especially important in this connection. (1) Although Matthew reflects the messianic secret (cf. ch. 16 : 20), he is not as concerned with it as is Mark. He does not feel the necessity of portraying the slowness of the disciples in perceiving Jesus' identity. Consequently he can state plainly the significance of Jesus' walking on the sea. With this stated, it is no longer necessary to continue the revelation of this theme as does Mark in connection with the feeding of the Four Thousand (ch. 8 : 14-21), where "the leaven of the Pharisees and Herodians" seems to be connected with it. Instead Matthew gives the figure of leaven a different and more directly religious turn by speaking of Sadducees rather than of Herod, and by defining the "leaven" as "the teaching of the Pharisees and Sadducees" (ch. 16 : 12). These differences are further evidence that he is conscious of what it means for his story to have stated clearly at ch. 14 : 33 that Jesus is "the Son of God." He probably has a specific purpose in making this statement, even though it seemingly detracts from the climactic nature of Peter's confession. (2) That the first evangelist can reveal Jesus' identity as early as he does is possible also because at this point he apparently is speaking with the voice of the church: it is "those in the boat," in the church, who recognize the meaning of this miracle and realize that Jesus is the Son of God. Viewed thus, Mt. 14 : 33 is hardly more inimical to the climax of Peter's confession than are Mark's broad hints at ch. 4 : 41; 8 : 21.

John 6 : 16-21.

The narrative of Jesus' walking on the water in the Fourth

---

[29] Cf. Dibelius (n. 8), p. 77, n. 2; E. Klostermann, *Das Markus Evangelium* (2d ed., 1926), pp. 75f.; Bultmann (n. 12), p. 231; E. Lohmeyer and W. Schmauch, *Das Evangelium des Matthäus* (2d ed., 1958), p. 241.

Gospel differs in a number of significant ways from its synoptic parallels. Here the story is told from the standpoint of the disciples on the sea, rather than from that of Jesus. The motif of the storm receives less emphasis, and the new miracle of a miraculous landing is introduced at v. 21. More important than these differences, however, is the setting of the story in John. The contextual connection with the mission of the Twelve, which we have noted in the Synoptics, is missing, but the relationship to the Feeding of the Five Thousand is maintained. The presence of this connection in John as well as in Mark and Matthew suggests that these stories were regularly combined in the oral tradition. Hoskyns and Barrett see this, along with the evangelist's need to bring Jesus back to the western shore for the sermon on the Bread of Life, as the reason for the preservation of our narrative in the Fourth Gospel in spite of the break it produces between the Feeding and its explanation in Jesus' sermon.[30] There is also an inner theological connection between these stories: in the one, Christ is the Giver of life; in the other, he appears to be the Conqueror over death. The former is fully explained in ch. 6 : 26ff., and in view of the clarity of this explanation, the evangelist could scarcely have been unaware of the implications of the latter. That he was alive to them is indicated, as Hoskyns has pointed out, by the fact that they form the subject matter of the farewell discourses in the Fourth Gospel.[31] Thus our narrative seems to be more than simply a transitional device between the Feeding and the sermon on the Bread of Life. It has an intimate theological connection with its context which suggests that it too, like the story of the Feeding, has a deeper meaning.

In the Johannine form of our narrative, the theme of the mission does not appear to be as pronounced as in the Synoptics. The story of the Feeding emphasizes christology from the standpoint of the eucharist. There is no mention of the ship in connection with that miracle, as there is in Mark and Matthew. This christological interest remains the leading motif of the story of Jesus' walking on the sea. Hence the figure of the ship here may suggest that our story deals primarily with relations between Christ and his church.

"It was now dark, and Jesus had not yet come to them" (6 : 17). This is the first, and unexpected, intimation that Jesus is coming.

---

[30] E. Hoskyns, *The Fourth Gospel* (1948), pp. 286f.; C. K. Barrett, *The Gospel According to St. John* (1955), p. 232.
[31] Hoskyns (n. 30), *loc. cit.*

It focuses on his coming to his disciples in the boat,[32] which may imply the return of Christ to his church. For the fourth evangelist this forms the point of our narrative. That "Jesus had not yet come" presupposes that the will come (cf. ch. 14 : 3). But now it was dark, and the disciples were without their master. Just as the Feeding reflects the eucharist, so the present point in our narrative seems to imply the period immediately following the crucifixion when the disciples were without their Lord.[33]

"The sea rose because a strong wind was blowing" (6 : 18). Wellhausen, Heitmüller, and Bultmann agree that this verse is a gloss because the stilling of the storm is not mentioned in our narrative, and because the particle τε and the genitive absolute as used here do not fit Johannine style.[34] However, if our understanding of the symbolism is correct, this verse plays a meaningful role in the narrative as it now lies before us, for it seems to portray the rise of the sea of death under the hand of demonic powers ("a strong wind") while Jesus is in the grave. It is not necessary that the evangelist should mention a stilling of this storm, for he has introduced the new miracle of a miraculous landing, which makes a reference to the stilling unnecessary. Thus, even if on stylistic grounds this verse is considered secondary, nevertheless it adds an important motif to the narrative.

"When they had rowed about three or four miles" (6 : 19a). This would place the ship in the midst of the sea.[35] Not only does this make Jesus' walking on the sea as miraculous as possible, but from the standpoint of the history of salvation, it seems to reflect the fact that with Jesus in the grave, the church was surrounded most fully by the sea of death.

"They saw Jesus walking on the sea and drawing near to the boat" (6 : 19b). This may symbolize the risen Lord in his post-resurrection appearances to his church. As in the Synoptics, his walking on the sea probably implies his conquest of death.

---

[32] R. Bultmann, *Das Evangelium des Johannes* (12th ed., 1952), p. 159; Hoskyns (n. 30), pp. 286f.

[33] In patristic exegesis this period extends until Christ comes to his church (the ship) at the end of the world; cf. Augustine, *In Joannis evang.*, XXV, 5; Cyril of Alex. (n. 7), *loc. cit.*; but it may be questioned whether this is in harmony with Johannine thought.

[34] J. Wellhausen, *Das Evangelium Johannis* (1908), p. 29; Bultmann (n. 32), p. 159, n. 1; cf. idem (n. 12), p. 231. Wellhausen notes that τε appears elsewhere only at ch. 2 : 15; 4 : 42, which he holds to be later additions.

[35] Cf. Josephus, *Jewish War* III, 506; Bultmann (n. 32), p. 159, n. 2.

"'It is I; do not be afraid'" (6 : 20). Ἐγώ εἰμι here probably equals אני הוא and shows that the whole episode is an epiphany. Dodd points out that this revelation of Jesus' divinity establishes a tie between it and the feeding of the Five Thousand. There the multitude recognizes Jesus as "the prophet who is to come into the world" (v. 14) and consequently attempts to make him king, but Jesus rejects this inadequate concept of his identity. The disciples are left in the "dark" and without Jesus (v. 17) until, coming to them across the water, he reveals through an epiphany who he really is.[36] For the admonition, "do not be afraid," cf. ch. 14 : 1.

"Then they were going to receive him into the boat" (6 : 21a). This passage (ἤθελον οὖν λαβεῖν αὐτὸν εἰς τὸ πλοῖον) has been translated in a variety of ways, the problematical word being ἤθελον.[37] As we have noted in another context, Riesenfeld has show that θέλω in the imperfect indicative expresses a wish or intention, the fulfillment of which in most cases is hindered by external circumstances.[38] This would suggest a translation such as we have proposed above, or as Barrett favors, "They wished to take him into the boat, but (adversative καί) found immediately that they had reached the shore."[39] The sequence in vs. 19-21 of fright, Jesus' reassurance, and the disciples' new attitude of welcome follows the pattern of the resurrection stories (ch. 20 : 19f.; 24-28; Mk. 16 : 8; Lk. 24 : 37-41) and seems to reflect them.

"Immediately the boat was at the land to which they were going" (6 : 21b). That a further miracle is intended here appears evident from the fact that the whole foregoing context is miraculous, and also because this last feature seems to be the counterpart in the Johannine narrative of the miraculous ceasing of the wind in the Synoptics

---

[36] Dodd (n. 6), pp. 344 f.
[37] A. Merx, *Das Evangelium des Johannes* (1911), p. 118, notes that the Sinaitic Syriac indicates that Jesus did enter the boat, while the other Syriac versions indicate that he did not. Cf. Bultmann (n. 32), p. 159, n. 7. C. C. Torrey, *Our Translated Gospels* (1936), pp. 105, 107f., suggests a mistranslation of Aramaic בעו (*bā'û*, "they rejoiced" having been taken wrongly as *be'û*, "they wished"; cf. *Rev. St. Vers.*, "they were glad"); this would find a parallel in the Johannine resurrection story where "the disciples were glad when they saw the Lord" (ch. 20 : 20).
[38] Riesenfeld (n. 19), *loc. cit.*
[39] Barrett (n. 30), p. 234; see above, Ch. V, n. 43. An alternative would be to take καί as hypotactic (cf. ch. 4 : 35; 11 : 55), reading, "Then they were going to take him into the boat, when immediately ...." Cf. Cyril of Alex. (n. 7), *loc. cit.*

(Mk. 6 : 51; Mt. 14 : 32).[40] Of particular importance in this connection is Ps. 107 : 29f.: "He made the storm be still, and the waves of the sea were hushed. Then they were glad because they had quiet, and he brought them to their desired haven."[41] From the standpoint of a later moment in the history of salvation, the typical eschatological outlook of the Fourth Gospel seems to be reflected here. When "Jesus had not yet come" it was dark (v. 17) and the ship was in the midst of the sea of death, buffeted by demonic winds (vs. 18f.). But as soon as the Lord who walks on the sea (triumphs over death) is present once more, those who are in the ship (the church) reach "the land to which they were going," eternal life (v. 21). This seems to anticipate ch. 14 : 3, "I will come again and will take you to myself, that where I am you may be also." That the believer should receive eternal life now in virtue of the resurrection of Christ is a thoroughly Johannine thought (ch. 3 : 3ff., 36; 4 : 10ff.; 6 : 32ff.; 11 : 25; 20 : 31; cf. 1 John 5 : 11f.). Closely connected with this is the fact that in the fourth evangelist's account the disciples receive the Holy Spirit directly from Christ immediately after the resurrection (ch. 20 : 22). Thus an eschatological application of v. 21 is in harmony with the viewpoint of the Fourth Gospel. At the same time however, the words "immediately the boat was at the land" do not necessarily imply a denial of salvation as a history. Both literally and symbolically our narrative sets forth a succession of events, a history, which climaxes in a new situation for the church: by virtue of the presence of the Risen One who has walked on the sea and conquered death, the ship – though the storm has not ceased – has already reached its desired haven.

With a keen sense of the tentativeness of our interpretation, we may summarize our conclusions regarding the story of the Walking on the Water as follows. In Mark the context of this story, and especially its relation to the Feeding of the Five Thousand, indicate that the voyage of the ship represents the church engaged in its

---

[40] B. Weiss, *Die vier Evangelien* (1900), pp. 491f., while agreeing that to the evangelist the landing is a miracle, explains that actually the disciples were no longer in the midst of the sea (as they thought, v. 19), but near the shore where they could see Jesus standing. Bultmann (n. 32), p. 159, n. 3, rightly rejects this explanation as "rationalistic."

[41] Hoskyns (n. 30), p. 291. Bultmann (n. 12), p. 253, n. 1, cites as parallel the Homeric hymn to the Pythian Apollo, 394ff., where a ship, once the god is on board, reaches its destination with miraculous speed. Further references, W. Bauer, *Johannesevangelium* (1933), p. 94; Bultmann (n. 32, *Ergänzungsheft*) p. 25 (n. to p. 159).

mission. The events of the voyage reflect the essential events that lie at the center of salvation-history and form the basis of its proclamation. Thus Jesus' absence from the disciples suggests his death, and their struggle alone with the wind upon the sea typifies their forsaken condition and discouragement while he was in the tomb. His walking on the waters to them proclaims him as Victor over death, just as the miracle of the Feeding shows him to be the Giver of life. Finally, the subsiding of the wind when he enters the ship represents the peace enjoyed by the church when he is in its midst, for by his death and resurrection he has conquered the demons.

In Matthew the chief difference from the Marcan story is the additional account of Peter's walking on the water. Taken in the context of the rest of the symbolism of the story, this would appear to reflect not only Peter's denial and reinstatement, but also the alienation of the whole group of disciples at the time of the crucifixion and the subsequent renewal of their commission. Also the implications of the story for the revelation of Jesus' identity as Messiah are more frankly stated in Matthew than in Mark, which seems to be connected with the fact that in the former the progressive revelation of the messianic secret does not play the central role that it does in the latter.

In John the theme of mission is superseded by a christological interest so that the focus of the narrative is upon the relation of Christ with his church. Even before the storm is mentioned, Jesus' return to his church is anticipated. In this account, Jesus probably does not enter the boat, but instead a new miracle is recounted, in which the ship immediately reaches the land when Jesus approaches. This is in harmony with the emphasis of Johannine eschatology.

If these interpretations are correct, each of the three evangelists who tells this story relates it, from his own particular point of view, to the central facts of the history of salvation.

CHAPTER VIII

THE STORIES OF A MIRACULOUS DRAFT OF FISH

Luke 5 : 1-11.

The setting of this miracle story is particularly significant. In recounting the beginnings of Jesus' ministry, Luke (3 : 21 – 6 : 11) follows the Marcan order of events (Mk. 1 : 9 – 3 : 6) with only two exceptions: (1) in place of Mark's account of the call of the first disciples by the sea (Mk. 1 : 16-20), Luke has the story of Jesus' rejection at Nazareth (Lk. 4 : 16-30); (2) following the account of a day at Capernaum (Mk. 1 : 21-45; Lk. 4 : 31-41), Luke inserts into the Marcan sequence the story of the Miraculous Draft of Fish. This includes a call to discipleship paralleling that narrated at an earlier point by Mark (Mk. 1 : 17; Lk. 5 : 10). It seems probable then that these two stories, inserted into the Marcan narrative at the very beginning of Jesus' ministry, have particular significance for the point of view from which Luke proposes to consider our Lord's life.

In both Mark and Matthew the rejection of Jesus at Nazareth constitutes a significant turning point in the evangelists' narratives (Mk. 6 : 1-6; Mt. 13 : 53-58), and probably symbolizes the rejection of Jesus by the Jewish nation. But for Luke, who recounts such a rejection almost at the beginning of his narrative, it cannot be a turning point; rather it introduces a *Leitmotiv*. As Lightfoot says, here "St. Luke probably invites us to see the future course of events, as it were, writ small, and indeed now forthwith foretold by Jesus."[1] Thus, in symbolizing the rejection of Jesus by the Jews at the very beginning of his career, Luke is able to anticipate the Gentile mission from the start (as he does in words of Jesus, ch. 4 : 25-27), and so to achieve a greater unity between his Gospel and the Acts. This unity is also enhanced by the fact that in anticipating Jesus' rejection from the first, Luke is able to remove all thought of tragedy from his portrayal of Jesus' career, and so can show one continuing plan and purpose throughout his two books.[2]

If it is correct that Luke's account of Jesus' rejection at Nazareth

---

[1] R. H. Lightfoot, *History and Interpretation in the Gospels* (1935), p. 207.
[2] Lightfoot (n. 1), pp. 199f., 203-208, who develops this point of view in detail.

is symbolic of a later and more important event in the history of salvation, it is also possible that the other story he has inserted into the Marcan sequence, that of the Miraculous Draft, is likewise symbolic and prefigurative. As the Nazareth story seems to foreshadow Jesus' rejection by the Jews and at the same time intimates the Gentile mission (as the positive aspect of the same situation), so the Miraculous Draft may symbolize that mission in greater detail and definiteness.[3]

"The lake of Gennesaret" (5 : 1). As we have seen in connection with the story of the Stilling of the Storm, this lake for Luke is not the center, but the boundary of Jesus' area of activity, which suggests that launching forth upon it symbolizes going forth beyond the geographical limits within which Jesus had worked (cf. Acts 1 : 8), and indeed beyond the bounds of Judaism. In the present context, the sea is presented without any of the sinister characteristics that are always associated with it in the stories of the Stilling of the Storm and Jesus' walking upon it. Rather, here the sea is depicted as a fruitful element. This suggests that in the present narrative the sea is to be interpreted not as a symbol of evil and death and the abode of demons, but as the nations of the world from whom a fruitful return in the proclamation of the gospel is to be expected.[4]

"One of the boats, which was Simon's" (5 : 3a). The introduction of Simon Peter at this point is significant for at least two reasons. (1) The fact that in this story Peter is essentially a fisherman implies (as is finally stated plainly) that he is to learn to be a fisher of men. Thus at the outset the understanding reader is given an indication that the story deals with the Christian mission. (2) As Conzelmann suggests, the leading part played by Peter in our story contrasts strikingly with the negative attitude of Jesus' own people in ch. 4 : 28f., and the two narratives taken together may reflect tension in the early church between a group led by relatives of Jesus and

---

[3] Cf. A. Loisy, *L'évangile selon Luc* (1924), pp. 28f., 51, 169.

[4] J. Mánek, "Fishers of Men," *Nov. Test.*, 2 (1957), pp. 139f., takes the sea in the present narrative as a symbol of sin, separation from God, and death; fishing for men involves rescuing them from these evils; accordingly the disciples fish during the day, rather than at night (with this might be associated the thought of John 9 : 4). However the specific indications of these motifs that are apparent in the Stilling of the Storm and the Walking on the Water are lacking here. Consequently we are also not so certain that the idea of baptism is present in the expression "fishers of men," as Mánek suggests. He sees this "because in early Christianity baptism was deliverance from waves of death in view of the Exodus" (*ibid.*, p. 141).

another centered about Peter.[5] Such tension may also be involved in the reaction of the "circumcision party" to Peter's baptism of Cornelius (Acts 11 : 2f.), and in the story of Peter's "dissimulation" at Antioch (Gal. 2 : 11ff.; cf. 1 Cor. 1 : 12). Reicke has shown that Peter's action there under fear of the "circumcision party" headed by James occurred at a time of renewed Jewish nationalism when the emergence of the Lord's brother as leader would fit the current atmosphere in Palestine. The increasing atrocities of the Zealots could easily have given pause to any Jew inclined to disregard Jewish particularism by fraternizing with Gentiles.[6] In view of this, the tensions behind Lk. 4 and 5 may reflect not only the immediate question of the Gentile mission (an internal question in the church), but also that question as seen against the whole ferment of Jewish nationalism and Zealotic violence in the 'fifties and 'sixties of the first century. Luke, a Gentile, may here be defending the stronger side of Peter's nature (cf. Gal. 2 : 12a; Luke is silent regarding the whole Antioch episode) against those of the "circumcision party" who would use the apostle's surrender to them as an argument against Gentile Christian freedom.

"He ... taught the people from the boat" (5 : 3b). Luke parallels the theme of Mk. 4 : 1 and may reflect the function of the church as the seat of the proclamation of the gospel.

"He said to Simon, 'Put out into the deep and let down your nets for a catch'" (5 : 4). Jesus' command to "put out" (ἐπανάγαγε, sing.) is directed to Peter as master of the boat, but the order to "let down" (χαλάσατε, pl.) the net includes the entire crew, for they must do this.[7] This seems to imply Peter's leadership of the church. He is to set forth into the world (cf. Acts 10 : 1-11: 18) as a founder of the Gentile mission, but the church as a whole (his crew) is to co-operate with him in this enterprise (cf. Acts 11 : 2-3).[8] Cullmann has seen Peter's role as the "rock" (Mt. 16 : 18) to be that of a founder: first as leader of the Jerusalem church (at that time the whole church), and when it was established and turned over to the care of James, then as leader in further mission endeavors.[9] This is the role of Peter

---

[5] H. Conzelmann, *The Theology of St Luke* (1960), pp. 42f.
[6] B. Reicke, "Der geschichtliche Hintergrund des Apostelkonzils und der Antiochia-Episode, Gal. 2, 1-14", *Studia Paulina* (Festschrift for J. De Zwaan, 1953), pp. 172-187.
[7] E. Klostermann, *Das Lukas Evangelium* (1929), p. 69.
[8] Loisy (n. 3), p. 174.
[9] O. Cullmann, *Peter: Disciple, Apostle, Martyr* (1953), pp. 223f.

in the present narrative: it is his boat from which Jesus teaches near the shore, it is his boat that Jesus sends out into deep water to catch fish.

The distinction between Peter's putting out first "a little from the land" (v. 3) that Jesus might teach the people on the shore, and then "into the deep" that the disciples might fish, seems to have symbolic meaning. As in Mk. 4 : 1, Jesus' teaching near the shore probably represents the Jewish mission. In terms of the symbolism of the sea as nations, launching out "into the deep" would appear then to refer to the world-wide mission to the Gentiles.[10] Jesus' instruction to Peter here may be a proleptic parallel to the lesson taught him in the conversion of Cornelius (Acts 10f.).

The figure of the net may be an extension of the figure for the church, particularly from the standpoint of its missionary enterprise. For the fisherman both net and ship contribute to the same end: the net carries the fish to the ship, and the ship carries them to land. The parable of the net (Mt. 13 : 47-50), where "the kingdom of heaven is like a net which was thrown into the sea and gathered fish of every kind," indicates the same symbolism, for in this parable the net is the church in its kerygmatic activity.[11] Similarly, the parallelism between nets and boats in vs. 6f. of our story indicates that they refer together to the church and its mission program.

"'Master, we toiled all night and took nothing!'" (5 : 5a). This suggests the comparative lack of success that accompanied the early Christian mission for the Jews as contrasted with the astounding success of the Gentile mission.[12] Since night was considered the best time to fish[13] Peter's reaction to Jesus' command may reflect the fact that from the standpoint of the earliest Jewish Christians, the Jews would have offered seemingly a more fertile field for mission endeavor than would the Gentiles.

"'But at your word I will let down the nets'" (5 : 5b). These words suggest that the Gentile mission is successful, not primarily because of Peter and the other apostles, but because they undertake it at the word of Christ, under his commission and power.[14]

---

[10] Bede, *In Lucae evangelium expositio* II, 5.
[11] Cf. Origen, *Scholia in Matthaeum* XIII, 47, where the net is the apostolic doctrine, and Bede (n. 10), II, 5, where it is the words of proclamation.
[12] Loisy (n. 3), p. 175.
[13] Aristotle, *Hist. anim.*, 8, 19, 602b5; Pliny, *Nat. hist.*, 9, 23, 56.
[14] L. Fendt, *Der Christus der Gemeinde* (1937), p. 68.

"They enclosed a great shoal of fish" (5 : 6a). This seems to represent the great success of the Gentile mission.

"And as their nets were breaking, they beckoned to their partners in the other boat to come and help them" (5 : 6b-7a). Several explanations in connection with the Gentile mission have been offered for this passage. One view sees the rupture of the net as an allusion to the controversy between Jewish and Gentile Christians in the early church. The disciples in the other boat would be the leaders of the "circumcision party" at Jerusalem, with whom Peter encountered repeated difficulties (Acts 11 : 2f.; Gal. 2 : 12); the unanimous recognition of Jesus' power in the miraculous catch would represent the ultimate acceptance by the church of the Gentile mission (Acts 11 : 18; 15 : 19ff.). While it seems probable that the tension between Peter and the "circumcision party" is reflected in this story, the absence of any indication of disagreement between the occupants of the two boats speaks against its being referred to this point. Lipsius suggests that the occupants of the first boat are Peter, James, and John. Those in the second boat represent other apostles later called to the Gentile mission. This also seems doubtful, for vs. 9f. may imply rather that James and John, as Peter's partners, operated the second boat (cf. Mk. 1 : 16-20; Mt. 4 : 18-22).[15] Loisy sees the breaking of the net as simply signifying the enormous quantity of fish caught, and so the large number of converts made from among the Gentiles.[16] This is entirely adequate for the interpretation of the narrative. However, the evangelist possibly intends more than this by his statement that the "nets were breaking" (v. 6) and that the boats "began to sink" (v. 7). These crises may reflect the fact that the success of the Gentile mission demonstrated the inadequacy and narrowness of the Jewish-Christian church to accommodate an influx of Gentiles.

"'Depart from me, for I am a sinful man, O Lord'" (5 : 8). Peter's confession of sinfulness in the presence of one who has just demonstrated supernatural power compares with Isa. 6 : 5, and is preparatory to his call to discipleship and proclamation.

"For he was astonished, and all that were with him... and so also were James and John" (5 : 9, 10a). The general astonishment finds an analogy in Luke's consistent portrayal of the attitude of the leaders

---

[15] A. Plummer, *The Gospel According to Luke* (5th ed., 1951), pp. 147f., rightly criticizes Lipsius' interpretation at this point; however the question of the identity of the occupants of the two boats is not essential to the basic symbolic motifs of the story.
[16] Loisy (n. 3), pp. 175f.

at Jerusalem toward the success of the Gentile mission as one of joy. (Acts 11 : 18; 15 : 23ff.; 21 : 17-20a; cf. Gal. 2 : 9).

"'Henceforth you will be catching men'" (5 : 10b). By giving here the words with which Jesus calls Peter, Andrew, and the sons of Zebedee in the other Synoptics (Mk. 1 : 17; Mt. 4 : 19), the evangelist clearly reveals that in the story of the Miraculous Draft, "fishing" implies the Christian mission. At the same time an important difference may be noted: according to Mk. 1 : 17; Mt. 4 : 19, Jesus promises to make his disciples "fishermen of men" (ἀλεεῖς ἀνθρώπων), while Luke has him say, "You shall be capturing men" (ἀνθρώπους ἔση ζωγρῶν). In ζωγρεῖν we meet another word with double meaning, both significances of which probably are here in play. Not only does ζωγρεῖν mean "to catch," "to capture," but specifically (and etymologically) "to capture alive," "to preserve alive" when capturing[17] (cf. Num. 31 : 15; Josh. 6 : 25). By extension it may even mean "to restore to life," "to revive."[18] Luke's deliberate choice of this word seems to imply that whereas Peter heretofore has caught fish alive, henceforth he will not only capture men alive, but in so doing will indeed bring them new life. The apparent double meaning at this point is an indication that the foregoing narrative, of which these words are the climax, has a double meaning throughout, bearing on the Christian mission.

Peter's position in the mission is also reflected in vs. 10f. Formally, Jesus' statement is directed to him alone: μὴ φοβοῦ ... ἔση (sing.), but the other disciples understand it to include themselves as well, and they too follow Jesus (v. 11). In this respect, vs. 10f. are the counterpart of v. 4, which is a further indication that in a deeper sense, both passages refer to the same thing. The pre-eminence of Peter here (as in vs. 4, 5, 8) is probably an intimation of his pioneer leadership in the Gentile mission, which Luke carefully notes later (Acts 15 : 7).

John 21 : 1-14.

The location of this story in the Gospel is significant. Whereas Luke places a similar story near the beginning of his Gospel, making the Gentile mission a pre-supposition of his entire work, the Fourth Gospel reserves such a story for an appendix at the end, as a post-resurrection appearance of Jesus. In this Gospel the Gentile mission

---

[17] Cf. J. H. Moulton and G. Milligan, *The Vocabulary of the Greek Testament* (1949), p. 274.
[18] *Iliad* 5, 697f.; Loisy (n. 3), p. 173.

is taken for granted from the beginning (ch. 1 : 9, 11-13); hence its introduction symbolically here can hardly be dictated by the desire finally to reveal a truth previously only hinted at, as in Mt. 28 : 19f. Regardless of the different locations assigned these stories in Luke and John, there is clearly an inner connection between them: the leading motif, as well as the point of both stories is the same. Both narratives deal with the disciples of Jesus making a miraculous catch of fish from their ship(s) at his bidding; both culminate in a commission.[19]

The structure and purpose of our story have received considerable discussion.[20] Bultmann speaks of it as presenting "such a remarkable confusion of motifs, that one can hardly say wherein its real point lies."[21] At the same time, when the story is considered from the standpoint of the purpose of the author, there seem to be indications of greater unity here, particularly in view of the resurrection narratives in Matthew and Luke. This we shall seek to point out in the exegesis that follows.

"By the Sea of Tiberius" (21 : 1). The Fourth Gospel is the only one to include post-resurrection appearances of Jesus to his disciples both at Jerusalem and in Galilee. Hoskyns sees this as a combination of the Matthean tradition (appearance only in Galilee) and the Lucan (appearances only around Jerusalem).[22] If this is correct, elsewhere also in our narrative the author may be motivated by the desire to round out his Gospel by bringing together ideas found in both the other traditions.

Galilee, as the locale of this narrative, probably has symbolic significance for the Gentile mission. In Mk. 14 : 28 (par. Mt. 26 : 32)

---

[19] On the relation of these stories in the sources, see the various views of Loisy (n. 3), pp. 173-175; R. Bultmann, *Geschichte der synoptischen Tradition* (3d ed., 1957), pp. 232, 246; ibid., *Das Evangelium des Johannes* (12th ed., 1952), pp. 545f.; Conzelmann (n. 5), p. 31, n. 3: M. J. Lagrange, *L'évangile selon St. Jean* (7th ed., 1948), p. 524; Plummer (n. 15), p. 147.

[20] For more than one source: J. Wellhausen, *Das Evangelium Johannis* (1908), p. 97; W. Bauer, *Johannesevangelium* (1933), p. 237; for the story as basically a unit: G. Bertram, "Le chemin sur les eaux considéré comme motif de salut dans la piété chrétienne primitive," *Rev. d'hist. et de phil. rel.*, 7 (1927), p. 526; R. Bultmann, *Das Evangelium des Johannes* (12th ed., 1952), pp. 543-545, 550; C. R. Gregory, *Wellhausen und das Evangelium Johannis* (1910), pp. 66f.; Lagrange (n. 19), p. 528; E. Hoskyns, *The Fourth Gospel* (1948), p. 555.

[21] Bultmann (n. 20), p. 550.

[22] Hoskyns (n. 20), *loc. cit.*; cf. C. H. Dodd, *The Interpretation of the Fourth Gospel* (1953), p. 431; R. H. Lightfoot, *Locality and Doctrine in the Gospels* (1938), pp. 107f.

just before his passion, Jesus declares to the disciples, "But after I am raised up, I will go before you to Galilee." As Hoskyns notes, the climax to which this statement looks forward is neither the cross nor the resurrection, but something beyond them, in "Galilee."[23] A mere return to Galilee, or even a resurrection appearance there would be anticlimactic; what is anticipated must be something greater. That it is the Gentile mission is suggested by the fact that the full name, גליל הגוים (Isa. 9 : 1 [8 : 23]; cf. Mt. 4 : 15), means "circuit, or district, of the Gentiles."[24] Also of significance in this connection is the double sense of προάξω, "I will go before," and "I will lead." Thus, as Jesus goes before (προάγων, Mk. 10 : 32), and at the same time leads his disciples to Jerusalem, so also his going before them into Galilee seems to signify his leading them into the world in behalf of the Gentile Mission.[25] Both the first evangelist and the author of John 21 appear to have been aware of this implication. In Mt. 28 : 7, 10, it is the angel at the tomb who sends the disciples to Galilee, and there they receive the commission to "all nations" (vs. 19-20). In John 20 : 11ff., the primary appearances of Jesus occur in Jerusalem; but for the symbolic portrayal of the Gentile mission, the scene changes to Galilee.

"Simon Peter, Thomas ..." (21 : 2). Bauer asks whether the fact that seven disciples are mentioned here has symbolic value.[26] If a symbolism is intended, it is probably that in these seven the whole apostolate is implied. Twelve would be impossible at this point, and any lesser number, except seven, would suggest incompleteness. The symbolism of the story applies to the entire apostolate, and by extension, to the whole church. Hoskyns notes a parallel with the Feeding of the Four Thousand, where seven baskets are gathered (Mk. 8 : 8, par.), suggesting seven disciples there (cf. the

---

[23] E. Hoskyns in *Theology*, Sept., 1923, cited by C. F. Evans, "I will go before you into Galilee," *Journ. of Theol. St.*, 5 (1954), pp. 4f.
[24] Origen, *Series veteris interpretationis commentariorum in Mattheum*, 87 (Migne, *Patr. Gr.*, XIII, 1738) quotes Isa. 9 : 2 in commenting on this verse; Cyril of Alexandria, Fragment 293 (J. Reuss, *Matthäus-Kommentare aus der griechischen Kirche* [1957], pp. 257f.): "... he promises to precede them into Galilee, by which he signifies that he is about to leave the Jews and go to the Gentiles." Evans (n. 23), p. 13, points out that this is the only instance where "Gallilee" appears on the lips of Jesus; elsewhere his references to geographical names also have more than a literal meaning (Mt. 11 : 21, 23; 23 : 37, pars.).
[25] Evans (n. 23), p. 11, however, takes προάξω here as meaning only "I will lead," and therefore as ruling out the idea of resurrection appearances in Galilee.
[26] Bauer (n. 20), p. 235.

twelve baskets and apparently twelve disciples in the Feeding of the Five Thousand, Mk. 6 : 43, par.). In view of the probable references to the eucharist later in the present narrative, the seven here may also have a eucharistic implication.[27]

"'I am going fishing'" (21 : 3). Is this action of Peter and the six other disciples a symbolic fulfillment of their original commission to fish for men, or is it an apostasy from that? In a sense it appears to be both. The elements of the Christian mission are present: the apostles, the ship of the church, the action of fishing from the sea of the world. The picture is probably that of the mission. But at the same time it is fruitless, because, on another level, the picture is also one of apostasy. The disciples are no longer fishing for men, but for fish. In returning to their old way of life, they have fulfilled ch. 16 : 32,[28] and so completely have they returned to it that they no longer recognize Jesus when he appears to them (v. 4).

"Just as day was breaking" (21 : 4). A comparison with ch. 20 : 1; Mk. 16 : 2; Mt. 28 : 1; Lk. 24 : 1, suggests that daybreak in association with the resurrection may imply the dawn of a new period in the history of salvation, a new time of successful activity in connection with the presence of the Risen One in and with his church.

"'Children, have you any fish?'" (21 : 5). The introduction of this question with μή (or μήτι) anticipates a negative reply.[29] Considering the disciples' situation as experienced fishermen who had worked all night, this is subtly ironical. It heightens the impression already received that their lack of success is not accidental, but is due to their apostasy and the consequent absence of Christ from their endeavors. This principle, the evangelist implies, is also applicable to the mission of the church. Bultmann sees Jesus' question here as a "novellistic" addition to the story, inasmuch as it seems to make the motivation of the miraculous catch to be the getting of food, whereas the original point of the story is a call to apostleship.[30] Whether or not this is so would seem to depend on the meaning here of προσφάγιον. Although basically this word means "something to eat," papy-

---

[27] Hoskyns (n. 20), p. 554.
[28] Hoskyns (n. 20), p. 552.
[29] So J. H. Moulton, *A Grammar of New Testament Greek* (3d ed., 1949), I, 170, n. 1; A. T. Robertson, *A Grammar of the Greek New Testament in the Light of Historical Research* (4th ed., 1934), p. 1168; however, F. Blass, *Grammar of New Testament Greek* (2d Eng. ed., 1905), p. 254, n. 2, thinks this passage "hardly lends itself" to this interpretation; but cf. similar uses in ch. 4 : 29; 8 : 22; 18 : 35.
[30] Bultmann (n. 20), pp. 545f.

rological evidence indicates that it "is best understood of some staple article of food of the *genus* fish, rather than of a mere relish."[31] Just as οψάριον, "relish," came to mean specifically "fish" (ch. 6 : 9; 21 : 9), so also προσφάγιον seems to have the particular sense of "fish" here (so the Revised Standard Version). This suggests the possibility that Jesus' question does not deal particularly with the disciples' lack of *food*, but with the fact that they have caught no *fish*.

"'Cast the net on the right side of the boat'" (21 : 6a). In the Gospels the right side is an omen of good (cf. Mk. 16 : 5; Mt. 25 : 33; Lk. 1 : 11).[32] Accordingly casting the net from the right side of the boat would imply success in the mission endeavor of the church.

"They were not able to haul it in, for the quantity of fish" (21 : 6b). Bauer sees the contradiction between these words and v. 11, where Peter lands the net singlehandedly, as an indication that two narratives have been combined.[33] However, Hoskyns says, "the narrative is bent this way and that under the subtle influence of the symbolism."[34] If the fish symbolize converts to Christianity, and the net the mission program of the church, the present passage may be a hyperbolical description of the unexpected measure of success that the Christian mission achieved. So regarded, it is not necessarily contradictory to v. 11, which seems to have a symbolic significance of its own for the Christian mission.

Augustine held the miraculous catch in Lk. 5 to represent the church in the world, from which the bad had not yet been separated from the good by the Last Judgment; therefore the net was not said to be landed, for, in analogy to Mt. 13 : 48ff., the shore represented the end of the world. The fish in the net, but still in the sea, he thought to be the righteous dead slumbering peacefully till the resurrection. Because in the Johannine narrative the net is brought to shore, he understood the catch here as the church triumphant.[35] However there seems to be no satisfactory basis for making such a distinction between the Lucan and Johannine narratives. In neither story does the shore appear to have particular significance. The difference seems rather to be determined by the position of Jesus: in Luke he is in the ship, and the fish are brought there; in John he is on land, and the ship,

---

[31] Moulton and Milligan (n. 17), p. 551.
[32] See also H. L. Strack and P. Billerbeck, *Kommentar zum Neuen Testament aus Talmud und Midrasch* (1922), I, 980f.
[33] See above, n. 20.
[34] Hoskyns (n. 20), p. 553.
[35] Augustine, *In Joannis evang.*, CXXII, 7; cf. *In Joannis evang.*, CXXIII, 2.

along with the net, is the means by which they are transported to him.

"That disciple whom Jesus loved said to Peter" (21 : 7a). The role played here by "the disciple whom Jesus loved" is typical of the place assigned him in the Fourth Gospel. Although the author consistently recognizes Peter's leading position among the disciples (ch. 1 : 40; 6 : 8, 67f.; 13 : 24; 18 : 10; 20 : 2; 21 : 3), nevertheless he is at pains to show that "the disciple whom Jesus loved" also had special claims to knowledge of Jesus that often exceeded even those of Peter. Indeed, this disciple's having enjoyed such proximity to Jesus and having had such insight into him is set forth as a credential of the Fourth Gospel (ch. 21 : 24). The present passage is quite in harmony with his role throughout. Here, while Peter is the *fisherman* (vs. 3, 11), that is, the pioneer of the Christian mission, this other disciple is the *identifier of Jesus*, not only in the present story but also and especially in the early church, for it is in the Gospel that derives from him, more than in any other New Testament writing, that the answer is given as to who Jesus really is. Amid the christological questions encountered by the mission, he points out to his fellows in the church the true identity of their Lord. Hence to mention "the disciple whom Jesus loved" at this point in our narrative seems not really to introduce a foreign element into the story, as Bauer suggests.[36] This disciple's identification in the present verse with the personality who stands at the source of the Fourth Gospel has significance for the story.

"Peter... sprang into the sea" (21 : 7b). Both this story and that of the walking on the water (Mt. 14 : 28-31) present similar pictures of Peter's reaction to an epiphany: his first impulse is to go to his master. However, the point of this motif in the Matthean narrative seems to be different from that here. There it implies walking above and sinking into the waters of death; here there is nothing miraculous. In the present passage probably we should seek no more than the general picture of Peter's enthusiasm upon learning the identity of his Lord. His being the first to reach Jesus is in harmony with the leadership he displays throughout.

"But the other disciples came in the boat, dragging the net full of fish" (21 : 8a). This is the counterpart to Lk. 5 : 7, where the partners in the second boat aid with the catch. Both passages suggest the co-operation of the apostles in the church in bringing their catch of converts to Christ. Both narratives seem to have the same point: the apostles bring converts to Christ; in one the church (the ship) is

---

[36] See above, n. 20.

the locus in which they encounter their Lord; in the other, it is the vehicle by which they are brought to him.

"About a hundred yards off" (21 : 8b). Bultmann is probably right in rejecting Carpenter's suggestion that this distance (two hundred cubits) symbolizes the cleansing of sinners in two stages.[37] We would prefer to take the figure simply as emphasizing that "they were not far from the land." In the Lucan story, the disciples were commanded to "put out into the deep" (ch. 5 : 4) for their catch; here they make it near the shore. If our understanding of the symbolism is correct, this may represent the thought that there Jesus was present in the boat, and as soon as the catch was made, the converts (the fish) were brought into the church (the ship) where they were in the presence of their Lord. Here, where the church is probably rather the vehicle by which souls are brought to Christ, their nearness to him is emphasized (cf. Eph. 2 : 13), once they are captured by the missionary enterprise of the church (the net attached to the ship).

"With fish lying on it, and bread" (21 : 9). In the fact that Jesus already had fish cooking when the disciples arrive with their catch, Bauer finds evidence that vs. 9ff. belonged originally to another story.[38] Bultmann sees the meal in these verses as a "novellistic" addition.[39] However it would appear that when the purpose of the author is taken into consideration, this part of the story may fulfill an essential role. That the meal described here is eucharistic has been widely recognized, not only because of the bread, but especially in view of the eucharistic language of v. 13.[40] This is suggested also by the fact that it seems to be provided by Jesus from the food he has at hand, rather than from the fish brought by the disciples.[41] We have already indicated

---

[37] Bultmann (n. 193), p. 548, n. 9, citing J. E. Carpenter, *The Johannine Writings* (1927), p. 246.

[38] See above n. 20.

[39] R. Bultmann, *Das Evangelium des Johannes* (12th ed., 1952), pp. 545f.

[40] Bauer (n. 20), p. 237; Bultmann (n. 20), pp. 549f.; Hoskyns (n. 20), p. 553; C. K. Barrett, *The Gospel According to St. John* (1955), pp. 481, 484. Note also the addition of εὐχαριστήσας in v. 13 by D d f g mm r sy^s. To our knowledge this meal is considered as eucharistic only twice in patristic literature: Augustine, *In Joannis evang.*, CXXIII, 2 (Migne, *Patr. Lat.*, 35, 1966): "The roasted fish is Christ who suffered (Piscis assus, Christus est passus). He is also the bread which descends from heaven"; and an anonymous work, *De promissibus et praedicationibus Dei*, 2, 39 (Migne, *Patr. Lat.*, 51, 816): "The great fish... satisfying from himself the disciples on the shore, and offering himself, the ἰχθύς, to the whole world." Cf. J. Wilpert, *Die Malereien der Katakomben Roms* (1903), pp. 290, n. 3; 384, n. 5.

[41] J. H. Bernard, *The Gospel According to John* (1948), II, 699, thinks that Jesus

the possibility that the Fourth Gospel (as including the appendix of ch. 21) is concerned in its post-resurrection narratives to unite and harmonize elements found in the Matthean and Lucan traditions, presenting appearances of Jesus both at Jerusalem and in Galilee. So also here, the themes of the commission to the world (Mt. 28 : 19f.) and the eucharist (Lk. 24 : 30f.) appear together. This is not a disharmonious combination, for the figure of the ship is closely related to the miraculous feedings (Mk. 6 : 32-52; 8 : 1-21; Mt. 14 : 13-33; 15 : 32-39; John 6 : 5-21), suggesting the thought that converts brought into the church encounter Christ there in the eucharist. Thus vs. 9ff., rather than introducing an element foreign to the point of the narrative, in reality may contribute to its unity and completeness.

"'Bring some of the fish that you have just caught'" (21 : 10). Does this command imply that the fish are to be eaten? Bernard thinks that it does.[42] In favor of this view is the fact that the disciples' fish only here are termed ὀψάρια (as are Jesus' fish, v. 9), the same word used for the fish of the meal in v. 13. Elsewhere the disciples' fish are ἰχθύες (vs. 6, 8, 11). Ὀψάριον appears in the New Testament only in the Fourth Gospel, and except in the present context, only in connection with the Feeding of the Five Thousand (ch. 6 : 9, 11). Thus it always is used in association with bread in a meal that appears to have eucharistic significance.[43] At the same time there seems to be intent behind the fact that Jesus tells the disciples only to bring their fish, and says nothing of eating them. As Hoskyns states, "the fish symbolize the converts to the Christian religion, and for this reason the natural imagery breaks down and becomes obscure at the crucial point. The disciples cannot eat the converts."[44] Thus while the fish here, as ὀψάρια, seem to have an intimate connection with the eucharistic meal, the whole significance of the story probably excludes their being used as food in it. The author may have been intentionally ambiguous at this point. His use of ὀψάρια may imply the intimate relationship between the converts of the Christian mission and the

invites the disciples to add their fish to a breakfast he has already prepared for himself. This explanation seems to overlook the general symbolism of the story, and especially the importance of the fact that the disciples are nowhere said to eat of their catch.

[42] See above, n. 41.
[43] Moulton and Milligan (n. 17), p. 470, provide a number of illustrations from secular sources of the coupling of ὀψάριον with bread.
[44] Hoskyns (n. 20), p. 554. Bultmann (n. 20), pp. 549f., agrees that the meal is not from the disciples' food, but from Jesus'.

eucharist, and yet the symbolism seems to forbid his carrying this figure to the extent of saying outright that the disciples ate these fish.

"Simon Peter ... hauled the net ashore" (21 : 11a). It is generally agreed that Peter's action here is symbolic of his leadership in the early church and its mission.[45] The other disciples had followed him to the shore to meet Jesus, and now he performs the definitive act of landing the catch. That he enters the ship[46] to accomplish this reminds us once more that the church, as the ship, appears here to be the vehicle by which converts are brought to Christ; it also suggests Peter's leading role in the church in general as well as in its missionary enterprise, which seems more particularly to be symbolized by the net. Furthermore, Jesus' command in v. 10, and Peter's action in the present verse are probably a symbolic counterpart to their conversation in vs. 15ff.[47] This would accord with the common Johannine pattern of symbolic action followed by literal explanation (cf. ch. 4 : 7ff.; 5 : 2ff.; 6 : 5ff., 25ff., etc.).

"Large fish, a hundred and fifty-three of them" (21 : 11b). A number of scholars deny that the figure 153 has any special significance beyond giving specific emphasis to the magnitude of the catch and the divine munificence it represents.[48] However, since early Christian times a wide range of attempts have been made to find symbolic meaning in this number. Among the various and ingenious solutions proposed by the Fathers,[49] two are of particular note and have found wide recognition in modern times. Jerome, commenting on Eze. 47 :

---

[45] Lagrange (n. 19), pp. 526, 528; E. Lohmeyer, *Galiläa und Jerusalem* (1936), p. 19; Bultmann (n. 20), pp. 545, 549f.

[46] Bauer (n. 20), p. 237, points out that ἀνέβη (v. 11) is ambiguous, for if taken in the sense in which it appears at v. 9 it would mean that Peter just now comes up out of the water on the beach, dragging the net, and that the other disciples have preceded him in reaching Jesus. On the other hand, ἀνέβη may refer to Peter's re-entering the ship (cf. Mk. 6 : 51; Mt. 14 : 32; Acts 21 : 6) to get the net attached there. Inasmuch as the latter interpretation fits the course of the story while the former does not, it seems to provide an adequate solution to the problem; cf. Lagrange (n. 19), p. 526.

[47] Lohmeyer (n. 45), *loc. cit.*; O. Betz, "Donnersöhne, Menschenfischer und der davidische Messias," *Rev. de Qumran*, No. 9 (Feb., 1961), p. 58.

[48] So B. Weiss, *Die vier Evangelien* (1900), p. 601; A. Schlatter, *Der Evangelist Johannes* (1930), p. 368; Bernard (n. 41), II, 699f.

[49] Origen (in Ishoᶜdad) takes 153 as 3 × 50 + 3 and proposes that it represents the Trinity, also noting that there are 153 psalms in the Law, Prophets and Psalms. Cyril of Alex., Ammonius (Cramer's *Catena*, 408 : 16), and Severus (Corderius' *Catena*, 468) divide the number into 100 = Gentiles, 50 = the Jews, 3 = the Trinity (see Bauer [n. 20], p. 237; Hoskyns [n. 20], p. 556).

9-12, says, "Writers on the nature and properties of animals, who have learned *Halieutica* in Latin as well as in Greek, among whom is the learned poet Oppianus Cilix, say that there are 153 different kinds of fishes."[50] On this basis, the 153 fish would represent all the various species, and by implication all the nations of the world. The miraculous catch would symbolize the success of the Christian mission among all nations.[51] However, as Lagrange is careful to point out, Oppianus Cilix (ca. A.D. 180) whom Jerome cites, actually gives no specific number for the different kinds of fish, but declares only that he believes them to be no less numerous than the kinds of land animals.[52] Jerome, of course, does not base his whole argument on Oppianus, but refers rather to a general opinion among the learned of his day. If this was a wide-spread idea in the first Christian century, it would seem to have significance for the figure here. However, in view of the lack of definitive evidence, this interpretation cannot be pressed.

The second important patristic interpretation of the number 153 is that of Augustine, who recognizes that 153 is the triangular number of 17 ($1 + 2 + 3 + ... + 17 = 153$). This latter number he divides into 7 and 10, and sees symbolized in it the believers who, under the sevenfold Spirit, keep the commandments.[53] Bultmann aptly characterizes this as "certainly no compelling thought."[54] At the same time, the basic recognition that 153 has special mathematical properties appears significant. The Pythagoreans laid great stress on the importance of triangular numbers, and the fact that four of these appear in the New Testament (120 [triangle of 15], Acts 1 : 15; 276 [triangle of 23], Acts 27 : 37; 666 [triangle of 36], Rev. 13 : 18) seems hardly accidental. By Pythagorean rule a triangular number had the same significance as its basic number (in this case, 17).[55] Exactly what the

---

[50] Jerome, *In Ezech.*, 14; quoted in English by Hoskyns (n. 20), p. 554; Latin text, Migne, *Patr. Lat.*, 25, 474.

[51] Among modern scholars who favor this interpretation (without necessarily endorsing it completely) are Bauer (n. 20), p. 237; W. Brandt, *Das ewige Wort* (3d rev. ed., 1940), p. 266; Hoskyns (n. 20), p. 554; Lagrange (n. 19), pp. 526f.; Lightfoot (n. 22), p. 103, n. 1; G. Spörri, *Das Evangelium nach Johannes* (1950), II, 213; H. Strathmann, *Das Evangelium nach Johannes* (1951), p. 265.

[52] Lagrange (n. 19), p. 526; the passage is Oppianus, *Halieutica* I, 88ff. Pliny, *Nat. hist.*, 32, 53, gives the number of kinds of fish as 144; in 9, 43, he makes a still smaller estimate.

[53] Augustine, *In Joannis evang.*, CXXII, 8.

[54] Bultmann (n. 20), p. 549, n. 1.

[55] F. H. Colson, "Triangular Numbers in the New Testament," *Journ. Theol. St.*, 16 (1915), p. 67.

number 17 may signify here is difficult to determine, but more than one possibility suggests itself. Barrett proposes that it be divided into 7 and 10, both of which indicate completeness and perfection: "the fish then represent the full total of the catholic and apostolic Church."[56] It may also be remarked that 17 is the number of nations represented at Pentecost according to Acts 2 : 9-11. Furthermore, 17 is the seventh of the prime numbers, while the number 153 is the sum of the cubes of its digits. It has also been suggested that in view of the similarities between this passage and Eze. 47 : 10, the latter may have been in the mind of the author of John 21. If so, it is perhaps not without significance that the two names given here (En)-gedi and (En)-eglaim have by gematria the numerical values of 17 (גדי) and 153 (עגלים). These mark the extent of the places from which "very many kinds" of fish are to be caught.[57]

Thus it is not impossible that our author may have recognized a whole group of ideas associated with this number: the mathematical interrelationship between 153 and 17 together with their other unusual characteristics, the possible connection of these numbers with a great catch of fish in Eze. 47 : 10, and the further association of this with a possible belief that the different kinds of fish total 153. Taken together, the special associations of the number 153 suggest that it does have symbolic value here, and that the catch of 153 large fish represents a marvellous, unique, and perfect success for the Christian mission.[58]

"And although there were so many, the net was not torn" (21 : 11b). Whereas in the Lucan narrative the nets break, here the net remains intact. Wellhausen explains this by saying that in Luke the

---

[56] Barrett (n. 40), p. 484; so also R. M. Grant, "One Hundred Fifty-three Large Fish," *Harv. Theol. Rev.*, 42 (1949), pp. 273ff.

[57] J. A. Emerton, "The Hundred Fifty-three Fishes in John XXI. 11," *Journ. Theol. St.*, 9 (1958), pp. 86-89.

[58] So Hoskyns (n. 20), p. 556; cf. Colson (n. 55), p. 74. Bultmann (n. 20), p. 549, finds no explanation of the number 153 satisfactory, but agrees that because it is not a round number, it must have some allegorical meaning. Other scholars have attempted a solution by gematria. Thus A. Merx, *Das Evangelium des Johannes* (1911), pp. 462-464, proposes העלם הבא. R. Eisler, *Orpheus – the Fisher* (1921), pp. 111ff., sees 153 to be composed of $\Sigma\ell\mu\omega\nu = 76$ and $\prime\iota\chi\vartheta\acute{\upsilon}\varsigma = 77$, meaning that Peter, who by putting on his clothing (v. 7), has put on Christ and by sprinting into the water has been baptized, has mystically become the Christ-Fish. Betz (n. 47), pp. 56ff., suggests בני אמן in view of the special role played in the Qumran literature by the letters aleph, mem, nun (cf. 1QS X, 1-4, and the frequency of the word $\dot{\alpha}\mu\eta\nu$ in the Johannine writings; note esp. Rev. 3 : 14; cf. Isa. 65 : 16).

nets are literal, while in John the net is symbolic.[59] However, both literal and symbolic meanings appear to be involved in each narrative, and the difference on the symbolic level is probably to be explained from varying points of view regarding the Gentile mission. For Luke the Gentile mission is still an issue, and on its validity he predicates his presentation of the gospel. His concern for the tensions occasioned by this mission, so clearly evident in the Acts, seems to be reflected in his notation that the "nets were breaking" (ch. 5 : 6). But in the Johannine writings the Gentile mission is no longer an issue; its validity is taken for granted. Looking back from a later point historically, our author can note that, notwithstanding the amazing success of this enterprise, it has after all not brought about a rupture in the church and its mission. The unity of the church has been preserved.[60]

"Jesus said to them, 'Come and have breakfast'" (21 : 12). Jesus is host, which suggests that it is he who provides the fish; at all events, he provides the bread, the staple of the meal.

"Jesus came and took the bread and gave it to them, and so with the fish" (21 : 13). The eucharistic theme, probably introduced at v. 9, seems to form the climax of our story. The focus is clearly on the bread, rather than on the fish. The ὀψάριον has become merely incidental to the ἄρτος. Hence the presence of fish should be no more disruptive to the eucharistic character of this meal than it is to that of the Feeding of the Five Thousand in ch. 6.[61] Indeed, the strongest evidence of eucharistic significance here derives from a comparison with the Feeding (ch. 6 : 11: λαμβάνειν, ἄρτος, διδόναι, ὁμοίως, ὀψάριον).

The question whether the fish at this point has symbolic significance has been answered variously. Barrett notes that "a fish occurs along with bread in some early representations of the eucharist; and fish-symbolism was very widespread in early Christianity."[62] Spörri goes even further and suggests that the disciples' eating the fish may have "the hidden meaning that in the bread we receive the Lord himself."[63] However, Bultmann points out that early Christian

---

[59] Wellhausen (n. 20), p. 15.
[60] That the unity of the church is symbolized by the untorn net is generally recognized; see Bauer (n. 20), p. 237; Bultmann (n. 20), pp. 549f.; Loisy (n. 3), pp. 175f.; Strathmann (n. 51), p. 265.
[61] On the eucharistic significance of the feeding of the Five Thousand, see especially O. Cullmann, *Early Christian Worship* (1953), pp. 93-102.
[62] Barrett (n. 40), p. 484.
[63] Spörri (n. 51), II, 213. Eisler (n. 58), pp. 238ff., also identifies the fish here

sources know no sacramental eating of fish, and when they do refer to the Christ-fish being eaten, as in the Abercius and Pectorius Inscriptions, it is a reference to the eating not of literal fish, but of the eucharistic bread and wine.[64]

Probably the earliest connection of the fish with the eucharist appears in the Roman catacombs in a painting in the crypt of Lucina.[65] Here two fish are depicted with baskets containing bread, and what are apparently glasses of red wine. Although the total picture probably has eucharistic significance (which it assuredly does if wine is really portrayed), the fish, bread, and baskets clearly point to the miraculous feedings, to which the addition of wine would indicate their having been understood as eucharistic. There seems to be no indication that the fish of themselves, any more than the baskets, are eucharistic symbols.

In the catacomb of St. Calixtus, on the left wall of the Chapel of the Sacraments, is represented the meal in John 21. Its location beside the painting of the fisherman, signifying baptism, as well as its general context in this chapel suggests a eucharistic interpretation. But again, this is an interpretaion of the scene as a whole, and not of the fish as an isolated symbol.

The earliest certain evidence of the fish as a Christian symbol is Tertullian's well-known reference to the abbreviation ἰχθύς (before A.D. 203).[66] At about the same time it appears in the Abercius Inscription, where the believer is said to eat the fish. Dölger concludes that since ἰχθύς = Christ, and bread and wine = the body and blood of Christ, then in this inscription the fish = the eucharist.[67] The Pectorius Inscription (2d-3d century) also uses the fish apparently as a reference to the eucharist.[68]

From all this we may conclude that our narrative is probably too early for the fish to have been intended as symbolic in its own right. Even if it were possible to carry Christian fish symbolism sufficiently far back to apply to our passage, we should then expect the word ἰχθύς rather than ὀψάριον. It seems more probable that the

---

as Christ, and sees a connection with the eschatological eating of Leviathan (*Apoc. Bar.* 29 : 4; *IV Ezra* 6 : 51).
[64] Bultmann (n. 20), p. 550, n. 2.
[65] Wilpert (n. 40), pp. 288f.
[66] Tertullian, *De baptismo*, 1. The date of the ἰχθύς-acrostic in *Sibylline Oracles*, 8 : 217-250 is uncertain; cf. Bultmann (n. 20), p. 550, n. 2.
[67] F. J. Dölger, ΙΧΘΥΣ, II (1922), 502.
[68] On the Abercius and Pectorius Inscriptions, see especially Dölger (n. 67), 492ff.

fish is a part of this meal simply because it was a part of the story as it came into the hands of our author (cf. the "broiled fish" in another resurrection story, Lk. 24 : 42). That he sees eucharistic significance in the meal and presents his narrative so as to express it (as in ch. 6), appears to be in harmony with his intention in the rest of the story: the apostles, in the ship of the church, by means of the net of its mission enterprise, bring a wondrous catch of souls to their risen Lord, whom they meet in the eucharistic meal.

In concluding this study of the stories of the Miraculous Draft of Fish, we may summarize our tentative conclusions as follows. The Lucan narrative, because of its position in the Gospel, appears to center on the Gentile mission. While Jesus' teaching by the shore would reflect the mission to the Jews, the voyage out into deeper water signifies that to the Gentiles. Peter's responsibility as master of the ship parallels his leadership of the mission. The nets seem to be a subsidiary figure for the mission enterprise, and their breaking may reflect the tensions experienced by the church in regard to the acceptance of Gentiles. Jesus' words of commission to Peter are significant for all the disciples, and provide the key to an understanding of the narrative.

In John a double, though not un-unified, focus seems to be present: the miraculous catch symbolizes the mission of the church, and this issues in a meal with eucharistic motifs. While Peter here plays a leading role similar to that in Luke, the "disciple whom Jesus loved" is also introduced, and it is he who points out the identity of Jesus, just as he has throughout this Gospel. That the net here does not break, as in Luke, parallels the fact that in this Gospel the Jewish-Gentile problem is not in view as it is in the Lucan literature. The number of the fish symbolizes, perhaps by a variety of associations, the wondrous number of converts brought into the church by its missionary endeavors. Finally, the meal presented by Jesus seems to reflect the fact that converts brought to him in the church encounter him particularly in the eucharist.

Few, if any, of these interpretations can claim more than probability. Many of the details we have presented must remain only possibilities. Yet it may not be unreasonable to conclude that in their general outlines, at least, all three of the stories we have studied have deeper significances for the history of salvation than might at first appear.

CHAPTER IX

THE SHIP IN THE ACTS, THE EPISTLES,
AND THE REVELATION

The ship appears specifically or by implication a number of times in the Acts, the Epistles, and the Revelation. Its one appearance in the Acts is in a narrative, much as in the Gospel stories. In the Epistles, on the other hand, it is more obviously a figure of speech, while in the Revelation it has apocalyptic associations. In the pages that follow we shall attempt explanations of these passages in terms of nautical symbolism.

The ship of Alexandria

"'Therefore I urge you to take some food, for this is essential for your being saved[1] so not a hair is to perish from the head of any of you.' And when he had said this, he took bread, and giving thanks to God in the presence of all he broke it and began to eat. Then they all were encouraged and ate some food themselves. (We were in all two hundred and seventy-six persons in the ship.)" (Acts 27 : 34-37).

This passage is a part of the familiar narrative of Paul's shipwreck on Malta. Commentators are divided on the question of its possible

---

[1] In translating the clause τοῦτο γὰρ πρὸς τῆς ὑμετέρας σωτηρίας ὑπάρχει we have departed from the *Rev. Stand. Vers.* ("it will give you strength"). This is the only instance in the New Testament of πρός with the genitive. In the LXX it usually has a local sense, "at", or "near" (e.g., Gen. 24 : 63; 1 Kings 26 : 7; Lam. 1 : 9), but in a number of cases it means "for", "in favor of" (Gen. 23 : 13; 29 : 34). In 2 Macc. 1 : 2 the desire is expressed that God may "be good to you and be mindful of His covenant πρὸς Αβρααμ καὶ Ισαακ καὶ Ιακωβ τῶν δούλων αὐτοῦ" (*The Second Book of Maccabees* [Dropsie College Ed., 1954], pp. 100f.). Here πρός seems to convey the basic idea of appurtenance (see A. T. Robertson, *A Grammar of the Greek New Testament* [1934], p. 493): the covenant is not simply with, but appertains to and is essential for, Abraham and his descendants. In the present passage πρός is probably used in much the same sense: the bread appertains to their salvation, and so is an essential factor in their being saved. See B. Reicke, "πρός", *Theol. Wörterb. z. N.T.*, VI (1959), 720.

symbolic significance.² However, as in Gospel narratives, the question of literal vs. symbolic does not seem necessarily to involve an either/or. Both may be present at different levels in the same narrative. As Reicke has shown, in the present story there are a number of indications that a significance beyond the strictly literal is intended.³

Throughout the narrative of this voyage, Paul is portrayed as being more than an ordinary man. Though a prisoner, he advises the captain and the centurion as one who speaks with supernatural insight and authority (v. 10, θεωρῶ [cf. ch. 7 : 56; 8 : 13; 9 : 7; 10 : 11]; v. 21, πειθαρχήσαντας; v. 23; v. 24). His utterances are filled with words that have meaning not only for the immediate situation (which in the first instance is certainly to be taken literally), but also for the Christian life and mission (vs. 10, 21, ὕβρις [cf. 2 Cor. 12 : 10], ζημία [cf. Lk. 9 : 25, par.; 1 Cor. 3 : 15]; vs. 10, 22, ψυχῶν, ψυχῆς; v. 24, κεχάρισται [cf. Lk. 7 : 42, 43; 2 Cor. 2 : 7, 10]; vs. 31, 34, σωθῆναι, σωτηρίας). As we have seen, in the Graeco-Roman world, the notion of sailing was a common figure for the course of the individual human life and of society. The figure of storm was used for the besetments of life, shipwreck for tragedy, and the shore for salvation. Shipmates were bound by the special ties of their common fate. Thus the present story of a group of men sailing together through storm, experiencing shipwreck, and yet all saved alive, could easily have suggested to the mind of an ancient Christian reader the vicissitudes of humanity and the question of its salvation.

From this point of view the utterances of Paul may be understood as the voice of God speaking to storm-tossed humanity. He warns against venturing out upon the sea, lest it result in ὕβρις, "injury," and ζημία, "loss," "damage," to their "souls" (ψυχῶν). Cf. Mk. 8 : 36, ζημιωθῆναι τὴν ψυχὴν αὐτοῦ (note also κερδῆσαι there and in Acts 27 :

---

² Literal only: H. H. Wendt, *Meyer's Kritisches exegetisches Handbuch über die Apostelgeschichte* (5th ed., 1880), p. 525; T. Zahn, *Die Apostelgeschichte des Lucas* (3d and 4th ed., 1927), p. 837; A. Steinmann, *Die Apostelgeschte* (4th ed., 1934), p. 305; E. Preuschen, *Die Apostelgeschichte* (1912), p. 153; K. Lake and H. J. Cadbury in *The Beginnings of Christianity*, IV (1933), 336; F. F. Bruce, *The Acts of the Apostles* (1953), p. 465; A. Wikenhauser, *Die Apostelgeschichte* (3d ed., 1956), p. 281. Symbolic: A. Loisy, *Les Actes des Apôtres* (1920), p. 918; O. Bauernfeind, *Die Apostelgeschichte* (1939), p. 275; B. Reicke, "Die Mahlzeit mit Paulus auf den Wellen des Mittelmeers Act. 27,33-38," *Theol. Zeitschr.*, 4 (1948), pp. 401ff. (also cites earlier literature); cf. idem, *Diakonie, Festfreude und Zelos* (1951), p. 11.

³ Reicke, "Die Mahlzeit" (n. 2), pp. 402f.

21). At sea, the ship is struck by a "typhonic" wind; by its derivation from Typhon, "the evil demon *par excellence* of magic"[4] and of the sea,[5] this expression suggests an attack by demonic powers upon humanity as it sails the sea of life.

At v. 21 Paul announces a new revelation to his fellow travellers, who have lost all hope of being saved (σώζεσθαι, v. 20). Although they have not heeded the voice of authority (πειθαρχήσαντας, v. 21) in their midst, yet because of Paul's presence among them[6] God has extended his grace to all (κεχάρισται, "forgiven" [?], cf. Lk. 7 : 42, 43; 2 Cor. 2 : 7, 10; Eph. 4 : 32; Col. 2 : 13; 3 : 13), so that not one soul (ψυχή) will be lost. This salvation is due to the fact that Paul has a divinely-appointed mission: he must "stand before" (παραστῆναι, v. 24) Caesar.[7] While παράστημι literally refers to an appearance before a judge (Rom. 14 : 10), here, as in the previous verse (and 2 Tim. 4 : 17), it also may mean "to stand beside" one in help and support and refer to Paul's proclamation of the gospel at Rome (cf. ch. 9 : 15; 23 : 11).

If Paul's words up to this point have implications for the Christian mission and message, his action depicted in vs. 34-37 may be similarly significant. Reicke notes that the food Paul offers to his companions is not just for nourishment, or to increase their chances of survival, for he already knows by revelation that they all will be saved.[8] The words πρὸς τῆς ὑμετέρας σωτηρίας would seem to imply more than their physical salvation.

Luke's language suggests that Paul's action in commencing this meal points to the eucharist. Three actions are particularly notable: "He took bread, and giving thanks... he broke it" (v. 35). In itself this is no more than the common Jewish ritual of beginning a meal.[9] Yet elsewhere in the New Testament, when these three actions are depicted together, eucharistic associations always seem to be present. These actions appear in all accounts of the institution of the Lord's

---

[4] J. H. Moulton and G. Milligan, *The Vocabulary of the Greek Testament* (1949), p. 646.

[5] H. Rahner, "Antenna Crucis," *Zeitschr. f. kath. Theol.*, 66 (1942), p. 101.

[6] The idea of a shipload of persons being saved for the sake of one man on board is the opposite of the familiar classical motif in which a ship and its passengers are lost because of the presence of one impious man (see above, Ch. II, n. 26; cf. the positive analogy in Rom. 5 : 15ff.).

[7] Bauernfeind (n. 2), p. 274.

[8] Reicke, "Die Mahlzeit" (n. 2), p. 404.

[9] See the references in n. 2 to the works of Lake and Cadbury, Steinmann, Bruce, and Wikenhauser. On the Jewish usage see H. Strack and P. Billerbeck, *Kommentar zum N.T. aus Talmud and Midrasch*, II (1924), 619.

Supper, in the miraculous feedings (John 6 : 11 mentions only Jesus' taking the loaves, giving thanks, and distributing them), and in the meal at Emmaus. It is improbable that Luke would be concerned to depict for his Gentile readers Paul's punctilious adherence to Jewish ritual, if he did not have a deeper, Christian, aim in view.[10] Nor does the lack of wine appear to rule out a eucharistic implication. As Reicke has shown,[11] on the principle *pars pro toto* the eucharist frequently was characterized simply as "breaking of bread." This seems evident from Acts 20 : 7, 11, and is probably true also of Acts 2 : 42[12] (cf. 1 Cor. 10 : 16). It is clearly so in Didache 14 : 1 and Ignatius, Ephesians 20 : 2. Wine is not mentioned in connection with the miraculous feedings, the meal at Emmaus, or that by Galilee, all of which probably have eucharistic implications.

That an association of our story with the eucharist was recognized at an early date may be suggested by the addition of ἐπιδιδοὺς καὶ ἡμῖν (614, 1611, 2147, sy^h sa) at the end of v. 35. This reading completes the series of actions that are specifically mentioned in all the synoptic accounts of the institution of the Lord's Supper. Its insertion here may have been an attempt to bring out more clearly the relation of our passage to the eucharist.[13] Like the miraculous feeding, the meal at Emmaus, and the breakfast by the sea, this meal may symbolize the eucharist. Unlike these, however, it is shared with heathen, but heathen whose "souls" God has already "granted" (κεχάρισται v. 24) to Paul in view of his mission. Just as throughout this voyage the apostle's dealing with his heathen shipmates seems to reflect his commission to the Gentile world, so the climactic meal here depicted may be symbolic of the central fact of his proclamation. The whole narrative appears to be suggestive of later successes to be expected for the Christian mission.[14] (Cf. v. 44, "all escaped to land" [πάντας

---

[10] Reicke, "Die Mahlzeit" (n. 2), p. 406.
[11] Reicke, *Diakonie* (n. 2), p. 14.
[12] See Strack and Billerbeck (n. 9), *loc. cit.*
[13] Reicke, "Die Mahlzeit" (n. 2), p. 410, notes further indication in the *Actus Vercellenses of Peter*, 5, where that apostle celebrates the eucharist on shipboard and then lands at Puteoli, the same port at which Paul ultimately arrives in our narrative (Acts 28 : 13). This suggests dependence of the Petrine story upon Acts.
[14] This point of view, expressed particularly by Reicke, "Die Mahlzeit" (n. 2), pp. 408f., answers effectively the complaint of Zahn (n. 2), *loc. cit.*, that to think of a eucharistic celebration here would contradict Paul's view of the relation between a meal to satisfy hunger and the Lord's Supper (1 Cor. 11 : 17-22). This was not actually a Lord's Supper, yet on the level on which it may refer to the eucharist, it is not concerned with physical nourishment.

διασωθῆναι ἐπὶ τὴν γῆν], with the common figure of a storm-tossed sailor's finally reaching land, representing the human soul's attaining the desired haven of salvation.)

The statement that 276[15] persons were aboard the ship seems out of place unless a particular significance for it in this context can be found. After the shipwreck a check was doubtless made not only of the prisoners but also of the whole group to ascertain possible losses, and from this an accurate count might have been obtained; nevertheless the presence and significance of the number at this point in our story remain to be explained.[16] As we have noted earlier, 276 is one of several triangular numbers in the New Testament.

Here it is the total of those "souls in the ship" (ψυχαὶ ἐν τῷ πλοίῳ) who have been fed by Paul and who are saved. This group seems to represent the wonderful number of Gentiles responding to the Christian mission. If this is correct, the ship *at this point* may represent the **church** in which these "souls" are found in communion with their Lord in the eucharist.

However, if the ship in v. 37 may be identified as the church, elsewhere in our narrative such an identification is not possible. If this symbolism were continuous throughout, the ship would not founder as it does. In this story we are dealing first and above all with a literal narrative of actual events, which appears now and again to have been stylized with theological implications in mind.

"Governments" in the church

In 1 Cor. 12 : 28, Paul lists two functions exercised in the church that appear nowhere else under the same terminology: "helps" (ἀντιλήμψεις), and "governments" (κυβερνήσεις). The latter of these is basically a nautical term denoting the act of piloting a ship. At an early date, however, it had come to have also the metaphorical sense of guiding, governing, and particularly of governing the state, which of course was frequently symbolized as a ship. Thus these two figures appear to have interacted in the course of their development. However, κυβέρνησις as "governing" became quite independent of the figure

---

[15] Variant readings: 275: A; 270: 69; "about 76": B sa; "about 70": Epiphanius. None of these is sufficiently well attested to be convincing; cf. J. H. Ropes, *The Beginnings of Christianity*, III (1926), 247.
[16] Luke may have inserted it at this point in analogy to the narrative of the miraculous feeding; Lake and Cadbury (n. 2), p. 337; Reicke, "Die Mahlzeit" (n. 2), p. 407.

ship = state (as in Prov. 11 : 14; 24 : 6; Susanna 5), and for this reason it is impossible to insist on Paul's having had in mind the symbolism ship = church when he wrote 1 Cor. 12 : 28.[17] At most we can say that κυβερνήσεις here is suggestive of that figure.[18]

Man "tossed to and fro"

According to Eph. 4 : 14, one of the purposes for which spiritual gifts have been bestowed upon the church is "so that we may no longer be children, tossed to and fro (κλυδωνιζόμενοι) and carried about with every wind of doctrine, by the cunning of men, by their craftiness in deceitful wiles." The verb κλυδωνίζεσθαι means "to be tossed about by a wave"; the author has drawn on the familiar classical and Hellenistic figure of a storm-tossed ship to represent a man, or men, beset by evil. Here the ship is threatened by both wave and wind. The wind is explained as doctrine, "every wind" being doctrines of various types and origins.[19] The symbolism of wind suggests that the author may mean to characterize these doctrines as demonic (cf. 1 Tim. 4 : 1, "doctrines of demons"). The figure of waves, implicit in κλυδωνιζόμενοι, probably refers to the difficulties in general that result from the proclamation of various false teachings – the waves would not exist if they were not stirred up by the wind.

While the figures of wind and wave seem clear enough, that of the ship, doubtless presupposed here, is not quite so easily interpreted. Does it refer to the individual, or to the church? From ch. 4 : 1 on, the author is concerned particularly with the unity of the church: in vs. 4-6 he directs attention to a series of unities on which this is based; with vs. 7, 8, 11, he considers the diversities of gifts within the church which yet contribute to its unity, and characterizes it as "the body of Christ" (v. 12); in v. 13 this unity of the church is likened to "mature manhood." With v. 14 such mature unity is contrasted with the condition of children, which then is described by our figure of a storm-tossed ship driven hither and thither by winds of variant doctrines. This contrast is essentially one between a united church and a divided one, the latter being likened to a ship in storm. Our passage appears to provide, implicitly, another example of the figure ship = church.

---

[17] K. Goldammer, "Das Schiff der Kirche," *Theol. Zeitschr.*, 6 (1950), p. 237.
[18] Cf. H. W. Beyer, "κυβέρνησις," *Theol. Wörterb. z. N.T.*, III (1938), 1035f.
[19] Cf. Hippolytus, *Elenchos*, 7, 13, who pictures Christians as sailing through a tossing sea of heretical teaching in search of a peaceful harbor.

At the same time, the church is these verses is made up of many individuals (οἱ πάντες, v. 13), who are given a variety of gifts (v. 11), and who, though now divided (v. 14), are yet to attain "to the unity of the faith and of the knowledge of the Son of God" (v. 13). The ship is an apt figure to illustrate such a point of view. In classical and Hellenistic usage, it represents the life course both of the individual and of the group. At times the two points of view merge, so that, as here, both appear to be mirrored simultaneously in the same figure (cf. *Syr. Apoc. Bar.* 85: 10f.).[20]

Shipwreck

"Holding faith and a good conscience; which some having thrust from them made shipwreck concerning the faith" (1 Tim. 1 : 19, *Am. Stand. Ver.*). The figure of shipwreck as used here of personal tragedy is familiar in classical and Jewish-Hellenistic literature.[21]

Particularly close to the present passage are a number of examples in which the ideas of shipwreck and allied figures have a religious application. In Sirach 33 : 2 the man who is hypocritical toward the law is likened to a ship in storm. In *Aristeas* 251, the invocation of God assures that the ship of life will be steered on a straight course, and thus will avoid shipwreck. In a number of instances, Philo compares the soul to a ship, and reason to its pilot which steers it away from shipwreck.[22] Especially significant for the interpretation of the present passage is *4 Macc.* 7 : 1f., where the ship is the pious soul, the sea is emotion, and the pilot is reason.[23]

In a detailed interpretation of the present passage, several questions present themselves. (1) What does the ship implied here represent? (2) What is rejected? (3) Does it have an implied place in the symbolism of shipwreck?

1. If the false teachers with whom vs. 3-20 are concerned have made shipwreck περὶ τὴν πίστιν, what does the ship which has foundered represent?

The translation of the Revised Standard Version, "certain persons have made shipwreck of their faith," implies that the ship is

---

[20] From the standpoint of the individual, Sirach 33 : 2 is a particularly close parallel; cf. also Isa. 57 : 20; James 1 : 6.
[21] C. Spicq, *Saint Paul: les epîtres pastorales* (1947), pp. 49f.; M. Dibelius, *Die Pastoralbriefe* (3d ed., 1955), p. 27.
[22] See above, Ch. III, nn. 21, 22.
[23] Cf. Tertullian, *De anima*, 52.

to be understood as faith, in the sense of an inner bearing which the false teachers have lost.[24] However the phrase περὶ τὴν πίστιν ἐναυάγησαν must be translated literally, "they suffered shipwreck concerning the faith," and most naturally suggests that faith is a goal which the people in question missed because of shipwreck. Important analogies to this are 1 Tim. 1 : 6; 6 : 21; 2 Tim. 2 : 18. Each of these passages seems to presuppose the idea of a journey. In ch. 1 : 5f. the persons referred to are thought of as moving toward a goal (τέλος), which is "love"; the medium or means of their journey is a "pure heart," a "good consent,"[25] and a "genuine faith." But some have "swerved" ἀστοχήσαντες) from the appointed path and so fail to reach their goal. Similarly in ch. 6 : 21 the individuals concerned are thought of as journeying, probably toward salvation (cf. 2 Tim. 2 : 10; 3 : 15); the medium again is faith, and once more some have missed (ἠστόχησαν) because of "falsely-called knowledge." The same thought is presupposed in 2 Tim. 2 : 16ff., where Hymenaeus and Philetus may be visualized as having been on the way to salvation, the medium of their journey being the "truth"; but they too, because of their ungodly "talk" have "swerved" (ἠστόχησαν) from their course and are lost.

The passage with which we are particularly concerned seems also to fit this recurrent pattern. The persons in question are pictured as having been on a voyage, their ultimate destination probably being salvation, their more immediate goal being faith. But because they have rejected a "good consent," they have "suffered shipwreck concerning the faith" and so fail to reach even this preliminary goal.

If this interpretation is correct, we should then refer the shipwreck in the present passage to individual persons. To an extent, this is an analogy to the familiar symbolism of the ship as the human soul. Here, however, the ship represents especially the soul of a Christian as it is characterized by faith (cf. *4 Macc.* 7 : 1-3, where the ship represents the soul as qualified by piety).

2. What is it that the false teachers of 1 Tim. 1 : 19 have "thrust from" themselves? Grammatically the pronoun ἥν, which stands as the object of this action, may refer back to both πίστιν and συνείδησιν (cf. ch. 1 : 6: ὧν [referring to καρδίας, συνειδήσεως and πίστεως] ἀστοχήσαντες). However in v. 19, ἥν refers only to συνείδησιν since πίστιν

---

[24] Cf. Chrysostom's interpretation (n. 30), contrasting faith with reason. H. Preisker, "ναυάγειν," *Theol. Wörterb. z. N.T.*, IV (1942), 896, discussing this verse, speaks of the "life of faith" (Glaubensleben) as having suffered shipwreck. Similarly G. Wohlenberg, *Die Pastoralbriefe* (1906), p. 100.
[25] See B. Reicke, *The Disobedient Spirits and Christian Baptism* (1946), p. 179.

plays quite another role here than does συνείδησιν. As the goal which the shipwreck has caused the soul to miss, faith can hardly have been rejected before the disaster occurs.[26] Only the "good consent" has been thrust away, and this is the cause of shipwreck.

3. May this "good consent" be seen as involved in the ship symbolism of 1 Tim. 1 : 19? Attempts have been made to find here a nautical counterpart for the conscience; it has been compared to an anchor[27] and to the cargo which keeps the vessel in balance.[28] J. Weiss rejects these suggestions as "artificial."[29] There is certainly no necessity of extending the nautical symbolism suggested by shipwreck to include other features of this verse. However, the frequency with which the figure of the pilot is associated in ancient literature with that of the ship, and especially with shipwreck, suggests that the "good conscience" here may be compared with it (cf. *4 Macc.* 7 : 1-3, where the "bark of piety" is piloted by "reason").[30] Similarly in a number of passages Philo, likening life to a ship, speaks of its pilot as the logos, the agency whereby man participates in the divine reason.[31] This characteristic way of thinking may also very well be applied to 1 Tim. 1 : 19. Here the "good consent,"[32] thought of as a positive attitude, would be that which orients the soul of a Christian to "the faith," as a pilot guides a ship toward its goal. When it is rejected, the soul founders as a ship without a pilot.

---

[26] H. J. Holtzmann, *Die Pastoralbriefe* (1880), p. 304.
[27] Wiesinger (in Olshausen's *Kommentar* [1850]) as cited by B. and J. Weiss, *Die Briefe Pauli an Timotheus und Titus* (6th ed., 1894), p. 106. This may be traced to Chrysostom who in this context compares faith and conscience to a ship and its anchor (see C. Spicq [n. 21], p. 50).
[28] Wohlenberg (n. 24), *loc. cit.*
[29] Weiss (n. 27), *loc. cit.*
[30] Chrysostom, *In Epist. I ad Timoth.* I, *Hom.* V (Migne, *Patr. Gr.*, 62, 527) employs the idea of "reason" quite differently in explaining our passage: "And some turn aside from faith, who seek out all things by reason: for reason produces shipwreck, and faith is like a secure ship."
[31] See above, Ch. III, nn. 21, 22.
[32] For this definition in the present context, see Reicke (n. 25), pp. 174-182, especially p. 179; cf. Dibelius (n. 21), pp. 16f., and the important excursus on "La bonne conscience et la foi" by C. Spicq (n. 21), pp. 29-38; however, this author speaks of conscience as "a right judgment which orients all his life toward God and inquires concerning the divine will" (pp. 36f.). On the typically Pauline sense of συνείδησις, see B. Reicke, "Syneidesis in Röm. 2, 15," *Theol. Zeitschr.*, 12 (1956), pp. 157-161.

Drifting away from the gospel

"Therefore we must pay the closer attention to what we have heard, lest we drift away (παραρυῶμεν) from it" (Heb. 2 : 1). This verse appears to draw on the familiar ancient symbolism of the ship as the soul. Failing to heed the gospel, it risks being washed from its moorings and may drift aimlessly away upon the sea of the world.

Recently this interpretation has been challenged by Spicq, who points out that the verb παραρρεῖν in secular literature is never the basis for such a metaphor. He favors instead the derived sense of "passing by" and so excluding oneself from salvation.[33]

The verb παραρρεῖν has, in general, three meanings: (1) "to flow beside, past," as of a river[34]; (2) "to slip off," "to go astray," "to pass by" with the implication that the subject is unnoticed;[35] (3) "to pass by" with the implication that the subject himself is unnoticing, careless.[36] For convenience we shall refer to these as (1) the basic, (2) the objective, and (3) the subjective meanings. All of these seem to be present in the LXX,[37] which suggests the range of possible interpretations of παραρυῶμεν in the present passage.

Patristic expositions emphasize that παραρρεῖν has to do here with the loss of the soul and its destruction. Chrysostom explains it, "that we may not perish, that we may not fall away."[38] Theodore of Mopsuestia emphasizes the personal responsibility of the Christian: "being on guard lest we are in some way turned aside from the better things."[39] Theodoret speaks of "something that slips away";[40] Hesychius defines παραρυῶμεν as "we might slip off";[40] Suidas, as "we might fall aside".[40] Oecumenius explains, "that is, we might

---

[33] C. Spicq, L'épître aux Hébreux, II (1953), 25.
[34] Xenophon, Cyrop. IV, 5, 2.
[35] Numerous classical examples in H. G. Liddell and R. Scott, Greek-English Lexicon (rev. ed., 1932), II, 1322.
[36] Clement of Alex., Paedagogus III, 11; Origen, Contra Celsum VIII, 23.
[37] Basic sense: Isa. 44 : 4; objective sense: Prov. 4 : 21 (Symm.), μὴ παραρρυησάτωσαν ἐξ ὀφθαλμῶν μου; subjective sense: Prov. 3 : 21 (παραρρυῇς, referring to υἱέ, could mean "get lost," but seems more probably to have the subjective idea, "pass by heedlessly").
[38] J. A. Cramer, ed., Catenae graecorum patrum (1844), VII, 140. Chrysostom thinks these words are taken from Prov. 3 : 21, which suggests that he probably understands that passage in the objective sense (see n. 37).
[39] Theodore of Mops., In epist. ad Hebr. fragmenta II, 1 (Migne, Patr. Gr., 66, 1953).
[40] Quoted by F. Bleek, Der Brief an die Hebräer, II : 1 (1836), 199f.

fall away from that which is proper and from the way to salvation."[41] Although it is not possible to make a clear distinction here between those who take παρρρεῖν in the objective and those who take it in the subjective sense, they all seem to understand this verb in these derived senses, rather than in its basic meaning on which alone a nautical symbolism may be postulated. To our knowledge, no ancient writer has sought to interpret παραρυῶμεν in the present passage in terms of the ship of the soul.

In more modern times, Luther saw a nautical implication here: "like a ship before its arrival slips off into destruction."[42] Michel adopts this, and similar nautical figures have been proposed by others.[43] Bauer translates, "so that we do not drift off"[44] which like the Revised Standard Version, "lest we drift away," clearly suggests the symbolism of the ship.

We may conclude that a reference here to the soul as a ship is possible in view of the basic meaning of παρρρεῖν and of the currency of this figure in ancient literature. However, considering that in both secular and religious literature this verb is more commonly used in derived senses which give no basis for nautical symbolism, it would appear more probable that the passage simply means, "lest we carelessly slip away and are lost."

The anchor of hope

"Which we have as an anchor of the soul, *a hope* both sure and stedfast and entering into that which is within the veil" (Heb. 6 : 19, *Am. Stand. Ver.*).

In this passage the figure of the anchor presupposes that of the ship. Two interpretations of this implied figure are possible: (1) The ship is the human soul. The words "anchor of the soul" cannot mean here that the anchor is the soul (*genitivus definitionis*), for the anchor is defined as hope. Apparently the anchor of hope has the same relationship to the soul as a literal anchor has to a ship, which would

---

[41] Oecumenius, *Comment. in epist. ad Hebr.* II (Migne, *Patr. Gr.*, 119, 292).
[42] Marginal gloss to Heb. 2 : 1 in 1546 ed. (not in those of 1522, 1524) of Luther's German Bible: Erlangen Ed., LXIV, 250; Weimar Ed., *Die deutsche Bibel*, VII, 349.
[43] O. Michel, *Der Brief an die Hebräer* (1949), p. 63; R. P. Médebielle, *Epître aux Hébreux*, in L. Pirot, ed., *La sainte Bible* (1938), XII, 297; B. F. Westcott, *The Epistle to the Hebrews* (2d ed., 1892), p. 37.
[44] W. Bauer, *Griechisch-deutsches Wörterbuch* (5th ed., 1958), col. 1132.

equate the ship with the soul. (2) The ship is the church, as it appears to be often elsewhere in the New Testament.

The church is not specifically mentioned in the present context. It is suggested, however, by the analogy between Christ and the high priest who entered the Most Holy Place on the Day of Atonement to make atonement "for all the assembly (קהל) of Israel" (Lev. 16 : 17). Furthermore the argument of the passage has just been grounded in God's oath to Abraham regarding the Chosen People (vs. 13ff.). The author seems to be concerned not only with Christ's relationship with the individual, but also with his relation to this people, his church. The implied figure of the ship may then represent the church, in which the soul may be thought of as a passenger. If this interpretation is correct, the ship/church is probably conceived as bearing souls through the waters of this world toward heaven, a theme that has its roots in classical thought and appears repeatedly in early Christian literature and art. The anchor is still "an anchor of the soul," but of the soul as one of the community of believers for whom Christ has gone as a "forerunner" (v. 20).

At the same time, as in classical literature there is a close relationship between the ship as an individual and the ship as a group, so here the meaning may oscillate between the ideas of the individual soul and the community of souls in the church. It is probably best to count on both possibilities.

The figure of the anchor as hope is also familiar from ancient literature.[45] Here the author has employed it boldly. As Chrysostom notes, while ordinarily an anchor is dropped in the depths of the sea, Christians place theirs in heaven.[46] Spicq suggests that the idea of an anchor in heaven may be connected with the Semitic cosmology in which there was a sea above the earth,[47] but this seems doubtful. In the immediate context of the present passage the concern is not so much with the fact that the anchor of hope is in heaven as such, but rather that it is fixed in the "inner shrine," in the very presence of God, where Jesus ministers as high priest. This gives point to the suggestion of a connection between the anchor and the idea, familiar in both paganism and early Christianity, that the voyage of the soul may terminate with a fortunate anchorage in the hereafter.[48] In

---

[45] See Ch. II, n. 40; further examples given by Spicq (n. 33), II, 164f.
[46] Cramer (n. 38), VII, 522.
[47] Spicq (n. 33), II, 164.
[48] Spicq (n. 33), II, 165, notes this connection and points out that in the Catacomb of Priscilla alone, some seventy anchors were discovered marked on graves.

hope the soul is portrayed here as already having cast anchor in the divine presence by virtue of the fact that Christ, its forerunner and high priest, is there (v. 20). In a sense, as Windisch notes, Christ himself is the anchor[49] (cf. 1 Tim. 1 : 1).

The ship and its rudder

"Look at the ships also; though they are so great and are driven by strong winds, they are guided by a very small rudder wherever the will of the pilot directs. So the tongue is a little member and boasts of great things" (James 3 : 4-5a).

This comparison between the rudder of a ship and the tongue is based upon the smallness of a cause as compared with the greatness of its effect (cf. v. 5b), a theme which appears repeatedly in classical literature.[50] Such classical figures are a characteristic of the diatribe form in which much of this epistle is framed.[51]

To what do "the ships" in v. 4 refer? The answer depends largely on the relation of this verse to its context. The chapter opens with an admonition that not many should aspire to the position of a teacher in the church, for such greater responsibility involves a greater judgment if the teacher fails. Next (v. 2) is a transitional verse in which it is pointed out that all make mistakes, but if anyone is able to keep from mistakes in what he says, he is also able to control "the whole body." Then follow two illustrations: (v. 3) that of a horse which can be turned about by the bit in its mouth; (v. 4) that of great ships that can be guided by small rudders. The next verse (v. 5a) applies these to the tongue: though small, it boasts greatly. This thought is intensified (v. 5b) by the figure of a small fire setting a great forest ablaze, which is driven home (v. 6) by the declaration, "And the tongue is a fire." Then follows a vivid and vigorous list of evils connected with the tongue. This devious chain of ideas and figures has given rise to a variety of attempts at analysis. The two main problems are (1) whether v. 1, with its admonition regarding teachers, can be connected with the figures and themes that follow, and (2) whether the pessimistic turn of vs. 5ff. can be applied backward to the figures in vs. 3f.

Hauck separates v. 1 from what follows by stating flatly that the

---

[49] H. Windisch, *Der Hebräerbrief* (2d ed., 1931), p. 59.
[50] See references in Windisch, *Die katholischen Briefe* (3d ed., 1951), p. 22.
[51] J. H. Ropes, *A Critical and Exegetical Commentary on the Epistle of St. James* (1916), pp. 10-16.

discussion of the control of the tongue as being important for the control of the whole self is to be taken "without further reference to the teaching office" (v. 1).[52] Huther breaks the line of thought between vs. 3 and 4, insisting that the reading εἰ δέ (v. 3),[53] as contrasted with ἰδού (v. 4), removes all reason for taking the figures of the horse (v. 3) and the ship (v. 4) as synonymous. He sees the figure of the horse (v. 3) to be connected with the previous verse as an admonition to control the tongue; but the figure of the ship (v. 4) he interprets in terms of the pessimistic attitude of vs. 5f. as an illustration of the destructive power of the tongue.[54]

Dibelius, while recognizing v. 2 as a transition between v. 1 and vs. 3ff., sees a gap between the admonition regarding teachers (v. 1) and the discussion of the evil of the tongue, for he cannot think that aspiring teachers in the church could be accused of such sins. He attributes the portrayal of these gross transgressions (vs. 6ff.) to diatribe style and warns against their being taken seriously as indicating the actual condition of the church. He holds the figures of horse (v. 3) and ship (v. 4) in parallel, and emphasizes that although they themselves are not pessimistic, they must be interpreted in terms of the pessimism of vs. 5ff.[55]

These analyses illustrate the variety of relationships that have been proposed between the various parts of our passage. If we are to understand its inner relationships correctly, we must place it in the total setting of the epistle and of the purpose of its author.

Reicke has shown good reason for seeing the epistle of James as directed against Zelotism and other restiveness in the church, particularly toward political authority, at the end of the first century.[56] In such a setting the excesses portrayed within the church and even

---

[52] Fr. Hauck, *Die katholischen Briefe* (1935), p. 22.
[53] εἰ δέ: BKL 69 pm ff vg; ἴδε: (ℵ*) CPK al sy sa arm; ἰδού: 36 pc TR. The reading ἴδε can have arisen through itacism, and ἰδού is obviously an accomodation to ἰδού in v. 4. However, Ropes (n. 51), p. 229, argues for ἴδε on the basis of sense, suggesting that itacism could have worked in the opposite direction, as B is not free from spelling mistakes.
[54] J. E. Huther and W. Beyschlag, *Krit. exeg. Handb. über den Brief des Jakobus* (4th ed., 1882), p. 160.
[55] M. Dibelius, *Der Brief des Jakobus* (1921), pp. 169f.; on pp. 173, 175f., he notes that it is a characteristic of diatribe to change the application of classical motifs and thinks that James accordingly has taken two originally optimistic figures and placed them in a pessimistic context; cf. H. Rendtorff, *Hörer und Täter* (1953), p. 53.
[56] Reicke, *Diakonie* (n. 2), pp. 339-347.

among its would-be leaders become quite believable. If the church at this time faced a serious threat from aspirant leaders motivated by an unscrupulous anti-Roman Zelotism, ch. 3 : 1-12 takes on a unity that transcends its devious inner relationships. The focus of the whole passage turns on the would-be teachers of v. 1, who are admonished that a greater judgment awaits them if they fail rightly to exercise the teaching office. The following verses are unified by a development of this theme: the one who speaks to and for the church, though small as compared with the total body, exercises a decisive influence over the whole; hence his greater responsibility and greater judgment. This emphasis upon teaching may be seen in v. 2 (ἐν λόγῳ), in v. 3 (the bridling of the mouths of horses), in vs. 5f. (the tongue). That it does not appear explicitly also in v. 4 is no indication of disunity in our passage. As Dibelius has amply illustrated, the motifs of horse – rider and ship – pilot are commonly paired in classical literature, and especially by Philo.[57] With such instances in mind the author, after introducing the figure of the bridled horse which perfectly illustrates his point, could easily add that of the ship and rudder without deflecting the direction of his thought. Huther's argument that the reading εἰ δέ in v. 3 breaks the parallelism between that verse and v. 4 (ἰδού) is hardly decisive, for ἰδού can as well be understood as introducing a further illustration of the point made just before (cf. *Rev. Stand. Vers.*: "Look at the ships also"). Nor does v. 5 introduce a thought that is really alien to v. 1, if the general background is taken into account. Rather the pessimistic turn taken by the discourse at this point (v. 5) reflects the unhappy situation that has given rise to the whole passage, and to the warning in v. 1 in particular. Thus there seems to be no necessity to propose a break in thought between either vs. 1 and 2, or vs. 3 and 4, or vs. 4 and 5. The ideas of control of the body by control of the tongue, and the disastrous effects of an uncontrolled tongue are complementary when considered in the light of the actual church problem with which our whole passage appears to be concerned.[58]

With the foregoing in mind, we may now return to the more specific question regarding the significance of the ship (v. 4) in this context.[59] Taken by themselves, vs. 2-5 would appear to focus on

---

[57] Dibelius (n. 55), pp. 174f.; Ropes (n. 51), p. 231.
[58] On the probable historical setting of this passage, see Reicke, *Diakonie* (n. 2), pp. 340f.
[59] The following exegesis is based upon lectures by Bo Reicke on the Catholic Epistles, at Basel, winter semester, 1957-1958.

the individual, with the thought that by mastering his tongue a man is able to control his entire body. But if we recognize an essential connection between these verses and v. 1, the tongue then relates to the specific work of teaching in the church. The author's concern is not merely with the problem of personal ethical development, but much more with the effect of the words of the teacher on his congregation. The responsibility of the teacher in view of his position as teacher and consequently toward his congregation is set forth in v. 1, and driven home by the figures in vs. 3f., where emphasis is on this very idea of responsibility, i.e., the great effect of a small cause.

That it is the church and its leaders, rather than the individual, which occupy the central focus here is suggested by a number of evidences. In v. 2 the man who is able to keep from error in his words is also competent to govern "the whole body" (ὅλον τὸ σῶμα, cf. v. 6). In view of v. 1, σῶμα seems to be suggestive of the church (cf. Rom. 12 : 5; 1 Cor. 10 : 16f.; etc.). The same thought is repeated in v. 3. The reference to blessing "the Lord and Father" (v. 9, cf. v. 10) suggests that the author has not only the church in mind, but especially the church engaged in divine worship (cf. ch. 1 : 19, 21; 2 : 2, 21; 3 : 6, 10; 5 : 13ff.).[60] It appears probable, then, that in v. 4 the figure of the ship once more represents the church. If this identification is correct, certain overtones of this symbolism such as the interdependence and common fate of shipmates, and especially the necessity of harmonious co-operation also fit the present context with its emphasis on patience and good will.

Within this frame of reference other figures in v. 4 suggest themselves. The rudder may be not only the tongue, but also the tongue of the church, the teacher. As long as the rudder/teacher is obedient to his pilot, Christ, the church advances toward its divinely appointed destiny. This figure takes on added meaning when we remember that in ancient times gods were thought to protect a ship by keeping special care of the rudder, it was thought to have a certain holiness, and it seems to have been considered to possess a *numen*.[61] The fact that the rudder was viewed with such importance seems to contribute to the emphasis that James places on the special significance of the teacher in the church. The "strong winds," which cannot deflect the ship as long as the will of the pilot is exercised upon it through the rudder, may represent powers of evil which the author sees exerted against the church, and especially "every wind of false

---

[60] Reicke, *Diakonie* (n. 2), pp. 340f., 345.
[61] See above Ch. II, nn. 9, 39.

doctrine" (Eph. 4 : 14) propounded to the church by unworthy teachers (cf. Mk. 4 : 37, pars.; 6 : 48, pars.).

The ark of Noah

"... the ark, into which a few, that is eight souls, were saved through water; which antitypical baptism now saves you ..."[62] (1 Peter 3 : 20b-21a).

The ark appears to be figurative here for several reasons.

1. The problem of interpreting v. 21a has usually been solved by one or another translation making baptism the "antitype." Whether v. 21a is taken as meaning merely that Christian baptism "corresponds to" the experience of Noah and his family (*Rev. Stand. Vers.*), or even less probably that it is the antitype of the waters of the Flood (*Am. Stand. Vers.*, margin), or, as we prefer, that Noah experienced an antitypical baptism and Christians now receive the foreshadowed reality,[63] a figurative relationship between v. 20b and v. 21a seems clearly to be present.

2. Repeatedly in the New Testament, Noah and his generation pre-figure the Last Day (Mt. 24 : 37-39; Lk. 17 : 26f.; 2 Pet. 2 : 5, 9; even Heb. 11 : 7 is in a sense eschatological).[64] Our passage implies

---

[62] This translation follows that of Reicke (n. 25), p. 145, for the clause ὃ καὶ ὑμᾶς ἀντίτυπον νῦν σῴζει βάπτισμα (v. 21a); cf. n. 79, below.

[63] For the English reader confusion is confounded by the ambiguity of the word "antitype": it may refer to the reality of which the type is a figure, or it may be only a figure of the original (cf. E. G. Selwyn, *The First Epistle of St. Peter* [2d ed., 1949], p. 204). The basic meaning of ἀντίτυπος, "struck back," suggests the latter definition, and in its only other appearance in the New Testament (Heb. 9 : 24) it clearly has this meaning (so also 2 Clem. 14 : 3). If, as appears probable, ἀντίτυπον in the present passage has the same sense, how can baptism be such an "antitype"? Certainly it is not a figure of the Flood! In view of this, Reicke has proposed that v. 21a be understood as a relative clause in which an appositional antecedent (βάπτισμα) has been incorporated ([n. 25], p. 145; on pp. 149-172 he presents numerous examples of this construction from Homer to late Hellenistic Greek), and that ἀντίτυπον be taken as an adjectival attribute to βάπτισμα. F. W. Beare, *The First Epistle of Peter* (1947), pp. 148 and S. E. Johnson, "The Preaching to the Dead," *Journ. Bibl. Lit.*, 79 (1960), p. 50, on the other hand, understand "antitype" in the sense of reality of which the Flood is a type.

[64] *Am. Stand. Vers.*; *I Enoch* constructs a similar relationship between the judgement of the Flood and the final judgment of fire: ch. 54 : 7-55 : 2; ch. 67 : 4 and chs. 52-55; cf. ch. 10 : 12f.; A. Dillmann, *Das Buch Henoch* (1853), pp. 205f.

the same thought.⁶⁵ When it declares that "baptism now saves you," this *now* clearly has the Last Day in view (cf. ch. 4 : 7). Moreover the clause, "when God's patience waited" (ch. 3 : 20; apparently superfluous to the sense of what precedes it) seems to find its significance in the thought that similarly God now is waiting in patience just before the coming of the judgment day⁶⁶ (cf. ch. 4 : 5, 7, 17; 2 Pet. 3 : 9). The participle ἀπειθήσασιν, applied in ch. 3 : 20 to the antediluvian "spirits," that is, the powers standing behind the pagan world, are in the context of vs. 13-16 a counterpart of the heathen to whom the Christian is to proclaim the gospel.⁶⁷ Inasmuch then as Noah's experience in the Flood, God's patience beforehand, and the disobedient spirits all appear to be figurative of the apostle's own time, the only other feature in the Flood story as narrated here, the ark and its eight passengers, may also have a typological significance.

What then is this typological significance of the ark? There is little direct evidence from pre-Christian literature to aid in making an identification.⁶⁸ Apart from the Flood story (Gen. 6-9), the ark of Noah is not mentioned in the Old Testament. In *1 Enoch* 67 : 2, God declares to Noah before the Flood, "And now the angels are making a wooden (building), and when they have completed that task I will place my hand upon it and preserve it, and there shall come forth from it the seed of life, and a change shall set in so that the earth will not remain without inhabitant."⁶⁹ Somewhat similarly, two passages in Wisdom refer to the ark:

> Ch. 10 : 4: And when for this cause [Cain's murder of Abel and ensuing crimes] the earth was drowning with a flood, wisdom again saved it, guiding the righteous man's course by a poor piece of wood (ξύλον);⁷⁰

> Ch. 14 : 3-7: Because even in the sea thou gavest a way, and in the waves a sure path, showing that thou canst save out of every danger, that so even without art a man may put to sea; and it is thy will that the works of thy wisdom shall not be idle; therefore also do men intrust their lives (ψυχάς) to a little piece of wood (ξύλῳ), and passing through the surge on a raft are brought safe (διεσώθησαν) to land.⁷¹ For in the old time

---

[65] W. Vrede, *Die katholischen Briefe* (4th ed., 1932), p. 109.
[66] Reicke (n. 25), pp. 137f., who notes parallels in *I Enoch* 9 : 11; 60 : 5; 93 : 3.
[67] Reicke (n. 25), pp. 130-132, 138.
[68] According to R. Mach, *Der Zaddik im Talmud und Midrasch* (1957), p. 232, the ark does not appear figuratively in rabbinical literature.
[69] R. H. Charles, *Apocrypha and Pseudepigrapha* (1913), II, 231.
[70] Charles (n. 69), II, 551.
[71] Reicke (n. 25), p. 139, notes that both ψυχαί and διασῴζειν reappear in 1 Pet. 3 : 20.

also, when proud giants were perishing, the hope of the world, taking refuge on a raft, left to the race of men a seed of generations to come, thy hand guiding the helm, for blessed was the wood (ξύλον) through which cometh righteousness.[72]

In each of these three passages, the ark is a means of salvation for humanity, and it is of wood. Thus the ark was looked upon as saving wood. In view of ch. 2 : 24, where ξύλον (= the cross; cf. Acts 5 : 30; 10 : 39; 13 : 29; Gal. 3 : 13) is connected with the gift of life and righteousness, the ark may possibly also be associated with the cross. At a later date Justin Martyr clearly makes this connection, comparing Noah, who "was saved by wood (ξύλῳ)," with Christians who have the mystery of the cross.[73] Cyril of Jerusalem similarly likens the wood of the ark to that of the cross and the waters of the Flood to those of baptism.[74]

The identification of the ark with the cross does not exhaust all the possibilities of our text. The phrase εἰς ἥν in v. 20 implies that the ark is something "into which" Noah and his family, and consequently Christians, enter to find salvation.[75] As the symbolism ship = church seems to have been live in first-century Christianity, it is probable that here again we are dealing with this motif.[76] Among

---

[72] Charles (n. 69), II, 557f. On this passage see also G. Bertram, "Le chemin sur les eaux," *Rev. d'hist. et phil. rel.*, 7 (1927), pp. 535f. Cf. 2 Pet. 2 : 5; Heb. 11 : 7.
[73] Justin, *Dialogue*, 138, 2 (Migne, *Patr. Gr.*, 6, 793); cf. F. J. Dölger, *Sol salutis* (2d ed., 1925), p. 273; P. Lundberg, *La typologie baptismale* (1942), pp. 86, 185f.,; Reicke (n. 25), p. 139. Note also that both for Justin and in 1 Pet. 3 : 20 the waters of the Flood appear to be a favorable, not an inimical, element.
[74] Cyril of Jerusalem, *Cath.*, 17, 10; others who see the ark as the cross are Hippolytus, *Arabische Fragmente zum Pentateuch, Fragm. IV zu Gen.* 8, 1 (*Gr. chr. Schriftst., Hippol.* I, 2, 91); Ambrose, *De Myst.*, 3, 11. Still others take the ship more generally, to symbolize the cross: Augustine, *Sermo* LXXV, 2; Prosper of Aquitaine, *Expositio:* Ps. 103, 25. Cf. also references to the cross as "the life-giving wood" on early Christian ampullae, H. R. Willoughby, "The Distinctive Sources of Palestinian Pilgrimage Iconography," *Journ. Bibl. Lit.*, 74 (1955), p. 67.
[75] Reicke (n. 25), p. 140, notes that 1 Peter "does not confuse εἰς and ἐν more than possibly in v. 12, which belongs to the special ending."
[76] Cyprian, *Epist.* 73, 11; 74, 15; 75, 2; Jerome, *Adv. Joviniam*, 1, interpret the ship here as the church. This identification raises the possibility that the idea of the ark as the church may also lie in the background of Lk. 17 : 26f., where εἰσῆλθεν Νῶε εἰς τὴν κιβωτόν stands along side of ἐξῆλθεν Λὼτ ἀπὸ Σοδόμων (v. 29). If the latter reflects withdrawal from the world, may the former imply entrance into the church?
The question of the interrelationship of the symbols ship = church and ark = church has been variously answered. E. Peterson ("Das Schiff als Symbol

patristic writers, the church is the most frequent symbolic meaning of the ark.[77]

Selwyn also understands the ark as a symbol of the church here, but from a different standpoint.[78] He proposes that in v. 20, ἀντίτυπον be understood as referring to the reality rather than the figure, and that it be taken in apposition to ὑμᾶς. Thus "you", the Christian congregations to whom the epistle is addressed, are an antitype of the eight souls saved in the ark. Selwyn explains the singular form of ἀντίτυπον as indicating that the "readers are thought of as a community" (cf. Phil. 3 : 17; 1 Thess. 1 : 7; 2 Thess. 3 : 9; Didache 4 : 11). Although the identification of the ark as the church does not depend on this exegesis of v. 20b, yet as Reicke has pointed out in regard to another problem, both biblical and Talmudic writers often present motifs with various possibilities of interpretation because the author intends to convey to his reader a variety of associated ideas.[79] On this basis, the "antitype" in v. 20b may be a link both between Noah's experience and that of the Christian in baptism, and also between the ark and the church (and/or the cross).[80]

der Kirche," *Theol. Zeitschr.*, 6 [1950], p. 77) is emphatic that "each of them has its particular origin and its own meaning." Lundberg (n. 73), p. 86, derives the figure ark = church from the figure ship = church, which he believes is older. Reicke (n. 25), p. 139, n. 4, warns against Lundberg's attempt to fix a priority among such typologies. To us it seems that these two symbolisms first appear in the New Testament at so nearly the same time, that it is impossible to establish one as being older than the other. The figure ship = church has a long ideological ancestry, which the figure ark = church lacks. Each figure draws on a somewhat different area of associated ideas, yet that which is essential to each symbolism they have in common (note the oscillation between the ideas of ship and ark in Wisdom 14 : 1-7). Certainly they must very quickly have overlapped and contributed to each other.

[77] E.g., Tertullian, *De baptismo*, 8; *De idolatria*, 24; Hippolytus. *Elenchos*, 9, 12 (who attributes the use of the figure to Calixtus I [A.D. 217-222]): Origen, *In Genesim Homilia* II, 3, 5; Chrysostom, *Laz.*, 7; Jerome, *Lucif.*, 22; Augustine, *De civit. Dei* XV, 26. In early Christian art, and especially in funerary inscriptions, the ark is frequently portrayed; see especially H. Leclercq, "Arche," *Dict. d'arch. chrét.*, I : 2 (1907), 2709-2732; Fr. Schmidtke, "Arche," *Reallex. für Ant. u. Chr.*, I (1950), 597-602; Fr. Sühling, *Die Taube als religiöses Symbol im christlichen Altertum* (1930), pp. 222-231. To what extent the ark in these inscriptions represents the church is difficult to determine.

[78] Selwyn (n. 63), pp. 204, 298f., 315, 332ff.

[79] Reicke (n. 25), p. 141. This appears to be true here not only of the ark, but also of the phrase "through water" and the figure of the eight souls.

[80] Reicke (n. 25), pp. 139f., notes a third possible interpretation combining the ideas of the cross and of a building (cf. ch. 2 : 5) in Ignatius, *Ephesians* 9 : 1. The cross and the church were united symbolically also by later Fathers in the

The figure ark = church also gives meaning to the mention of "eight souls" saved. In the first instance, these "eight souls" emphasize the smallness of the church in contrast to the pagan world about it.[81] Beyond this, the symbolism of the number eight in ancient thought offers a variety of associations of ideas connected with baptism and the resurrection.[82]

The reference to baptism here is also significant for the identification of the ark as the church. The close relation between baptism and the church is mirrored in the association of flood and ark. Noah's experience is essentially one of being saved from and coming out of his wicked environment [83] (cf. Lk. 17 : 26f.) "into" the ark; his salvation takes place "through (διά) water." The preposition διά may have either a local or an instrumental sense, and in view of its implications both for Noah's experience and for Christian baptism it possibly is to be understood in both ways.[84] Leaving his evil world, Noah was saved by entering the ark and passing *through* water. Here the ark and the Flood are complementary; the water seems to be looked upon as a favorable, if not actually a saving element.[85] So the Christian leaving the world, enters the church and is saved by baptism, in the sense of v. 21.[86]

If the Flood is a favorable element here, does it have an eschatological implication as we have noted elsewhere? The eschatological nature of the church derives from its being a refuge not simply from the final cataclysm, but also from the world, over whose demonic rulers Christ has shown himself victorious and will one day be finally and completely conqueror. Just as New Testament eschatology

figure of ship (= church) and mast (= cross): Justin, *Apol.* I, 55, 3; Hippolytus, *Dem. de Chr. et Antichr.*, 59; Minucius Felix, *Octavius*, 29, 8; Ambrose, *De virginitate*, 18, 118.

[81] Selwyn (n. 63), p. 332; Reicke (n. 25), p. 140.
[82] Reicke (n. 25), pp. 140f.
[83] Reicke (n. 25), p. 143.
[84] Lundberg (n. 73), p. 113; Beare (n. 63), pp. 147f.; Reicke (n. 25), p. 142; cf. Vrede (n. 65), pp. 109f.
[85] Selwyn (n. 63), p. 329. Bertram (n. 72), p. 526, on the other hand, sees the Flood here as the waters of death, "but without it salvation could as little be effected as without the betrayer Judas or without the pillory of the cross."
[86] Lundberg (n. 73), pp. 76, 84f., notes other associations of ark and baptism: (1) The *Odes of Solomon*, 38, presents the Christian as entering the church, in the form of a vehicle, by means of baptism. Cf. J. H. Bernard, *The Odes of Solomon* (1912), pp. 123f. (2) A poem of Ephrem Syrus (*Opera*, VI, 355) declares: "Baptism shall be for me a ship that shall not sink." (3) Cyril of Jerusalem (*Procat.* I, 16) speaks of baptism as "a vessel to heaven."

characteristically oscillates between the two points of this tension, so also the eschatological typology of the Flood here appears to have in view primarily the Christian's present deliverance from the world and its dominating powers (as also in 2 Pet. 2 : 5, 9), whereas elsewhere (cf. Mt. 24 : 38f.) it focuses more directly upon the parousia.[87]

Rocks and waves

"These are they who are hidden rocks in your love-feasts when they feast with you, shepherds that without fear feed themselves... wild waves of the sea..." (Jude 12f., Am. Stand. Vers.).[88]

This passage is one of two instances in the New Testament in which ἀγάπη clearly refers to the sacred meal observed by the early church.[89] This, together with the fact that almost the whole epistle is directed against false teachers who slip into the congregation to lead it astray (cf. v. 4), means that the author addresses his readers as the church.

Two figures used here to describe false teachers appear to have a nautical basis: "hidden rocks" and "wild waves." However, the word σπιλάς here translated "hidden rock," may also mean a spot on a surface, a spot of dirt, a blemish. In this latter sense it may be used adjectivally as well. The evidences for each translation are as follows:

1. σπιλάς as a rock in or near the sea is an old Greek word that appears first with Homer.[90] Both the older and a number of modern exegetes have interpreted it in this way in the present passage.[91] An even more specialized meaning of this type is given by the *Etymologicum magnum*, which offers "underwater rocks" (αἱ ὕφαλοι πέτραι),

---

[87] Lk. 17 : 26ff. seems to present a problem from this point of view because it sees Noah delivered from his evil generation, as does 1 Pet. 3 : 20, but at the same time focuses on the parousia more than on the situation of the church during the period between the resurrection and the end. However, the essential difference between Lk. 17 : 26ff. and 1 Pet. 3 : 20 seems to be that in the one the Flood is a cataclysm which destroys the evil world; in the other it is the antitype of the baptism by which Christians are saved. The former points to the parousia; the latter, to the present period of the church. See above, n. 76.
[88] On the translation of this passage, see G. Wohlenberg, *Der erste und zweite Petrusbrief und der Judasbrief* (1915), pp. 311f.
[89] Reicke, *Diakonie* (n. 2), pp. 12, 353; the other passage is John 13 : 1; next earliest references are Ignatius, *Rom.* 7 : 3; *Smyrn.* 6 : 2; 7 : 1; 8 : 2.
[90] Homer, *Odyssey* III, 298; V, 401.
[91] Oecumenius, *Comment. in Epist. Judae*, 2; Bauer (n. 44), col. 1510, cites the following commentators as favoring this interpretation: De Wette, Mayor, Wordsworth, Chase.

a definition of σπιλάδες which it appears to attribute to the fifth-century lexicographer Orion.⁹² The participle κατασπιλάζοντες it defines as "hiding: from the metaphor of underwater rocks, which, hidden beneath the water bring danger to those who unforeseeingly strike against them."⁹³ Knopf complains that this definition appears nowhere in ancient literature, and that there is nothing in the context of Jude 12f. regarding shipwreck.⁹⁴ However, an unsupported definition in the *Etymologicum magnum* ought not to be rejected completely for lack of further evidence, since it may rest on documents no longer extant. Regardless of whether σπιλάς can refer to *underwater* rocks, its reference to rocks in the sea and on the shore, upon which ships may be wrecked, is well attested. Although there is nothing specifically of shipwreck in our context, the reference to "wild waves of the sea" (v. 13) is suggestive.

2. σπιλάς in the sense of a spot, a stain, also appears in classical literature,⁹⁵ and the majority of modern commentators on our passage have accepted this meaning.⁹⁶ In its favor is the parallel in 2 Pet. 2 : 13, σπίλος, which can only mean "a spot," "a blot." If 2 Peter is secondary to Jude, σπίλος would appear to be its author's definition of Jude's ambiguous σπιλάς. With this may be compared Eph. 5 : 27, where the church is to be without σπίλον.

No final decision can be reached as to which meaning is intended for σπιλάς in the present passage. However, a number of considerations lead us to favor the idea of some kind of rock upon which a ship may founder, rather than that of a spot or blemish. A comparison between our passage and its parallel in 2 Pet. 2 : 13-17 is essential to an understanding of the problem, but the comparison must be made between the two passages as a whole, and not merely between σπιλάς and σπίλος. The passage in 2 Peter is obviously not an attempt to define the words of Jude. Whether the author of 2 Peter wrote with Jude's epistle

---

⁹² *Etymologicum magnum* (ed. T. Gaisford, Oxford, 1848), p. 724. This work derives from a tenth-century Greek lexicon compiled by an unknown author from various ancient sources, a number of which are no longer extant. Cf. K. Krumbacher, *Geschichte der byzantinischen Literatur* (2d ed., 1897), pp. 574f.
⁹³ *Etymologicum magnum* (n. 92), p. 495.
⁹⁴ R. Knopf, *Die Briefe Petri und Judä* (1912), p. 232.
⁹⁵ E.g., Orpheus, *Lithica*, 614. A. Bailly, *Dictionnaire grec-français* (11th ed., n.d.), s.v., derives this second definition by analogy from the first.
⁹⁶ Bauer (n. 44), col. 1510, cites the following: Spitta, B. Weiss, Kühl, Bigg, Hollmann, Zahn, Wohlenberg, Vrede, O. Holtzmann. Bauer himself offers no judgment.

before him, or they both worked from a common source, each handled his material with independence. Thus in the series of figures constituting our passage, whereas Jude has "waterless clouds, carried along by winds" (v. 13), 2 Peter has "waterless springs, and mists driven by a storm" (ch. 2 : 17). The differences here between "clouds" and "springs," and between "winds" and "storm" would suggest that one cannot depend on σπίλος as a certain definition of σπιλάς, if there is good reason from the context of the latter word for interpreting it differently. An examination of the context in Jude seems to provide such a reason. Verses 12f. present a series of figures describing the threat of false teachers to the church; each of these figures is vigorously presented to depict a scene of action: carrousing shepherds, driven clouds, uprooted trees, tossing waves, wandering stars. As compared with these, σπιλάδες, if it means merely "blemishes," "spots," is weak and colorless. But if it is taken as "reefs," immediately the picture of a foundering ship is suggested to the mind, a picture of the same dramatic stature as the other figures in this passage. It may not be impossible that Jude, in working out this compact and graphic series of figures, intentionally changed the σπίλος preserved in 2 Pet. 2 : 13, to σπιλάδες, as the latter fits better the context in which he places it. The corresponding figures in 2 Peter are neither as graphically developed nor as succinctly presented, and there σπίλος is quite in place. Similarly 2 Peter has not preserved the related figure of "wild waves" found in Jude 13.

If the foregoing judgment is correct, our passage may be seen as implying the figure of the ship. Jude's concern is with the threat of false teachers to the church as a body. These he likens to "reefs." The object which is threatened by a reef is, of course, a ship. Hence by implication, the ship would once more be a figure for the church. Such an identification, of course, can only be tentative in view of the problem in defining σπιλάδες.

The figure of "wild waves casting up the foam of their own shame" (v. 13) also fits the idea of the church as a ship, which we have seen repeatedly portrayed in storm. As false teachers, the waves may have a certain demonic implication (cf. v. 6; Eph. 4 : 14).

Thus Jude portrays graphically the danger of false teachers who have slipped secretly into the church (v. 4). The implied figure of the ship of the church may be thought of as making its way through stormy seas, threatened to be dashed to pieces on reefs in the sea or against cliffs on the shore.

A third of the ships in the sea destroyed

"The second angel blew his trumpet, and something like a great mountain, burning with fire, was thrown into the sea; and a third of the sea became blood, a third of the living creatures in the sea died, and a third of the ships were destroyed" (Rev. 8 : 8f.).

Our central problem here is the meaning of the statement, "a third of the ships were destroyed." In the old exegesis, these words were taken as symbolic. Following a classical figure, Oecumenius declares: "He calls the souls of the saints, figuratively, ships." The destruction of one-third of the ships he sees as a warning that "some are likely to be led astray from those who have laid hold of salvation."[97] However, such an interpretation can hardly be correct if the total context of our passage is taken into account.

The destruction of a third of the ships is a part of the judgment that descends upon the sea when the second of the seven angels with trumpets sounds. This judgment is preceded by one upon the earth (v. 7) and followed by plagues upon rivers and fountains (vs. 10f.) and the heavenly bodies (v. 12). Lohmeyer points out that some of the elements in this series appear to be expansions of eschatological motifs in the synoptic apocalypses, particularly in Lk. 21 : 25ff.[98] Such passages as Isa. 13 : 10; Joel 2 : 10; Zeph. 1 : 3, 15, and above all the first plague on Egypt (Ex. 7 : 14ff.; cf. Ps. 78 : 44) show that the present series of judgments is rooted in Old Testament typology. The repetition of an almost identical series of judgments upon the earth, the sea, the rivers and fountains, and the sun when the first four of the seven last plagues are poured out (Rev. 16 : 2-8) indicates that our passage deals with eschatological portents.[99] A characteristic idea of the Old Testament is that the natural world undergoes convulsions at the Day of the Lord. Consequently it would seem that the figures of the present passage should be interpreted in terms of Old Testament, rather than classical, symbolism.

Even on this basis, it is tempting to assign the sea some such meaning as that of the demon-possessed world, and to understand judgment as descending upon it. This would be tenable in terms of Old Testament symbolism, but consistency then would seem to demand an interpretation of the whole series of judgments (at least through v. 12) on a similar basis, and this does not appear possible. Hence

---

[97] Oecumenius, Ἐξήγησις εἰς τὴν Ἀποκάλυψιν, 23, in Cramer (n. 38), VIII, 305
[98] E. Lohmeyer, *Die Offenbarung des Johannes* (2d ed., 1953), p. 75.
[99] Cf. *Sibylline Oracles* 4 : 76f.; 5 : 55-60.

the safest procedure is probably to understand the sea simply as one part of a series that includes all the features of the natural world: earth, sea, flowing waters, and heavenly bodies (cf. ch. 14 : 7; 16 : 2-9). Judgments poured out upon them imply the disarrangement and convulsion of the whole of nature.

The destruction of one-third of each of the elements named is a characteristic of this series of judgments. Of fifteen things stricken by plagues, in twelve instances one-third of each is affected. Division by thirds to represent partial judgments is found in Old Testament prophecy (Eze. 5 : 2, 12; Zach. 13 : 7-9)[100] and in the present passage may be taken to mean that a part, but not all, of the sea is involved.

If it is the world of nature that is attacked by these plagues, why are ships, man-made objects, included? The suggestion that a great loss of ships brings about serious disconcertion of Mediterranean commerce and travel[101] seems to introduce an element foreign to the tenor of the passage. Bousset understands the ships to mean the men travelling in them, and Swete sees in the plural διεφθάρησαν after τὸ τρίτον τῶν πλοίων an attribution of "quasi-personal life to the ships, in view of their human masters and crews."[102] A parallel to such an interpretation is the statement under the next plague that "many men died of the water" (v. 11).

Without denying the possibility of this interpretation, we would suggest that primarily the ships here are considered as inhabitants of the sea, much as they appear to be in Ps. 104 : 25f.; Prov. 30 : 19.[103] The description of this judgment then would be in almost exact parallel to that of the first (v. 7), where the fire burns one-third of the earth and of the two things that grow on it, trees and grass. So here a third of the sea and its two types of denizens, "living creatures"[104] and ships, are destroyed. Thus the destruction of ships appears to be primarily a part of the eschatological convulsion of nature.

[100] Cf. *Babba Mezia* 59b.
[101] C. Brütsch, *Die Offenbarung Jesu Christi* (1955), p. 45.
[102] W. Bousset, *Die Offenbarung Johannis* (5th ed., 1906), p. 296; H. B. Swete, *The Apocalypse of St. John* (3d ed., 1951), p. 112.
[103] Oecumenius (n. 107), *loc. cit.*, connects our passage with Ps. 104 (103).
[104] The destruction of fish has eschatological significance in Zeph. 1 : 3; cf. R. H. Charles, *The Revelation of St. John* (1920), I, 234.

CHAPTER X

CONCLUSION

Retrospect

In concluding this study, we may pause for a moment to look back over the way we have come. Virtually from the dawn of human civilization, the ship has been a significant figure in man's thoughts about life and destiny. In Egypt it was connected with the voyage of the soul to the hereafter; in Mesopotamia, with a divine drama of salvation. In classical literature nautical figures took on a variety of meanings. Charon transported the dead to the next world by a ship. Quite apart from this a series of other symbolic meanings show a logical, if not a chronological development: the human being (and/or the soul) was conceived of as a ship, storms portrayed the difficulties of life, and the port was the hereafter; then the ship became a community of individuals, and particularly the state, its pilot was the ruler, and storms were international problems; finally the ship was also the world (or the universe), with the pilot representing God.

In the Old Testament the ship presents quite another figure: there it is associated chiefly with foreigners and enemies of Israel. However in the wisdom and the lyric literature of the Old Testament, a variety of other applications appear, derived from particular characteristics of the ship viewed as an object in itself or against the background of nature. In deutero- and extra-canonical Jewish literature, the familiar classical themes were adopted; here the ship was a human being, or the whole world, or the Jewish nation. In the immediate environment of the New Testament, all these motifs were present.

Thus the possibility arises that nautical figures may also be significant in the New Testament. We have thought to see a deeper, symbolical meaning in at least some Gospel stories. In the three narratives of Jesus' performing miracles on the sea of Galilee – the Stilling of the Storm, the Walking on the Water, and the Miraculous Drafts of Fish – there may be symbolic meanings that relate these narratives more directly to the central events of salvation-history. An important factor in such an interpretation is the ship as a figure for the church. This symbolism would seem to be related to the ship of Israel in Jewish literature, and is well attested in Christian sources from at least the early third century onward.

It is impossible, of course, to prove much of the symbolism we have thought to see; hence these suggestions must remain tentative. But taken as a whole, the evidence seems to make reasonably probable that the symbolism of the ship as the church has its origin in the New Testament.

Prospect

The figure of the ship, particularly as it represents the church, reaches its full expression in post-biblical Christian literature and archaeology.[1] The fact that this symbolism seems never to be presented consciously as a new idea suggests that it already may have been known from the New Testament.

In the paragraphs that follow we can consider only a few of the earliest examples of our symbol in post-biblical literature. Possibly the first evidence for it outside the New Testament is in the *Testament of Zebulon* 6 : 1-8,[2] in so far as this passage may be considered from a Christian point of view:

> I was the first to make a boat to sail upon the sea, for the Lord gave me understanding and wisdom therein. (2) And I let down a rudder behind it, and I stretched a sail upon another upright piece of wood in the midst. (3) And I sailed therein along the shores, catching fish for the house of my father until we came to Egypt. (4) And through compassion I shared my catch with every stranger. (5) And if a man were a stranger, or sick, or aged, I boiled the fish, and dressed them well, and offered them to all men, as every man had need, grieving with and having compassion upon them. (6) Wherefore also the Lord satisfied me with abundance of fish when catching fish; for he that shareth with his neighbor receiveth manifold more from the Lord. (7) For five years I caught fish and gave thereof to every man whom I saw, and sufficed for all the house of my father. (8) And in the summer I caught fish, and in the winter I kept sheep with my brethren.

---

[1] For studies of the ship as a figure in patristic literature, the reader is referred to the works cited in Ch. I, n. 6. For the ship in Christian archaeology, see especially G. Stuhlfauth, "Das Schiff als Symbol der altchristlichen Kunst," *Rivista di archeologia cristiana*, 19 (1942), pp. 111ff., H. Leclercq, "Navire," *Dict. d'arch. chrét.*, XII : 1 (1935), 1008-1019; Fr. Sühling, *Die Taube als religiöses Symbol im christlichen Altertum* (1930), pp. 239-250.

[2] R. H. Charles, *Apocrypha and Pseudepigrapha* (1913), II, 330. Verses 4-6 appear only in part of the extant mss.

As we have seen, the *Testaments of the Twelve Patriarchs* underwent a long process of development, so that it is impossible to date this passage. In origin it may be pre-Christian, but if so, at an early date it came into Christian hands. Accordingly the interpretation proposed here is one which Christians may have seen implied in it. Possibly the following meanings are involved: ship = church; mast = cross; rudder = administration of the church; fishing = missionary activity; giving fish to eat = giving the eucharist(?); "catching fish for the house of my father until we came to Egypt. And through compassion I shared my catch with every stranger" = missionary activity for the Jew first, and also the Greek; fishing in summer, shepherding in winter = missionary and pastoral work of Christian leaders. So understood, these words would symbolize the mission program of the early church.

A further hint of this may lie in *T. Zeb.* 5 : 4f.:[3]

> For the sons of my brethren were sickening and were dying on account of Joseph, because they showed not mercy in their hearts; but my sons were preserved without sickness, as ye know. (5) And when I was in the land of Canaan, by the sea-coast, I made a catch of fish for Jacob my father; and when many were choked in the sea, I continued unhurt.

In view of the apparent connections of the figure of Joseph with Jewish Hellenism in the early church,[4] this passage might reflect the tension between the first-century Christian mission and Jewish Zealotism.

The earliest nearly datable evidence for our figure, though here it is only implied, is in Ignatius' *Epistle to Polycarp* 2 : 3 (ca. A.D. 110). Exhorting the bishop of Smyrna regarding his episcopal duties, Ignatius declares: "The times call for thee, as pilots do for the winds, and as one tossed with tempest seeks for the haven, so that both thou [and those under thy care] may attain to God."[5] Here the idea of the church as a ship may be presupposed.

The first explicit statement of the equation ship = church is probably that of Tertullian, who declares of the disciples' ship in the storm on Galilee: "But that little ship did present a figure of the Church, in that she is disquieted 'in the sea,' that is, in the world, 'by the waves,' that is by persecutions and temptations; the Lord, through patience, sleeping as it were, until, roused in the last extremities by the prayers of the saints, He checks the world, and restores

---

[3] Charles (n. 2), *loc. cit.*
[4] B. Reicke, *Glaube und Leben der Urgemeinde* (1957), pp. 414f.
[5] *Epistle of Ignatius to Polycarp*, 2 (A. Roberts and J. Donaldson, eds., *The Ante-Nicene Fathers* [1895], I, 94).

tranquility to His own."[6] Inasmuch as Tertullian just before has referred to a traditional interpretation of the story of Jesus' stilling the storm, it may be assumed that he draws the figure ship = church also from tradition. He makes no apology for it but takes for granted that his readers will understand.[7]

Soon afterward, and probably from opposite ends of the Roman world, come two elaborate developments of our figure.

Hippolytus, writing from Rome at the beginning of the second century, gives an extensive catalogue of the various parts of the ship, and assigns each a spiritual meaning in harmony with the basic notion of the ship as the church. Thus "the sea is the world, in which the Church is set, like a ship tossed in the deep, but not destroyed."[8] The pilot is Christ, the mast is the cross, the bow is the east,[9] the stern the west, the hold the south, the tillers are the two Testaments, the girding ropes are the love of Christ which binds the church, her net is baptism which renews the believers, the position of the wind represents the Holy Spirit, the anchors are the commandments of Christ, the sailors are the angels, the ladder leading to the mast is the imitation of the sufferings of Christ which draw the believer toward heaven, the top-sails are the prophets, martyrs, and apostles at rest in the kingdom of Christ.

At approximately the same time as Hippolytus,[10] but probably in Syria and from a Jewish-Christian background, the *Epistle of Clement to James*, a part of the pseudo-Clementine literature, presents another elaborate figure based on the equation ship = church. Here Peter, in consecrating Clement bishop, is made to declare:

> For the whole business of the Church is like unto a great ship, bearing through a violent storm men who are of many places, and who desire to inhabit the city of the good kingdom. Let, therefore, God be your ship-master; and let the pilot be likened to Christ, the mate to the bishop, and the sailors to the deacons,[11] the midshipmen to the catechists, the

---

[6] Tertullian, *On Baptism*, 12 (Roberts [n. 5], III, 675).
[7] E. Peterson, "Das Schiff der Kirche," *Theol. Zeitschr.*, 6 (1950), pp. 77f.
[8] Hippolytus, *Treatise on Christ and Antichrist*, 59 (Roberts [n. 5], V, 216).
[9] F. J. Dölger, *Sol salutis* (2d ed., 1925), p. 286, shows that the easterly direction of the ship indicates it is bound for paradise, inasmuch as it was thought to be located in the east; cf. Fr. Sühling (n. 1), pp. 244f.
[10] O. Cullmann, *Le problème littéraire et historique du roman pseudo-clémentin* (1930), p. 157; cf. p. 143, dates the part of the pseudo-Clementine literature with which we are concerned here between A.D. 220 and 230.
[11] The Eng. Translator (see n. 12) apparently has overlooked some words at this point; the texts of Migne (*Patr. Gr.*, II, 49) and P. de Lagarde (*Clementina*

multitude of the brethren to the passengers, the world to the sea; the foul winds to temptations, persecutions and dangers; and all manner of afflictions to the waves; ... In order, therefore, that sailing with a fair wind, you may safely reach the haven of the hoped-for city, pray so as to be heard. But prayers become audible by good deeds. Let therefore the passengers remain quiet, sitting in their own places, lest by disorder they occasion rolling or careening. Let the midshipmen give heed to the fare. Let the deacons neglect nothing with which they are entrusted; let the presbyters, like sailors, studiously arrange what is needful to each one. Let the bishop, the mate, wakefully ponder the words of the pilot alone. Let Christ, even the Saviour, be loved as the pilot, and alone believed in the matters of which he speaks. And let all pray to God for a prosperous voyage.[12]

Peterson has sought to connect this passage, and particularly the motif of the salvation of the ship/church from storm through prayer, with the *Testament of Naphtali* 6, which portrays the ship of Israel saved from the eschatological tempest by the prayer of Levi.[13] This connection is made even more possible by conclusions derived from the Qumran discoveries. The presence of a fragment of the *Testament of Naphtali* among the Qumran manuscripts makes it probable that the figure ship = Israel, together with the motifs of storm and salvation from it by prayer, were current in that community. As Cullmann has shown, it is also probable that after A.D. 70 the Qumran sect was absorbed by Jewish-Christianity in Transjordan.[14] Within this Jewish-Christian milieu a century and a half later these same motifs reappear, applied to the Christian church. The elaboration with which the author of the Epistle of Clement to James develops them suggests that the basic equation ship = church was not his invention, but that for this, as with so much of his work, he drew on older traditions current within his circle. Thus the figure ship = Israel/church possibly may be traced from Qumran into the post-biblical Jewish-Christian community. However, the ship as a representation of the church was not the exclusive property of Jewish Christianity. The elaborateness of Hippolytus' metaphor presupposes that for him and his readers the figure ship = church was traditional. The basis of this tradition we believe we have found in the New Testament.

[1861], pp. 10f.) read οἱ ναῦται πρεσβυτέροις. οἱ τοίχαρχοι διακόνοις, οἱ ναυστολόγοι τοῖς κατηχοῦσιν.
[12] *Epistle of Clement to James*, 14f. (Roberts [n. 5], VIII, 220f.).
[13] Peterson (n. 7), pp. 78f.
[14] O. Cullmann, "Die neuentdeckten Qumrantexte und das Judenchristentum der Pseudoklementinen," in *Neutestamentliche Studien für Rudolf Bultmann* (1954), pp. 35f.

From the third century onward, the figure of the ship, especially representing the church, is one of the more frequent Christian symbols, both in patristic literature and in art. This leads us beyond the limits of the present study. These rich materials from patristic sources are being exhaustively studied by H. Rahner.[15]

It remains to summarize the implications which the figure of the ship may have for the general theological concept of the church.

For the very reason that the ship is never explicitly stated in the New Testament to represent the church, but only seems to function thus by inference, we tread dangerous ground if we attempt to derive elaborate doctrinal conclusions from such symbolism. However, our symbol may illustrate theological insights based on other, explicit evidence. We suggest the following implications:

1. Basic to the figure of the ship is the idea of the relationship between the individual and the corporate body. In Greek and Jewish-Hellenistic literature, the ship was often a figure for the individual soul; by extension it represented groups of persons. Implicit in the thought of the group was that it was composed of individuals bound together by the necessity of co-operation, by a common fate, and by a common goal. These ties meant that chief emphasis fell on the corporate nature of the ship's company. This corresponds to the nature of the church as set forth in the New Testament. It is composed of individuals, yet of individuals considered as a body whose members must work with harmonious co-operation and obedience to authority if their common goal is to be achieved (Rom. 12 : 3ff.; 1 Cor. 12 : 12ff.). The ship aptly illustrates this, as appears from James 3 : 4 and from the context of Eph. 4 : 14.

2. Closely related to the foregoing is the idea of the ship as a divinely-protected refuge from danger. Ancient man stood in awe of the sea, and in the fact that "men also trust their lives even to a little wood, and passing over the waves, by ship, are saved" (Wisdom 14 : 5), both pagan and Jew perceived divine power. As a figure for the church, the ship thus reflects the thought that the church is a divinely-guided and protected refuge from the world and the evil forces that dominate it (cf. Mt. 14 : 32). This thought seems to be associated in the New Testament particularly with the ark in 1 Pet. 3 : 20 and possibly also in Lk. 17 : 27; it may appear in Mt. 14 : 32.

3. The figure of the ship implies a mission. A ship does not

---

[15] References in Ch. I, n. 6.

sail out upon the sea without a purpose for its voyage. Similarly the church puts forth on a mission to the world (Mk. 4 : 35ff.; Lk. 5 : 2ff.). On the other hand, it is also directed toward an eschatological goal, as in Heb. 6 : 19 (cf. the implications of 1 Tim. 1 : 19).

4. The close association of the ship with motifs that appear to pertain to the sacraments (John 6 : 1-59; 21 : 1-14; Acts 27 : 34-37; 1 Pet. 3 : 20f.) provides an illustration of the essential relation that exists between the church and baptism and the eucharist.

5. Finally, the fact that the ship is repeatedly connected with events that seem to reflect the central happenings of salvation-history (e.g., Mk. 4 : 35ff.; 6 : 45ff.; pars.) suggests that these are significant not only for the individual, but also for the church. Hence the church plays an essential role in the history of salvation.

SELECTED BIBLIOGRAPHY

Ambrosch, J. *De Charonte etrusco.* Vratislaviae, 1837.
Bertram, G. "Le chemin sur les eaux considéré comme motif de salut dans la piété chrétienne primitive," *Revue d'histoire et de philosophie religieuse,* 7 (1927), pp. 516ff.
Betz, O. "Donnersöhne, Menschenfischer und der davidische Messias," *Revue de Qumran,* No. 9 (Vol. 3 : 1, Feb., 1961), pp. 41-70.
Bonner, C. "Desired Haven," *Harvard Theological Review,* 34 (1941), pp. 49-67.
— "The Ship of the Soul on a Group of Grave-Stelae from Terenuthis," *Proceedings of the American Philosophical Society,* 85 (1941), pp. 84-91.
Bultmann, R. *Das Evangelium des Johannes.* 12th ed., Göttingen, 1952.
Colson, F. H. "Triangular Numbers in the New Testament," *Journal of Theological Studies,* 16 (1915), pp. 67-76.
Conzelmann, H. *The Theology of St. Luke.* New York, 1960.
Cullmann, O. *Christ and Time.* London, 1951.
— *Early Christian Worship.* London, 1953.
— "Der johanneische Gebrauch doppeldeutiger Ausdrücke als Schlüssel zum Verständnis des vierten Evangeliums," *Theologische Zeitschrift,* 4 (1948), pp. 360-372.
Cumont, F. *After Life in Roman Paganism.* New Haven, 1922.
Dölger, F. J. ΙΧΘΥΣ. 5 vols., Rom, Münster, 1910-1943.
— *Sol salutis.* Münster, 1925.
Eisler, R. *Orpheus – the Fisher.* London, 1921.
Eitrem, S. "De servatore mundi navis gubernatore," *Coniectanea neotestamentica,* 4 (1940), pp. 5-8.
Emerton, J. A. "The Hundred Fifty-three Fishes in John XXI. 11," *Journal of Theological Studies,* 9 (1958), pp. 86-89.
Goldammer, K. "Das Schiff der Kirche," *Theologische Zeitschrift,* 6 (1950), pp. 232ff.
Goodenough, E. R. *Jewish Symbols.* 8 vols., New York, 1953-1958.
Grant, R. M. "One Hundred Fifty-three Large Fish," *Harvard Theological Review,* 42 (1949), pp. 273-275.
Gunkel, H. *Schöpfung und Chaos.* 2d ed., Göttingen, 1921.
Hoskyns, E. *The Fourth Gospel.* 2d ed., London, 1948.
— and N. Davey. *The Riddle of the New Testament.* London, 1931.
Kahlmeyer, J. *Seesturm und Schiffbruch als Bild im antiken Schrifttum.* Diss. Greifswald, 1934.
Kaiser, O. *Die mythische Bedeutung des Meeres in Aegypten, Ugarit und Israel* (Beiheft zur *Zeitschrift für die alttestamentliche Wissenschaft,* 78), Berlin, 1959.
Kaufmann, C. M. *Die sepulkrale Jenseitsdenkmäler der Antike und des Urchristentums.* Mainz, 1900.

Kees, H. *Totenglauben und Jenseitsvorstellungen der alten Aegypter.* Leipzig, 1926.
Lagrange, M. J. *L'évangile selon St. Jean.* 7th ed., Paris, 1948.
Leclercq, H. "Arche," "Navire," *Dictionnaire d'archéologie chrétienne.* Paris, 1907ff.
Lidzbarski, M. *Das Johannesbuch der Mandäer.* 2 vols., Giessen, 1905, 1915.
Lightfoot, R. H. *History and Interpretation in the Gospels.* New York, 1934.
— *Locality and Doctrine in the Gospels.* London, 1938.
Lundberg, P. *La typologie baptismale dans l'ancienne église* (Acta semin. neotest. Upsal. X). Uppsala, 1942.
Mach, R. *Der Zaddik im Talmud und Midrasch.* Anhang I: "Die nautische Symbolik in der rabbinischen Literatur." Leiden, 1957.
Mánek, J. "Fishers of Men," *Novum Testamentum,* 2 (1957), pp. 138-141.
May, H. G. "Some Cosmic Connotations of Mayim Rabbîm," *Journal of Biblical Literature,* 74 (1955), pp. 9-21.
Mitzka, F. "Symbolismus als theologische Methode," *Zeitschrift für katholische Theologie,* 67 (1943), pp. 21-35.
Moortgat, A. *Tammuz: der Unsterblichkeitsglaube in der altorientalischen Bildkunst.* Berlin, 1949.
Niewalda, P. *Sakramentssymbolik im Johannesevangelium?* Lahn, 1958.
Peterson, G. "Das Schiff als Symbol der Kirche," *Theologische Zeitschrift,* 6 (1950), pp. 77-79.
Rahner, H. "Antenna crucis," *Zeitschrift für katholische Theologie,* 65 (1941), pp. 123-152; 66 (1942), pp. 89-118, 67 (1942), pp. 196-227; 68 (1943), pp. 1-21; 75 (1953), pp. 129-173, 358-410; 79 (1957), pp. 129-169.
— "Navicula Petri," *Zeitschrift für katholische Theologie,* 69 (1947), pp. 1-35.
Reicke, B. "Die Bedeutung des Gottesvolks-Gedankens für den neutestamentlichen Kirchenbegriff," *Kirchenblatt für die reformierte Schweiz,* 111 (1955), pp. 258-262.
— *Diakonie, Festfreude und Zelos.* Uppsala, 1951.
— *The Disobedient Spirits and Christian Baptism.* København, 1946.
— "Einheitlichkeit oder verschiedene 'Lehrbegriffe' in der neutestamentlichen Theologie?" *Theologische Zeitschrift,* 9 (1953), pp. 401-415.
— "Die Mahlzeit mit Paulus auf den Wellen des Mittelmeers Act. 27, 33-38," *Theologische Zeitschrift,* 4 (1948), pp. 401ff.
Reymond, P. *L'eau, sa vie, et sa signification dans l'Ancien Testament* (Supplement to *Vetus Testamentum,* Vol. IV). Leiden, 1958.
Richardson, A. *The Miracle Stories of the Gospels.* London, 1956.
Selwyn, E. G. *The First Epistle of St. Peter.* 2d ed., London, 1949.
Stuhlfauth, G. "Das Schiff als Symbol der altchristlichen Kunst," *Rivista di archeologia christiana,* 19 (1942), pp. 111ff.
Sühling, Fr. *Die Taube als religiöses Symbol im christlichen Altertum.* Freiburg i.B., 1930.
Widengren, G. *Mesopotamian Elements in Manichaeism* (*King and Saviour* II; Uppsala Universitets årsskrift, 1946, No. 3).
Wilder, A. N. "Scholars, Theologians, and Ancient Rhetoric," *Journal of Biblical Literature,* 75 (1956), pp. 1-11.
Witzel, M. *Tammuz-Liturgien und Verwandtes* (Analecta Orientalia, X). Roma, 1935.

www.ingramcontent.com/pod-product-compliance
Lightning Source LLC
Chambersburg PA
CBHW050824160426
43192CB00010B/1885